JOYride

*How My Late Wife
Loved Me Back To Life*

. . . .

◆

I. J. Weinstock

JOYride
How My Late Wife Loved Me Back To Life

ISBN 978-0-9829322-1-6

For information write:

DreaMaster Books
DreaMasterBooks@gmail.com
www.IJWeinstock.com

Layout & Design by EditWriteDesign.com
Original Cover Graphic by aloha_17, iStockPhoto.com
Printed in the United States of America

Author's Note: Some names in this book have been changed to protect peoples' privacy.

For Joy,
A million Thank You's for the Love AND the Loss,
and for gifting me with a love story for the ages.

♦

To My Friends and Family,
A community of wise, generous and loving souls,
who supported and ministered to me in whatever way I needed.
Thank you for loving me through this dark passage
so I could testify to the remarkable story contained in these pages.

In Roman myth, Baucis and Philemon were an old married couple who were favored by the gods and granted one wish. Though poor, they didn't ask for wealth; though old, they didn't ask for youth; though infirm, they didn't ask for health. Their one wish, above all others, was to die at the same time so that neither would have to suffer the loss of the other and go through the torments of grief.

* * *

"We do not need to proselytize either by our speech
or by our writing.
We can only do so really with our lives…
Let our lives be open books for all to study."
— Mahatma Ghandi

CONTENTS

I SPRING

II SUMMER

III FALL

IV WINTER

Introduction

Like all great love stories ours is about sex and death and the eternal nature of love.

Joy was the love of my life—we were soulmates. As you'll discover, we were literally a *match made in heaven*. After experiencing such a profoundly fulfilling love, I felt I could die happy. But when she finally succumbed to breast cancer, I was so grief-stricken, *I* wanted to die. I couldn't imagine living without her.

A blonde, blue-eyed beauty, Joy began her professional life as a fashion model and ended her life as a role model of how to live joyfully despite cancer and blindness. She was an extraordinary woman who in life communicated with souls on the Other Side and when confronting death spent her last weeks planning her "graduation" party.

At her "Celebration of Life" memorial, a poem she'd written two days before her Good Friday "transition" was read, at her request, to the hundreds of assembled guests. In her poem Joy offered to be their spirit guide.

In the devastation of her passing, I stood alone and bereft in the ruins of our love. A part of me had died. I was desolate, grief-stricken. If anyone needed a spirit guide it was me.

i

But something extraordinary happened. In the depths of my grief, Joy began communicating with me from the Afterlife. She guided me on an incredible healing journey. Ultimately, like the final scene of the movie, *Ghost*, she found someone—a willing medium—through whom she literally loved me back to life.

Many people will be shocked by our story; others may be inspired. Some will find it ridiculous; others miraculous. Of course, there will be those who consider it blasphemous. Most, however, will find it hard to believe. I can't blame them. I'd heard of life-after-death, but *sex*-after-death? If I hadn't experienced it myself, I wouldn't have believed it either. But this is a true story.

A Deal with God

The only reason I can testify to the unbelievable love story you're about to read is because years ago I heard a voice, a disembodied voice, a voice that wasn't mine, asking me a question...the kind that changes your life.

It's said that the ancient Egyptians believed that when you die, your soul is asked two questions about the life you lived: Did you give joy? Did you find joy? The question I was asked *led* me to Joy.

But first I made a deal with God.

It was 1994 and I was in the conference room of a law firm during two weeks of exhausting, mind-numbing depositions in a lawsuit over the new cable network I'd created. As often happens in business, the big fish eat the little fish. As the creator, I was the little fish. My media partner and now adversary, a major cable network, was the big fish. I'd given the launching of my baby, The Game Channel, everything I had. Now I was a David against Goliath, outgunned financially and outmaneuvered legally, fighting for my financial and creative life.

So I was sitting in that conference room on the eighth floor of an office building in Norfolk, Virginia surrounded by teams of lawyers staring out the floor-to-ceiling window onto a Chesapeake Bay dotted with naval ships. I must have been daydreaming and everyone else must have taken a break because suddenly I was alone.

That's when I heard the Voice ask me that fateful question. *"What will you regret on your deathbed?"*

I was stunned.

"What will you regret..?" the Voice asked again.

My life flashed before me....

There'd been so many paths not taken: deciding *not* to become a doctor, to the horror of my parents, both of whom were Holocaust survivors, and choosing instead to go into the theater and pursue a life in the arts (I wanted to be Fred Astaire rather than Dr. Kildare); then instead of heading off to Broadway and Hollywood with classmates like Albert Brooks, leaving the most prestigious drama school in the country to live abroad in Jerusalem; and finally awakening in that holy city to a spiritual quest which propelled my life further and further off the beaten path.

You'd have thought I would have had a lot of regrets at the age of forty-six. But only one regret emerged with any certainty. And it surprised me.

The one thing that popped into my mind in answer to the question *"What will you regret on your deathbed?"* was a visionary dream, a "burning bush" of a dream that I'd had several years earlier about sacred sexual love. The French mystic and philosopher Teilhard de Chardin suggested the inexpressible beauty of that dream when he wrote, *"Some day, after we have mastered the winds, the waves, the tides and gravity... we shall harness...the energies of love. Then, for the second time in the history of the world, man will have discovered fire."*

At the time, I knew I'd been graced and that I needed to share my vision with the world. But I was reluctant to take up the call. Years later, alone in that law office, surveying my heart for my ultimate regret, I remembered my dream and knew instantly that my profound regret was a reflection of my as-yet-unfulfilled soul's purpose.

I was being called again. This time I couldn't say no.

So I said to the Voice, "Okay. Here's the deal. Get me some money from this lawsuit and I vow to devote myself to communicating this vision with whatever gifts I possess." At the time it was a pretty safe bet, since it appeared to be all over but for the Fat Lady Singing.

Lo and behold, miracles occurred and suddenly the Big Fish found itself legally cornered and on the hook for tens of millions of dollars. Two weeks before trial they settled.

Now I had some money and no excuse. After the lawyers took their well-deserved forty percent and splitting what was left with my partners, I didn't have forever money, but it gave me a window of opportunity.

It wasn't easy for me to walk away from Hollywood. The temptations were many. I'd been speaking at interactive media conferences as the creator of The Game Channel. These were the early days of the Internet and many opportunities were open to me. But I'd made a contract. A soul contract. I wasn't simply honoring my obligation, I also felt this pull, a kind of yearning, like love—call it a certainty, an inevitability, perhaps my soul's destiny.

So once again I stepped off the beaten path. I left Hollywood and all the potential riches it held, and nine months later I found a priceless treasure—Joy.

From Job to Joy

When I met Joy she had already lived a life filled with enough challenge and loss to have destroyed most people. But rather than crush her, all that pressure had, over time, forged a diamond-like jewel.

In the beginning she was like everyone else, except that her mother was on a "spiritual quest" long before people knew what that meant. She had Joy baptized by Ernest Holmes, the founder of Religious Science and the author of *The Science of Mind*, which, based on the metaphysical principles of the perennial wisdom, brought together religion, philosophy, and science into the quintessential spirituality for the New Age. This "New Thought," as it was called at the time, was the basis for much of the human potential/self-help movement of the past half-century. As a child in the Sunday School where her mother taught, Joy learned the principles of *The Secret* and the Law of Attraction sixty years before they became a cultural phenomenon. Joy was fortunate to have been raised with the principles of *The Secret* because they helped her navigate the many challenges that lay ahead.

She married her high school sweetheart, only to discover he was a pathological liar and compulsive gambler who would wind up in prison for writing bad checks. With her second husband she had to walk on eggshells for more than a decade until she was literally paralyzed by her unexpressed anger and realized that her "perfect marriage" was over. She claimed her third husband was a flat-out mistake that didn't last two years. And her fourth husband was addicted to cigarettes even though he was dying of emphysema. The "secrets" she'd learned as a child became instinctive ways of being and habits of thinking that allowed her to eventually bless all these relationships for the lessons she learned and the gifts she received.

Perhaps the most telling measure of Joy's level of consciousness was the way she dealt with the death of her first two children—her first at eleven months and second at eleven years. They say that what doesn't kill you makes you stronger. In Joy's case, rather than becoming embittered by these tragedies, she found a way to transform her unimaginable pain into yet another opportunity for growth. In contrast to most parents for whom the loss of a child typically scars them for life, when I encountered Joy decades after her children's deaths, she was the happiest person I'd ever met. A true embodiment of her name.

When I found Joy I became deliriously happy. I'd never experienced such a fulfilling love. And I had no idea there would be such an enormous price to pay for having made that deal with God.

Ten Things You Should Know About Joy

1. Born in Cincinnati, Ohio, her family moved to Los Angeles where, at ten months old, she made her stage debut as Baby Jesus with her mother playing Mary.

2. As a child her family moved a lot. She loved moving! It taught her not to be afraid of change. By the age of forty-five, she'd lived in thirty-two homes.

3. In sixth grade, she wrote, produced and directed her first play, and promised herself that she would be a singer when she grew up. By the time she graduated high school, she dreamt of becoming the editor of a fashion magazine.

4. At the age of twenty, she lived for three years in Lubbock, Texas where her first husband worked as a radio announcer and she opened a modeling school. Regarding Lubbock, she agreed with Kris Kristofferson's song, "Happiness is Lubbock in my rear-view mirror."

5. She adored her brother, sixteen months older, whom she described as her "hero and mentor." His drowning at age twenty-four—when a rogue wave swept him into the ocean while fishing off the rocks at Laguna—devastated her.

6. Of her four children, two died in childhood. Her daughter, Terri Nunn, became a rock star and her son, Elliot Anders, became a musician and composer.

7. During the '60's she was secretary to Groucho Marx when he was hosting the TV show *You Bet Your Life*. Groucho, old enough to be her grandfather, often chased her around the desk telling her she had the "best legs of any secretary I've ever had." She also worked for Jack LaLanne when his TV show aired in sixty-five cities. In those days she smoked like a chimney and ate donuts with her morning coffee.

8. She devoted more than fifty years to astrology, appearing on forty-two TV shows and over seventy radio shows. She counseled over 5,000 clients (some of them famous.) Among her many accurate astrological predictions, she predicted the Oscar nomination of her daughter's song, "Take My Breath Away," from the movie *Top Gun* six months before it was announced.

9. According to Joy, she dated thirty-two men, married five and lost three. Her two favorite Halloween costumes were Scarlett O'Hara and Howard Stern. She wrote two books—one about astrology and sex; the other about talking to dead people.

10. In her most recent book, *LOVE EVER AFTER: How My Husband Became My Spirit Guide*, she chronicled her almost daily conversations with husband #4 *after* he died and how he gave her a 12-Step program to find new love, which she used for six weeks to find her soulmate—*me*!

I

Spring

❧ 1 ☙

The Secret

For nearly a year I'd been secretly crying in the shower—the love of my life was dying of breast cancer. Every morning I'd sob in the privacy of my bathroom, my wails drowned out by the thundering water. I'd rest my head against the cool tile as the hot shower patted my back. *There...there....* I cried in the shower so I could put a smile on my face at breakfast and say, "Honey, how are we going to enjoy the day? How do you want to play?"

In the comforting embrace of the hot water, all my hidden and unexpressed emotions—fear, despair, grief, pain—welled up inside me and poured out. In the storm of tears I didn't know *who* I was crying for. Joy? Me? I couldn't stand to think of her suffering, her decline, her dying, her death. And I couldn't bear the thought of losing her.

I kept Joy's terminal condition a secret for almost a year to honor her wishes. She'd told her oncologist that she didn't want to know the "truth" of the tests that were regularly done because she'd reached a point where she wasn't going to do anything about it. Until she felt symptoms, she didn't want to be preoccupied with her cancer. She didn't want to deal with other people's worries and fears. She didn't want every conversation to be about her illness. She didn't want cancer to become her identity. As long as she felt good, she was going to be true to her name and enJoy life.

1

At first I didn't confide in anyone. Joy was "fine" as far as anyone else was concerned. She meant so much to so many people. They depended upon her for guidance and looked up to her as a model of inner joy and happiness no matter what the outer circumstances. She was for many a blonde, blue-eyed guru. To learn she was dying would be a devastating blow to them. And, despite their best intentions to keep the secret, she would discover the terrible news.

As the year went by, it became increasingly difficult for me to keep this secret. It was festering inside me and began to ooze out of my pores. At a party a friend remarked that lately I seemed to have a wall up. It was true. I was afraid that if I shared the slightest intimacy, it might crack the dam and all hell would break loose. But I was cracking anyway. And *leaking*, too.

My friend wanted to know what was *really* going on. "You don't really want to know," I heard myself say. Horrified that the dam was about to burst, I excused myself to get a drink. That's when I realized I needed some help.

A few days later, I was sitting across from the therapist who'd helped us cope with Joy's cancer, her sudden blindness due to macular degeneration, and the stress of my care-giving, I revealed my secret—Joy's cancer was now terminal and she was dying. I told the therapist how I'd struggled to keep the secret and how crying in the shower every morning helped. The therapist said I was protecting Joy the way a husband protects his pregnant wife, only now I was helping Joy birth her own death.

My relief at having shared my secret, however, was short-lived. The secret came out a few days later during our monthly appointment with Joy's oncologist. Dr. D was the perfect oncologist for Joy since he understood and respected her desire not to do any chemotherapy whose side effects would diminish her quality of life. Initially, he'd offered her a mild chemo protocol—a pill and a weekly injection—that wouldn't have adverse side effects. It was an offer she couldn't refuse. We'd go to the hospital every Tuesday morning for her chemo injection and in the evening we'd go dancing. And it seemed to work.

And then her tumor markers began going up. Dr. D recommended a more intensive chemo regimen that he warned would have significant side effects, like losing her hair or having a low-grade fever several days a week. Since she was feeling fine, Joy decided she wasn't going to do anything that made her sick. "I'm interested in *quality* of life, not quantity," she told him. "And I'm not afraid to die. I'll come in every month for the tests. And *you* worry about them. Since I'm not going to do anything about it, I don't need to know...until I feel something."

And that's what we did for nine months.

On February 15th, a few days after I'd shared my secret with our therapist, Dr. D asked Joy how she was feeling. Her response wasn't her usually upbeat, "Fine." Instead, she said, "I'm tired. It's been over two months since the radiation, but I can't seem to get my energy back. What's going on?"

"Do you really want to know?" Dr. D asked.

Joy took a deep breath and nodded. "Yes."

"You're terminal. The cancer has spread to your liver."

Though I knew it was coming, I felt as if I'd been hit with a sledge hammer.

"The good news," he continued, "is that it's one of the most painless ways to die from cancer. You'll get tired. You'll sleep more and more...until you finally slip into a coma."

"How long?" would have been the next likely question. But for some reason we didn't ask it. We were in shock. I figured we had at least six months, maybe a year. After all, we'd been dancing a month earlier.

We drove home from the hospital in silence, my mind racing. I didn't know what to say or do. Even though I'd known Joy was terminal, I was stunned by the news. I kept looking over

3

at Joy trying to imagine what she must be feeling. Desperate to say something that would comfort her, I stopped at a red light a few blocks from home, turned to her and said, "Honey, I think this calls for some ice cream. Would you like some?"

Half-smiling, she nodded. Going to Baskin & Robbins for a single scoop of Jamoca Almond Fudge in a sugar cone had become a rare and special treat. Since her breast cancer diagnosis, she'd cut down on sugar. For the past six years, an ice cream cone had taken on an almost mythic, holiday specialness. Like Christmas! If ever there was a time for a little Christmas cheer it was now.

Joy didn't feel she could eat an entire cone by herself, so we split one. Seated at a table by the window, we passed the cone back and forth. There was something about licking ice cream from a cone that we both felt was more satisfying than spooning it from a cup. Licking around it, catching any that dripped. It was primal, animal, wonderfully childlike. As we took turns licking our ice cream cone, I savored it, knowing that this was probably the last ice cream cone Joy would ever eat...and, of course, the last we would share.

She asked me how long I'd known about her condition. I told her how difficult it had been to keep the secret all that time, and the irony that I'd gone to our therapist just a few days earlier for help. And now the secret was out.

For the rest of the day Joy was unusually quiet. She wept a little and told me she wasn't afraid or sad about dying. She wasn't worried about her children. Her daughter, Terri, a rock star with an Oscar-winning song, and her son, Elliot, an Emmy-nominated composer, would be fine. Her greatest sadness was not being there to see her two-and-a-half-year-old granddaughter, Natalie, grow up and her stepson, Bruce Lisker, who'd spent nearly a quarter of a century in prison for a crime he didn't commit, finally exonerated and released.

Just then, I suddenly remembered that more than a dozen people were coming over that evening for our monthly Wisdom

Circle. I asked Joy if she wanted to cancel. She said *No*. But she wasn't up to playing hostess. When people started arriving, she stayed in the bedroom until the Circle was ready to begin.

We'd started our Wisdom Circle more than ten years earlier with a dozen or so friends and had been meeting every month since. We used a "talking stick," passing it around the circle, Native American style. Each month we discussed a topic or question and shared our wisdom about it. Whoever had the stick had the floor. Over the years we'd explored many fascinating topics—money, relationships, sex. We'd worn masks during an October Circle and experienced how they can be both liberating or imprisoning. We sat in complete darkness during one Winter Solstice Circle to understand what "the dark" meant to each of us. Ironically, the subject for that night's Wisdom Circle was "Planting New Seeds for the New Year."

Once people had arrived and the Circle was about to begin, I went into the bedroom and got Joy. She sat next to me in our living room and held my hand, uncharacteristically quiet the entire evening. After everyone else had contributed the subjects they wanted to explore in the coming year, Joy was asked to share. She declined, saying she was tired.

After our goodbyes were done and we had finally closed the door, I turned to Joy and we embraced as always, happy to be alone together once more. Holding her in my arms, I couldn't shake the awful irony that we'd "planted seeds" for the future without her because she wouldn't be here to harvest them.

The next morning I was surprised to find Joy upbeat. In her morning meditation, her guides had told her that "dying is a great adventure." Besides her sarcastic aside—"Another fucking adventure!"—she seemed buoyed by this guidance. She'd come to terms with dying in less than twenty-four hours. I, on the other hand, sank like a rock into the depths of despair.

ℰ 2 ℭ

The Promise

No longer having to hide my feelings did not make me feel better. I was so full of desperate and dark emotions I could barely speak. The "happy face" mask I'd hidden behind for the past year after my morning cry eluded me. For once I was thankful that Joy, in her blindness, couldn't see me. But I'm sure she could hear the sorrow in my voice. And, of course, my silence spoke volumes.

I'd been hiding from Joy, but also from myself. I hadn't realized how much comfort and refuge I'd taken in her hope and optimism. Now that she'd confronted and accepted her impending death, I had no place to hide.

Joy's children came by that Saturday and, as Terri and Elliot were told the news, my gloom only grew. Strangely, I wasn't crying in the shower anymore, but throughout the day I was tearing up and melting down at the slightest provocation. Anything and everything set me off.

The change in me was pretty obvious...even for a blind psychic. Joy's response? "We have to talk."

That was the *last* thing I wanted to do.

Joy wanted to know what I had gone through all those many months keeping such a terrible secret. And, more importantly — what was I feeling now?"

I told her, "I can't burden you with my feelings."

Her blue eyes filled with tears. "You have to."

I shook my head. "I *can't!*"

"If you don't, then I've already died. *We've* died. Our intimacy has ended. So I have to know."

"But—" I protested. *Now that she knows she's dying*, I thought, *how can I burden her with my anguish and grief?*

"I can handle it," she insisted as if reading my mind.

"I can't do it to you. For all these years I've loved you, taken care of you, protected you, tried to ease your journey, to hide my burdens and lighten yours."

"I know, sweetheart, and I don't know how I would have gone through it all without you. But I need to know. And you need to tell me."

"You won't want to hear what I have to say." The truth was *I* didn't want to hear myself say it. I'd cried for a year about the tragedy that was unfolding, but I'd never said it aloud, never given it the concreteness of words. I was afraid to give it voice and thus an even greater reality. And beyond that, I realized, there were two secrets, really. The one I knew about was her terminal condition. The one I didn't want to acknowledge was the unfathomable abyss of grief that awaited me.

"I have to hear it," she insisted. "Whatever it is. Please. For me. For us."

Our marvelous relationship had flourished in the face of some of life's greatest challenges—cancer and blindness— because it was based on intimacy and communication. I couldn't let it flounder now at the very end. She was right, so I promised to tell her everything.

The next day after breakfast we sat on the couch in our living room as we had thousands of times before. I looked around the room and took in the sky blue walls and sand-colored carpet, the marble tables, the pyramid-shaped mirror, the slabs of

Egyptian hieroglyphics on the wall, the side-by-side portraits of a pharaoh and his wife. Here I was with my dying Queen, faced with her one request—that I show her my darkest shadow. This was going to be one of the most difficult things I'd ever done. But for Joy I would have walked through fire.

I'd prepared a bottle of vodka and now poured myself a stiff drink. I'm not a drinker—an occasional vodka tonic or glass of red wine socially, and sometimes a beer with an infrequent pizza. But at ten in the morning I gulped the stuff down. It burned, but I needed help to act against my prime directive of protecting Joy, to override six years of vigilance, six years of care-giving since her diagnosis for breast cancer and macular degeneration.

I drank because I needed courage. I was afraid that what I was being asked to reveal—the truth of my grief—would be too much for her. Perhaps too much for me. But I had no choice—*not* revealing myself and my deepest, darkest truth would break her heart.

Downing more liquid courage, I began tentatively. I told her about my morning cries in the shower. I told her that I couldn't imagine life without her...that I didn't want to live without her...that our love was so fulfilling I could die happy. I choked up, I wept, I wailed.... Once the floodgates opened I couldn't hold back.

When we first met I'd confessed to Joy that my deepest desire was to be known. She had fulfilled that desire in ways I couldn't have imagined. Before we parted she would know it all

I stood and, in a delirium, shared all my fears. Tempests of grief swept me from one corner of the room to another. I was spun around like a tornado as I confessed.... *WE'D* been my life for the past six years. What would I do when WE DIED?!

I sat back down, caught my breath and took another drink. Then, like a cloudburst, I was wracked with sobs. Through my tears, I told her all the ways I loved her and all the ways I'd mourn her. And that I didn't think I could survive losing her. If our love was so great, how would I survive so great a loss? On my knees looking up at her, tears running down my cheeks, I told her that I felt like I was tied to a railroad track and a speeding train was bearing down on me and would tear me into a million pieces.

Joy listened intently in a way only she could. Her eyes watered, but she kept her composure. I wondered if she was protecting me so I wouldn't see what I feared most—that my anguished truth was too much for her to bear.

In the calm after the storm I tried to catch my breath. I stayed on the floor surrounded by a sea of used tissues, the debris of my tear-filled confession.

Finally, she broke the silence. "Thank you." She took my hand in both of hers and said, "I know you feel that your life will be destroyed without me. It won't. I've been there. I know. But there's no way you can know."

She'd lost many loved ones—two children, a beloved brother, both parents, husbands, friends. The only loved one I'd lost was my father two years earlier, at 92, and he'd been bedridden for several years, so his passing was a blessing. Joy had built up an emotional muscle that could handle loss. I was still a novice.

She began to weep. Distraught, I handed her a tissue.

She dried her eyes and collected herself. "If your life is destroyed by my death, then our love is a poison pill! If the price of our love was ultimately your life, then it's too great a price. We both know how wonderful our love and life together have been. Our love is a life-giver, not a life-taker. I don't want to destroy your life. I love you so much. Please promise me you'll make a new life. Promise me you'll believe there is a great purpose yet for you. And that a wonderful new love awaits you when you're ready. The legacy of our love can't be your destruction. You fear the unknown. But after all we've been through—the cancer, my blindness—it wasn't as bad as you might have feared."

"It was wonderful in spite of —"

"Maybe *because* of...."

She was right. We were always amazed at how facing cancer and blindness had deepened our love.

Yet I silently protested — *But we went through it together! We could go through anything together!*

I laid my head in her lap and whispered, "I don't want to live without you."

She stroked my head and then lifted my face so that I was looking up at her. "How can my soul move on with the karma of having destroyed your life? If you won't live for yourself, live for my sake. Live for me. Love for me. You've loved and protected me all these years. Don't stop after I'm gone. Promise me you won't grieve a second more than you absolutely have to. Promise me that the legacy of our love will be that you experience an even greater love and more joy. Promise me. Not for you. For *me*."

I looked up at her. Tears were streaming down both our faces. With my heart breaking I said weakly, "I promise." I would continue to take care of her even after she was gone.

She was so wise, leveraging my great love for her and redirecting it to me. She'd given me my next mission, my next adventure, my next quest: to love and care for myself the way I'd loved and cared for her. For her sake.

Like an infected boil that had been lanced, all my unspoken fears which had been festering inside me were released. In the days and weeks that followed my "promise," a feeling of peace and acceptance descended upon me.

Many months later, however, in the depths of my grief, when I wanted to give up, when I didn't want to live, when I didn't care anymore what happened to me, I remembered my promise to Joy and took the next step forward towards life and love — for *her*.

℘ 3 ℃

A Match Made in Heaven

⊢————————————————————⊣

On April 15, 2007, I stood before a crowd of over 200 mourners on a crisp spring Sunday in Los Angeles. My knees shook, my hands trembled, my heart pounded. My throat felt constricted, as though a hangman's noose was wrapped around my neck. To steady myself, I white-knuckled the podium as the seated mourners waited for me to give a eulogy for my beloved wife, Joy, who'd died a week earlier.

A brisk wind swept through the Pickwick Gardens and rattled the green canopy beneath which the memorial service was being held. There had already been several eulogies and musical performances from Terri and Elliot. My eulogy was to be the last.

One of Joy's last wishes was to throw a party. She planned every last detail of her "Celebration of Life" party—from the musical selections to the centerpieces to the menu for the "champagne brunch." She didn't believe death was an end but rather a "transition" to another plane of existence. Her experience had taught her that we were eternal souls who incarnate on earth to learn and grow. So she wanted those whom she left behind to treat her "death" as a "graduation." The invitations instructed, "Dress for joy, not for sorrow."

From the day of her transition on Good Friday, a week earlier, I was so busy with all the arrangements that the only

11

time I could find to write my eulogy was late in the evening. Though I wanted to give a eulogy, I wasn't sure I'd be able to. But when the time came, I looked out over the gathering of family and friends, and was buoyed by their love for us both. For that moment, love won out over grief.

> I know it's not usual for the spouse to speak at the memorial service. But I have to speak today, I have the rest of my life to cry. I've been the luckiest man in the world. Right now, and for the time being, I'm the saddest.
>
> Joy and I used to joke that I love to overdo things. According to her, my motto is: *"If it's worth doing, it's worth overdoing!"* And I'm going to over do it, so bear with me. I want to share our Love Story. And it begins with **my** blindness. Sometimes we can't see what's right in front of us.
>
> When I met Joy I was 49 and she was 68. That's right— a 19 year age difference. When I was born she was already *married*. I joined a spiritual group she was leading and for many months attended regularly. I liked the group, I liked her, but there was no inkling of anything romantic. Though a strikingly beautiful woman, she was from a different generation.
>
> When I learned that she was a renowned astrologer, I asked her for a reading. We made an appointment and I went to her home where she proceeded to look at my horoscope and tell me things about myself only I knew. At one point she told me that I was "about to fall in love...to find the love of my life...to love like I never had before...and to learn what love really is." Neither of us had any idea that it was *her*.
>
> I wrote her a check and was leaving...
>
> She'd told me earlier during the reading that she could see from my chart that I liked to dance. I told her I loved to dance. She told me she liked ballroom dancing. I said I'd like to learn someday.

...So I'm standing at the door saying goodbye when out of the blue she announces, "I'm going dancing tomorrow. Would you like to come?"

I was taken aback, but mumbled, "Sure."

The very next evening we're at this club taking a lesson in the mambo. Here's one of those synchronicities—I'd been humming an old tune all week called "*Besame Mucho.*" I'd heard it as a child in the '50's and couldn't get it out of my head. Joy and I must have danced well together because at the end of the lesson we were picked to demonstrate the steps. What song did we dance to? *Besame Mucho!*

Funny, but we didn't dance much that night. Instead, we talked. And the more Joy told me about her life, the more I realized she wasn't Doris Day. No, she was Madonna. She was much, **much** wilder than I'd imagined.

And so began a friendship.... I say "*friendship*" because there was no hint of a romantic connection. We talked occasionally on the phone. We had lunch. I liked being with her but I was still blinded by the age difference.

The turning point came weeks later. I showed her an article I'd written in a Tantra magazine. For those of you who aren't familiar with Tantra, it's the yoga of sex. An ancient spiritual tradition, Tantra harnesses sexual energy for spiritual purposes to expand consciousness.

Joy read my article and saw an ad for a Tantra workshop which she said she felt compelled to attend. As fate would have it, I was at this weekend workshop, too. Here she wasn't the group leader. And this was the first time I'd seen her dressed so informally in jeans. Looking back, one has to be impressed with the courage it took to attend a workshop where she was by far the oldest person. Throughout the weekend I had the opportunity to do exercises with her as well as all the other women. I was stunned—Joy's energy was extraordinary. She felt like the *youngest* woman there!

But the real parting of the veil came when I saw her feet. She was often barefoot and had high arched, perfectly manicured, beautiful feet. Throughout the weekend, I found my gaze drawn to her feet. You see, her toes were constantly moving, pawing the air, as if beckoning. There was something very sensual about it...and I began to see beyond our age difference. When I told her she had beautiful feet, she smiled and agreed. They were, she felt, her best feature. So we agreed about her feet and from then on almost everything else....

The workshop deepened our "friendship" and weeks later, when I told her "I love you," she said, "But I'm 19 years older." To which I replied, "So what."

We'd never even kissed.

When we finally did kiss...and consummate our love...I have to admit I was nervous...about what I'd find beneath her clothes. Yes, her feet were beautiful, but she was almost 69! I knew I loved her, I just hoped I'd be turned on.

Joy, on the contrary, was totally confident. She didn't dim the lights...or hide behind a negligee. She didn't try to cover any insecurity. She seemed totally confident. And I was amazed!

So let me get to it...enough foreplay. The first time we made love, she whispered in my ear, "Welcome Home!" And that's exactly how I felt in the depths of my soul. I'd come home!

She claimed that she'd *manifested* me. After her previous husband, Bob, died, he helped her from the Other Side find a new man in her life and gave her a 12 Step program to attract new love.

The first of the 12 Steps is *knowing what you want*. So Joy wrote a very short list with only three things on it. She wanted a man who danced, who was free to travel and…(this sounds better when she tells it)…who was good in bed.

We had four glorious, magical and carefree years. We danced, we traveled and we made lots of love. On her 70th birthday, I wrote Joy a card. We'd been together a little over a year. I'll quote a few lines to give you an idea of how happy we were.

> *"…Your 69th year was a fine year, an essential and sensual year, a mature and fruity year with more than a hint of abandon to titilate the most knowing palates.*
>
> *You are the youngest woman I've ever known, both the wisest and most innocent, the most playful and most sensual, the most spontaneous and yet the most prepared and organized woman on the planet."*

Joy had a magic purse. Anything you ever needed she could find in there. If you had a flat tire on the freeway, she could probably pull out a jack!

Just one more quote from that card I wrote to Joy:

> *"You told me once that you felt you were my Guardian Angel who'd loved me so much you incarnated into a human body so you could be with me physically. You must be an angel because when I'm with you, I'm in heaven."*

We were very happy. Unbelievably happy. Deliriously happy!

Since Joy had experienced several past lives already, I wasn't surprised when she told me that she'd had a vision of **our** past life thousands of years ago in the Middle East. She said I was the king and that the queen had been a political match and there was no love between us. Joy had been been my favorite at the court. She remembered planning great feasts and parties and celebrations for us and the court. A lot like in this life. But as a king, she said I was spoiled and didn't know how to love.

15

Joy had an effect on people like the sun has on plants—they blossomed in her radiance. She blessed them with her non-judgment. It wasn't that she was polite and hid her judgment. She looked for and therefore saw only the good. Everyone blossomed beneath her love and acceptance. Her son. Her daughter. Her friends. And, of course, me.

During the ten years we were together I don't remember her ever criticizing me. Not that I'm an angel. Far from it. Just ask some of our friends. And yet I found nothing to criticize about her. (Except maybe her fondness for the music of Yanni and Neil Diamond.) Everything about her delighted me. And after ten years I was just as much in love. But now I was in awe, too.

I want to read the last birthday card I wrote Joy three months ago.

> *Dear Joy,*
>
> *You are my:*
> - lover
> - healer
> - oracle
> - keeper
>
> *You are my:*
> - muse
> - midwife
> - editor extraordinaire
>
> *You are my:*
> - playmate
> - helpmate
> - angel so rare
>
> *You are my:*
> - doctor
> - daughter

- student
- teacher

You are my:

- beloved without compare

You are my:

- coach
- mentor
- admirer
- reward

You are my:

- joy ride
- theme song
- social director
- way to belong

You are my:

- winning lottery ticket
- dream come true
- my joy
- my prize
- my one and only you

Joy taught me the greatest lesson of all—*How to Love! How much I could Love!!* Her prediction 10 years earlier that I would meet the love of my life and learn what love really was came true. She blessed me with a love so fulfilling that it's not a once in a lifetime love, it's once in a thousand lifetimes. She was the Joy in my life...and despite the depths of grief I haven't even begun to feel...I was blessed to share a portion of my life with her.

I don't want to only sing Joy's praises as a wife and lover. I also want to tell you that we had a Great Being in our midst. She wasn't clothed in robes and didn't retreat to a mountain ashram with a following to start a new religion. She was cloaked by her beauty, her modesty, her kindness. She came

19

to us in the form of an elegant woman, a wonderful mother, a dream wife and a best friend. But she was more.... As her stepson, Bruce Lisker, said—she was a GREAT ONE.

There's a tradition among Jews that you can tell who's a *Tzaddik* or Righteous Individual because they often die on a holiday. When Joy passed over it was Passover...*and* Easter. That's like Double Jeopardy or triple-word score in Scrabble. But *noon* on Good Friday, too!

And lastly there's her feet. Even as she lay on her deathbed, her feet were beautiful. No calluses, no blemishes, no sign of the wear and tear of her 79 years walking upon this earth. Those of us who were with her at the end marveled that her feet looked as if they'd never touched the ground. Indeed, they were the feet of an angel.

Joy had a recurring dream of flying...actually *dancing* in the sky. She *loved* that dream! She was a sky-dancer! In the great Eastern spiritual traditions, there are celestial beings called "skydancers." Here in the West we call them "angels."

On Wednesday morning, two days before she transitioned, Joy awoke and told me she wanted to write a poem that she had in her head. I gave her a pad, propped her up in bed and in a few minutes she was done. She titled it *"Opening to Joy"* and asked me to read it to you today. Many people have asked Joy to communicate with them from the Other Side, to give them guidance, to be *their* guide. Joy intends to continue her mission of teaching and extends this invitation to you.

"<u>Opening to Joy</u>"

I have not left you,
I did not die.
I will speak to you in the sacred silences
Of your days and nights.

Listen for my voice
And trust what you hear.
Ask your questions and I will tell you the Truth.

I look forward to sharing
All the wisdom I will be learning
From the Other Side.

So Open To Joy and let it fill
Every moment of your life.

My eulogy finished, I hung on to the podium for dear life. I blew a kiss toward the painting of Joy that stood on an easel, then, dazed, staggered from the stage. On shaky legs I stumbled down the stairs and was immediately swept up into a sea of hugs. Tossed from one set of arms into another. Rolling on the waves of this ocean of love. And sympathy. And grief.

The rest was a blur.

In hindsight I don't know how I could have given such a lengthy eulogy. I'm a pretty emotional guy. I wasn't able to get through my marriage vows without repeatedly choking up. Yet somehow I stood before all these people and spoke for nearly half an hour, inspired by our love and life together, and by Joy's glorious Good Friday transition. This was not the time to allow my loss and personal grief to silence me. Rather it was the moment to announce the "good news" that a Great Love had blossomed for a time and that a Great Being who'd walked among us had passed on. I'd have the rest of my life to grieve.

After the formal service in the gardens, the guests made their way to a banquet hall for the champagne brunch that followed. There were more live performances, slideshows and even a hilarious clip from Joy's '70's TV show in which she spoofed astrology by telling viewers "what's *wrong* with your sign."

By the time desserts were served, I'd received hundreds of hugs accompanied by words of condolence. To my surprise, *I* wound up comforting many of our grief-stricken friends. Other people cried—I didn't. Not yet. I was still in an exalted state from having witnessed Joy's grace-filled exit.

And then a strange thing happened—I became punch drunk on so much sympathy. With each hug I began to feel as if I was being injected with *everyone else's* grief. I reached a point when I couldn't receive another condolence. No more grief-stricken hugs. I had to get away.

Across the banquet hall in front of the stage I noticed my granddaughter, Natalie, playing as only a two-and-a-half year old can. She was totally captivated blowing bubbles. I excused myself from the line of mourners and sat down with her on the empty stage, hoping to find some refuge in her innocent play.

At her request I blew bubbles, grateful for a respite from the torrent of condolences, grateful to escape for even a few moments from my awful adult reality into her carefree child's world. I blew stream after stream of bubbles into the air. Her face lit up with wonder. "Bubbles!" she exclaimed, as if I'd performed some miracle, like raising the dead. Her gaze, fascinated by the rainbow-flecked bubbles floating in the air, suddenly fixed on Joy's portrait resting on an easel on the stage. Pointing up at it, she smiled and said sweetly, "Nana!"

That's when I fell apart.

℘ 4 ℘

The Elephant in the Room

Alone at home later that day I wandered from room to flower-filled room, but couldn't escape the gloom. I was overwhelmed by the perverse irony that I was surrounded with so much beauty, yet filled with so much sorrow. Rather than appease my suffering, the stunning floral arrangements seemed to mock me — their beauty accentuating the loss they were meant to console.

Exhausted, I soon found myself lying in bed, fully dressed with the curtains drawn. Joy's portrait, which I'd brought home from the service, now leaned against the bureau. It was large — more than 2' x 3' — and when I walked in, without thinking, I'd propped it up against the bureau that lined one bedroom wall. Now it stared back at me.

The larger-than-life-size portrait, which the artist had brought as a surprise to the memorial, captured Joy's timeless beauty, but he outdid himself painting her radiant blue eyes. I found myself fixated by those eyes as I descended into a grief-fueled delirium remembering the way we were.

I'd surface from these daydreams to get a glass of water or drop off into a fitful sleep. Then I'd wake with a start, sit up in bed only to confront Joy's portrait. As day turned into night, her portrait became the touchstone for my time-travels, her unblinking gaze transporting me into the past. And when I returned from the joyful memory, her piercing gaze welcomed me back to my joyless present.

As the evening (or was it night) wore on, Joy's portrait seemed to grow larger, as her persistent, penetrating gaze raised the question I was afraid to ask. The portrait's "provenance" (the story of its making) involved a "contact from Joy," and so it became the elephant in the room—its very existence begged the question: Would Joy contact *me*?

At the memorial service, the artist had told me how Joy had inspired him. "I hadn't painted in years," he said. "But I felt compelled to put my gift to work for her memorial service. I had only one week and the first five days were horrible. When I woke up on the fifth day and viewed my work, I was mortified. So I called a buddy and asked him to meet me at a local hangout for happy hour. I was depressed—there was no way I was going to finish the surprise portrait in time. Suddenly, a Tina Turner song began to play and I started to bebop to it. Then I heard Joy—*There ya go! I want you dancing and singing in front of the canvas. Get rid of all of that maudlin crap you've been listening to and celebrate.* I almost dropped my drink. I went home and changed all of the heavy music *and* my attitude and completed the painting in a really short time. It's miraculous, but Joy gave me back my mojo."

That's Joy! I thought, *continuing to guide and counsel people even from the Other Side.* And that wasn't the first "contact" either.

Easter morning, less than forty-eight hours after Joy's passing, I was showering when I thought I heard Joy's voice in my mind say, *"Dress for Joy. Not for Sorrow,"* in reference to the Celebration of Life memorial service we were planning for the following Sunday. But I immediately questioned it. I knew Joy's feelings about "mourning." Maybe this was my way of reminding myself to include a note in the invitation for people to dress for a party, not a funeral.

After I got dressed, I noticed the red light flashing on my answering machine. It was our therapist. *How strange,* I thought.

Though we'd known her for many years, we'd never socialized. So I wasn't prepared for a phone message in which she said matter-of-factly, without a trace of irony, that as she lay in bed on that Easter morning, listening to the birds outside her bedroom window, she heard a voice say, *"And on the third day she rose..."*

Later that Easter Sunday I attended a family brunch Terri hosted. Despite our grief, we gathered together for the sake of Terri's daughter, Natalie, so she could experience her first Easter egg hunt, which Joy, over the years, had made a family tradition.

During the meal I shared my shower "message" so we could incorporate *"Dress for Joy. Not for Sorrow"* in the invitations that were going out on Monday. Jackie, Joy's best friend, shocked me when she said, "I got the same message." Maybe I wasn't imagining it after all.

A week later, alone in my bedroom, Joy's portrait confronted me with the "fact" that she was communicating with people from the Other Side. I knew three individuals—the artist, the therapist and Joy's best friend—who claimed to have had contact. I didn't include myself. Not yet. I needed something more dramatic, something irrefutable.

At the memorial service, mourners were invited to take a JoyStone—one of the hundreds of blue agate stones Joy had prepared in a brass bowl—to help them focus their attention and quiet their mind, so they could hear her voice in the "sacred silences." Everyone took a JoyStone but me. I didn't need one. Joy was everywhere—etched in my heart, emblazoned on my psyche, branded in my soul.

I'd given her a gold anklet for our first Valentine's Day engraved with the words *Joy & Jerry* on the outside and *Ecstasy* on the inside. In the ten years we were together she never took it off. Now I wore the anklet as a bracelet on my left wrist. Besides the sentimental reason, the anklet was filled with Joy's energy and I hoped it might act as an antenna for contact from the Other Side.

In my pocket I carried Joy's custom-made brass pendulum, which I called "Dr. P," with which she used to answer people's questions during psychic readings. I looked at her pictures, touched her clothing, sniffed her jewelry to revel in her scent. I had all kinds of relics: her toothbrush, her lipstick, her love notes. Our home was filled with things Joy loved. Our bedroom displayed couples in loving embrace—porcelain swans, wooden Balinese dancers, pewter dolphins—that mirrored our love. Relics of Joy? I was drowning in them!

I reached for the memorial service program on the night table. The insert with Joy's poem fell out. I re-read it, but now certain lines seemed to shout at me.

I have not left you,
I did not die.
I will speak to you in the sacred silences
Of your days and nights.
Listen for my voice
And trust what you hear....

She'd offered to be everyone's spirit guide. But what about me? *Will she speak to me?* I wondered. *Will I trust what I hear?*

ℰ 5 ℂ

A River Runs Through Me

As busy as I was before the memorial service, the Monday after was quiet—the calm *after* the storm. I was no longer producing the Celebration of Life party. And I was lost. I went through the motions of living—I showered, dressed and fed myself—but I was in shock, walking between worlds.

Just going through the motions, I did a load of wash. As usual I took the clothing out of the dryer and dumped it on the bed for sorting. I'd done this for years because of Joy's blindness. I was separating out Joy's socks and underwear when suddenly I froze. *What the hell am I doing? Folding her pajamas? Sorting her socks?* I couldn't bear to answer the question. *I can't deal with it now!* I thought. So I continued to fold her clothes and put them away in her drawers. For now, simply "going through the motions" was comforting.

By the afternoon I was lying in bed again communing with Joy's portrait. I was confronted once again with the nagging question—*Was Joy going to communicate with me? Would I receive messages the way she'd received messages from her late husband Bob?*

I remembered Joy describing in her memoir how Bob first spoke to her from the Other Side. For the 72nd time in four years, he was rushed to the Emergency Room because of emphysema. As usual, Joy got into her car to follow the ambulance. "As I slid behind the wheel and started the engine," she wrote, "I began to feel a strange energy around me, as though I wasn't alone. At that moment I heard a voice saying, *I figured I could help you more from over here than from there.* Instinctively, I turned to see if someone was in the backseat, but I was alone." At the hospital Joy learned that Bob had died in the ambulance.

In *Love Ever After*, Joy chronicled her almost daily conversations with Bob after he died. At her many book signings, talks and radio appearances, the most frequently asked question was how to contact loved ones on the Other Side. Joy's answer was that "believing it's possible is the first step." One's belief primes the pump. If you don't believe it's possible, then it's much more *unlikely* that you'll be receptive to communication from the Other Side.

Though I'd never experienced it, I believed it was possible. But I wasn't sure it was possible for *me*. Hearing about other people's contacts with Joy gave me hope, but also put pressure on me. And, to be totally honest, it elicited a tinge of envy, a touch of jealousy. *Why them and not me?*

For the ten years we were together, Joy's ongoing communication with Bob was a part of our lives. Since neither of us smoked, the faint smell of cigarettes in our home would signal Bob's presence. Joy would sit down, close her eyes and go within to listen for a message. After a few moments, a knowing smile would spread across her face. Then she'd tell me what Bob had told her.

Joy told our friends that the scent of gardenias—one of her favorite flowers—would be a sign of her presence. I sniffed around. No gardenias. Then I had an idea. I found Joy's favorite perfume—Opium—and sprayed it into the air. Closing my eyes I walked through the cloud of perfume hoping to hear her voice. I inhaled the fragrance, *her* fragrance, hoping for some vision, some communication. Instead I was bombarded with memories of our life together.

As if in an opium dream I laid down on the bed, grabbed her satin-covered pillow and hugged it like a child hugs a teddy bear. And I began to remember…and weep…eventually crying myself to sleep.

The phone rang a lot. Except to talk with the immediate family who checked in on me daily, I didn't answer. Everyone left loving messages. I just couldn't talk to them. I didn't want to answer the same question a hundred times—*How are you doing?* To those few I did speak to, I replied, "Okay, I guess." What could I say? Especially since I didn't really know myself.

By Tuesday I had to get out of the house. I decided to drive to the mortuary in Burbank, a half hour away, to pick up Joy's ashes. I went alone. Neither I nor Joy's children had any attachment to her ashes. No one intended on keeping them in a special urn to be put on display.

When hospice sent a social worker over to see what sort of funeral arrangements Joy wanted, Joy told her she wanted to be cremated. The social worker consulted her files and informed us there were several mortuaries to choose from. Acme Mortuary cost $600. A Better Way Mortuary cost $900. *Why?* we asked. *No difference really*, she replied. Joy wondered if it was because of the name. The social worker was about to give us a third option when Joy waved her away. "Acme is fine," she said. "Just burn me and let's have a party."

At the mortuary I was handed a shoe box–sized carton wrapped in brown paper with a label that read "the cremated remains of Joy Mitchell." I felt nothing. It was surprisingly heavy. After signing some papers I got in the car and put the ashes on the seat next to me, where Joy always sat.

As I drove home with Joy's ashes riding shotgun, I found myself talking to her as if she were sitting beside me in the car. I wanted to have a conversation. I waited. And waited. *Don't be a jerk*, I scolded myself. *She's not in the ashes!*

At home I didn't know what to do with her ashes—I hadn't thought that far ahead—so I put the box on the floor in the bedroom in front of her portrait.

It was dark outside when I woke up from a nap. I checked the clock—nearly 8 p.m. I didn't feel well. A slight nausea, like seasickness. Stomach cramps got me out of bed. I hurried to the bathroom. Diarrhea. I made several trips to the bathroom that evening before realizing I had a severe case of the runs. It got worse—so bad, in fact, that sometime after midnight I got in my car in an attempt to find an all-night pharmacy where I could score some Kaopectate.

Mission accomplished, I downed the mint-flavored stuff. It didn't work. I had the runs the next day, too, and seemed to get worse in the evening. I was barely eating and yet fluid clear as water was gushing out of me. I'd finished the entire bottle of Kaopectate but it didn't help. I didn't know what to do.

Friends brought over food I couldn't eat and homeopathic remedies that didn't work. I grew weaker, too weak to do much or even think much. I laid around the house—listless, lightheaded, in a twilight zone. By Saturday morning I was worried. I calculated that since Tuesday—the day I'd picked up Joy's ashes—I'd had severe diarrhea for almost five straight days. Years ago I'd lived in the Middle East and tangled with dysentery, but I'd never experienced anything like this. I googled "diarrhea" and learned that after three days it can be dangerous due to dehydration. I considered taking myself to the emergency room, but since I'd been in hospitals so often with Joy, the idea of going to one now filled me with dread.

In desperation I asked Joy for help. That's when I noticed my desk calendar and that I had a doctor's appointment on Monday. It had been made months ago, when Joy was still alive. By Sunday morning I was somewhat better and I decided to wait until Monday to see a doctor.

On Monday morning, despite being lightheaded, I managed to drive to the doctor's office. After examining me he said I was "a pint low" and gave me an IV drip of minerals and electrolytes to replenish what I'd lost. For an hour I sat in a room with other patients who were receiving IV cocktails for various health reasons. The drip in my arm reminded me of all the times I'd sat with Joy when she was the one getting the IV.

From the easy conversation between some of the patients I could tell they were regulars. At one point they turned to me and introduced themselves.

I was dazed and my disorientation wasn't solely due to being "a pint low." This was the first time I'd been outside since picking up Joy's ashes nearly a week ago, and my first introduction to strangers since Joy's memorial.

When I introduced myself to these well-meaning, IV-ing strangers, I did so with these four words—"I lost my wife."

I was stunned by my own words. Not only had I lost my wife, I'd lost my identity. With those words, I'd proclaimed my new one. No name, just pure archetype—*widower*.

As my minerals and electrolytes were replaced, I realized that I wasn't in the same place I'd been when I'd sat before Joy's portrait, sniffed clouds of her perfume, picked up her ashes and was swept away by seven days of the runs. I'd survived a flood. My life had been washed away, destroyed by a tsunami. I'd been literally "swept away" by a river of sorrow. The river that ran through me all week swept away everything about my life with Joy. Like some biblical flood, it had destroyed my world.

And now that the rains finally stopped and the flood waters receded, I found myself shipwrecked, thrown up onto dry land. In a new world. Homeless. A refugee.

The moment I introduced myself as man without a name, I realized I *was* someone else, and I'd arrived somewhere else, too. I'd been transported to a place I began to call "Planet Grief."

℘ 6 ℰ

Planet Grief

They talk about the *fog of war*. There's also a *fog of grief*. I began to compulsively jot down thoughts so as not to forget.

> In the weeks preceding Joy's death, I saw myself tied to railroad tracks as on oncoming train bore down on me. As it turned out, the metaphor of a train wreck wasn't accurate. A more apt metaphor was a flood, a *tsunami* that washed everything away. *Tossed on turbulent seas of sorrow, I'm wracked by relentless waves of grief.*

Like a captain's log, I recorded the rocky coastline, the pounding surf and the dangerous currents of my new uncharted journey on the Sea of Sorrow.

> I've begun to keep a journal to help me navigate these rough seas. A journal helps mute the awful loneliness. With Joy I felt so TOGETHER. Now I feel so ALONE. I'm shipwrecked. A castaway talking to my journal—like Tom Hanks talking to his soccer ball "Wilson"—in a desperate attempt to save my sanity.

Journaling was an instinctive effort to grab and burn as many memories into my psyche as possible. Above all, it was a way to not let Joy go. Journaling was a way to still be with her. In those awful first weeks, I wrote these entries:

> During the Easter brunch at Terri's, I instinctively reached for Joy to guide her through the buffet and help fill her plate with food as I'd done for the past 6 years of her blindness. Realizing she wasn't there anymore and that I was free to go through the buffet line alone nearly brought me to my knees.
>
> I feel like a child that's fallen down or awoken from a terrifying nightmare. All I want is to be held and comforted. My very cells are crying out—"*Hold me!*"
>
> *What's it like to be without Joy?*
> I'm lost....
> I died...and yet I walk around...I feel like a zombie.
> I'm heavy...leaden...everything has dimmed.
> I'm raw...vulnerable...fragile....
> I've lost my witness. I'm ALONE!
> I'm so empty...so sad...so dead....
> I'm a ghost in my life.

Like the character in the movie *The Sixth Sense*, I'd died but didn't know it. Certainly a part of me had "died," though my body walked around going through the motions of "living." But as the days wore on, the enormity of what had happened caught up with me.

I had trouble sleeping. It was so strange to sleep alone and not wrap my arms around Joy. Though I was constantly exhausted, I had to take pills to get some sleep. Meanwhile, my waking life took on the quality of a dream. Every morning I'd wake up to the nightmare of my Joy-less day, wishing I was dreaming.

I went to lunch with Terri and we compared notes. She lost not only her mother, but her "hero." Terri told me she was doing better than she expected, thanks to Natalie. Besides her musical career, her daughter was the light of her life and gave her a reason to live.

I wept as I told her how my grief wasn't easing, but rather increasing. Every day I discovered new ways I missed Joy.

I told Terri that I was now living on Planet Grief, where the gravity is ten times that of Earth. I felt denser, heavier, and moved more slowly. Everyone else—the people on Earth—were lighter, quicker to smile and laugh. Living on Planet Grief was exhausting.

"Are you afraid?" Terri asked, fixing me with her blue eyes that so reminded me of Joy's.

"Yes," I told her, "I'm afraid of the silence, afraid of losing my self."

She placed her hand gently over mine. We looked at each other with eyes brimming with tears. She's lost her mother, I've lost my life.

Food was difficult in the beginning.

Shopping for food was something Joy and I did together because of her blindness. So shopping alone was a painful reminder that she was gone. The first few times I was greeted at the checkout by a cheery clerk's, "How's your day going?" I couldn't even respond. After a week or two I finally managed to mutter, "My wife just passed." It would be several weeks before I could answer the perfunctory query about my day with a feeble "Okay."

At first I shopped as we had before, partly out of habit and, quite honestly, partly out of a desire not to have to come back soon to shop again. It was just too painful. But shopping for two resulted in throwing out a lot of food. Gradually, I learned to shop for one.

Then one day while shopping at the supermarket I had a revelation. In the checkout line I noticed how "dead" I felt compared to how I felt with Joy. The difference? I'd be kissing her cheek, stroking her back, joking, talking, *loving* her. And that made all the difference. I was too busy loving her to notice that we were standing in line or waiting in a doctor's office or anything else...even dying of cancer. Loving Joy made all the difference.

We were blessed in many ways, one of which was to live next to a recreation area of parks, tennis courts, playgrounds, a golf course and a man-made lake. Lake Balboa was literally right around the corner. Almost every day Joy and I walked its mile and a half perimeter and watched ducks waddle, geese fly in formation, pelicans float regally, and snowy egrets balance on tree branches while blue herons stood on one leg at the water's edge. For a few weeks in early spring the cherry blossoms that surrounded Lake Balboa created a fantasy world of pink enchantment.

Sometimes we'd walk the lake in the morning, sometimes during twilight. Joy would always begin walking with a brisk pace and I'd begin by strolling and have to ask her to slow down. Gradually I'd speed up so that at a certain point she'd ask *me* to slow down. Most of the time we'd hold hands. During these walks we'd share our dreams of the night before or inspirations from our morning meditations. We'd catch each other up on our conversations with friends and family and prioritize which of their "problems" needed our attention. As we'd feed the ducks we'd brainstorm ideas for our many creative projects and often come up with topics for our monthly Wisdom Circle. We'd people watch, sing songs and picnic. And we'd laugh, tickling each other's funny bone in ways only intimate lovers can.

We'd sit on a bench, hugging and kissing like teenagers. Or we'd sit on a hill overlooking the water and share our soul's deepest longings. In spring we'd sit on benches shaded by wooden trellises covered with wisteria vines whose purple blossoms were so fragrant they were literally intoxicating. The lake was a part of our day, a part of our life, our garden, our backyard. We'd walk, we'd sit, we'd talk, we'd kiss. We'd lie in each other's laps and even take naps.

> I walked around the lake and cried. I sat on a bench and realized that I've lost my purpose. With Joy I had a powerful purpose: to save her, to love her, to take care of her. Now I've lost that purpose. Now I have to save, love and take care of *me*. But I haven't the strength, nor the will.

• • • •

I discovered that you can't dance on Planet Grief.

Joy and I loved to dance. She was a ballroom dancer who had two pairs of custom-made dance shoes, the kind pros wear so she could dance all night. Since she grew up in the Swing Era, she was used to being led. As part of the Rock & Roll generation, I danced primarily alone. So we took dance lessons—I learned ballroom so I could lead, and Joy studied belly dance to learn to dance alone. We danced at parties, clubs and rock concerts. Even at home. If the right song played on the radio while we prepared a meal, I'd sweep her into my arms and we'd dance in the kitchen. We danced in the living room and, of course, in the bedroom.

After Joy's mastectomy we went dancing as soon as we could because her post-surgical pain disappeared while she danced. To celebrate Joy's recovery from her mastectomy, we rented a dance floor and hosted a Valentine's Day party. Dancing was how we celebrated life.

On the day Joy went to the hospital for her weekly chemotherapy, we went dancing in the evening. Dance Home was a dance studio where people came to do their thing— freestyle. For Joy, dancing on those chemo days was about Life giving Death the finger.

At the urging of some friends I went to Dance Home. It was very hard to be there without Joy. I wept as I danced. It was hard to dance on Planet Grief. I felt so heavy. And though I appeared normal, I was anything but. People on Earth were partying, but I couldn't join the party. I realized that when I was home alone,

I missed Joy. But when I was out among people, like at Dance Home, I missed myself.

Someone at Dance Home mentioned there was a grief formula for the loss of a spouse—for every year of being together there would be a month of intense grief. That put me at about a *year*!

As I drove home, I wondered when, if ever, I could return to Dance Home. I even wondered if I would ever dance again.

• • • •

If finding a soulmate is like winning the lottery or finding the pot of gold at the end of the rainbow, then losing a soulmate is indescribable agony, unbearable pain. Joy had always said we were greater together than apart, like the two wings of a greater being she called the JoyousOne. Individually we were good but earthbound. Together, the JoyousOne *soared*!

Life with Joy healed me. My imperfections, flaws, weaknesses, shadows, shames and inadequacies were healed by our love. I came to see the *perfection* of my imperfections, and any last shred of "not being enough" was transformed into "*more* than enough."

Living without Joy, I was the JoyousOne no more. Like the mythological Greek figure Icarus who'd flown too close to the sun, I was falling...falling...falling back to earth. As I fell, all my old doubts, fears and not-being-enough's rose up to meet me. *Will I mourn well enough? Will I be able to keep my promise to Joy? To live again? To love again?*

Ironically, the last six years of caring for Joy were both her ultimate gift to me and my ultimate healing because I was tested in so many ways. Now, living without Joy, would be my final exam. I would find out what I was really made of.

I was in free-fall....

In the same way Joy had filled up my life these past ten years, especially the past six, now her loss rushed in to fill the vacuum. The blessing of the freedom from worldly obligations that Joy and I had enjoyed now turned out to be a curse. I didn't have a career to go back to or work to distract me. I was free and totally at the mercy of my grief

In my journal I wrote: "It's only been a few weeks and there's no understanding...just enduring. My loss can't be put into words. Indescribable! It's HUGE! I'm constantly measuring my grief. Each time it's larger. Compared to my grief, my identity is small. And yet.... I know...hope I will recover. People say Time heals all wounds. For now Time unfolds it rather than heals it."

My grief was compounded by my lack of contact with Joy. I tried rereading her book, hoping to find inspiration. "According to Bob," she wrote, "it's not difficult to connect with someone when love is present on both sides, since emotions are the bridge between dimensions."

There was no lack of emotion. Perhaps the problem was trust. Joy wrote about the importance of trust. "The fact that I already trusted the process was an enormous help in opening me to receive Bob's messages. Without personal experience, you can't really *know* that this kind of connection is possible, but your *belief* in the possibility will go a long way in allowing it to happen."

Instead of finding inspiration from Joy's book, the ease with which she communicated with Bob only stoked my feelings of failure. I was already *wild with grief,* and my failure to communicate with Joy was rubbing salt into the wound.

I was at my lowest point when I received an invitation that would change everything.

℘ 7 ℭ

Opening To Joy

Over the years Joy and I had created a wonderful community of kindred spirits. Our friends were there for us during Joy's illness and were there for me after she was gone. Now I was in seclusion, but even so, word got out that I wasn't doing well. I was informed that I'd be visited by a group of friends on Friday afternoon for some emergency TLC. I protested that I wasn't up to a social visit, but was told I had no choice.

I dreaded Friday's intervention. Yet I was aware that Friday was exactly thirty days since Joy's passing. In the Jewish tradition, the thirty-day mark is a significant milestone for the mourner. I wondered if it would be significant for me.

As Friday approached I recalled how I'd been surprised a year earlier when one day the phone rang—Genevieve was downstairs waiting to be buzzed in. Joy feigned ignorance but she knew what was about to happen. To my surprise, in marched a dozen friends carrying bags of food and wine. Genevieve unrolled a parchment and formally read a proclamation with all the requisite "Hear Ye, Hear Ye's" announcing that, in recognition of his selfless service to Queen Joy, it was officially King Jerry Day.

I was completely taken aback. Food was set out and drinks poured. I was presented with several gifts, one of which was a t-shirt on which was printed an original design for a coat of arms that read, "King Jerry, the Beneficent." For the next several hours I was literally waited on hand and foot. While one friend gave me a manicure, another gave me a foot massage and someone else gently massaged my scalp and ears. This pampering not only soothed my body, it touched my heart. I'd been caring for Joy for years. Receiving our friends' tender care moved me to tears.

On Friday afternoon my home was once again overrun by friends. They brought food, which they fed me, and songs, which they sang to me. I was cared for and pampered, sung to and entertained. I was toasted and lavished with gifts. But the highpoint of the evening was yet to come. It had been decided that in honor of her poem, we'd all "open to Joy" in a group meditation, then share whatever guidance we received.

We closed our eyes, went within and invited Joy to speak to us in "the sacred silence."

I didn't expect to hear anything. I'd tried so many times in the past few weeks and had been so disappointed that I'd just about given up. Buoyed by my friends, I figured I'd try one last time. So I offered up a silent prayer. "I'm desperate, Sweetheart. I'm drowning. I'm lost. Please help me! What can I do to heal this unbearable grief?"

I waited and listened.

And then I heard a voice. From deep within I heard the words *Fill your life with joy!*

I was elated—it was Joy! Immediately I understood why I hadn't been able to communicate with her before this—I couldn't hear her over the roar of my grief. Basking as I had for the past few hours in the love of my friends had been so uplifting it had literally raised my vibration so that I could hear Joy.

There was more to her guidance which I wrote down immediately after the meditation. *"Don't expect to have a plan,"* I heard her say. *"Whatever you come up with can't match what's unfolding. Trust in the process and move towards joy. Be patient. You must crawl first."*

Of course! Without Joy, I had to fill my life with different *kinds* of joy.

Easier said than done.

In an attempt to "fill my life with joy," I attended the performance of a Native American drum team at the Onion, a dome-like structure that was a favorite venue for spiritual events. I'd belonged to this drum team many years earlier and had been moved by the chants we sang as we sat around a large drum and in unison beat out the hypnotic, heartbeat-like rhythms. It had been many years since I'd heard the drum team perform and, since I knew several of its members, I looked forward to it.

The drum team's purpose is to inspire people to dance, and normally I would have been the first to get up and dance around the drum. But I felt too heavy to move. Other people got up and danced while I sat there. Soon everyone was dancing but me. Finally, someone took me by the hand and pulled me onto my feet. I was literally forced to dance. That had never happened to me. This was another sign how depressed and depleted I was. A stranger to myself.

I left soon as I could. I'd tried to "fill my life with joy" but was more miserable than when I'd arrived. Driving home, I wondered if I'd misunderstood what Joy had said. Or worse still, maybe I'd imagined it all.

A few days later I tried again to "fill my life with joy" by going to a rock concert that Terri and her band, Berlin, were headlining. She was performing in front of several thousand people at the annual Gay Pride Festival in a park in West Hollywood. When she strode onto the stage the crowd went wild. This was the first time I watched Terri perform without Joy by my side.

I stood alone in the crowd with tears running down my cheeks as Terri spoke about losing her mother. She dedicated her Oscar-winning song, "Take My Breath Away," to Joy. As usual, when performing this anthem of love, one of the biggest hits of the 80's, she stepped off the stage onto her husband Paul's shoulders and rode through the audience while singing her signature song. It's always a magical moment as she appears to float above the crowd, hovering like an angel, as her fans reach up to her. Holding her mike in one hand, she'd reach out with the other to touch their outstretched hands as she floated by.

Above the darkened sea of captivated fans with only a spotlight on her, Terri sang her heart out. She wove her way through the crowd of thousands and somehow came right up to me. I was stunned—neither she nor Paul knew where I was in that large crowd. She was shocked, too. As she sang, she reached down and took my hand. It was...*miraculous*. This had to be a sign from Joy.

೮) 8 ೮೩

A Mantra from Joy

More than anything I wanted to experience another contact from Joy. She'd promised to meet me "in the sacred silences." And if I was going to "meet" her, I'd have to raise my vibration. I had to "lighten up."

Joy's guides had given her a simple yet powerful philosophy of life. She called it *"The 5 Ls"—Live, Laugh, Love, Learn & Lighten Up. Live your dreams. Laugh and have fun. Love with all your heart. Learn from your life. And for God's sake, lighten up!"*

Yoga and meditation would help me lighten up. They always did. I had done some version of a morning spiritual practice—consisting of tai chi, yoga and meditation—since my twenties. My practice began to collapse when I discovered Joy was terminal. I hadn't had a consistent morning practice in over a year. I rededicated myself to my yoga practice.

I usually meditated in my office after yoga since it was my spiritual as well as creative sanctuary. Besides an L-shaped desk with computer and phone, there was a comfortable recliner where I read and often napped. The walls were lined with bookshelves and art objects. It was an eclectic mix—a Native American dreamcatcher (a birthday gift from Joy) hung from the ceiling, while Tibetan tangkas and Hindu mandalas— art used for meditation—shared a wall with African masks and tribal rattles. On top of a double filing cabinet I'd created an altar to nature—seashells, feathers, pine cones, corals and crystals. On a bulletin board a bumper sticker read, *LOVE is our soul purpose.*

After a gentle yoga workout I did some *pranayama*—breath work in preparation for meditation. And as I sat in the sacred silence, I began to feel Joy's presence. I was stunned, too stunned to ask a question. But my concerns must have permeated my being: *Was I doing the right thing? Was I on the right path?*

"*Trust your process,*" were the words I heard. My heart leapt! This was confirmation that Joy would meet me in the sacred silence of meditation. I fervently hoped this was just the beginning of our communication, that as I *lightened up*, I'd experience a greater and greater connection with her.

Yes and *No*, like the gas pedal and brake, are the two main levers with which we navigate our life journey. Joy and I used to joke that one of the reasons I came into her life was to teach her how to say "No." How ironic then that her leaving my life would teach me how to say "Yes."

Inspired by the "sign" I'd received at Terri's concert, I devoted myself to yoga and meditation with a renewed intensity. During one morning meditation, as I sat eyes closed on the oriental rug in my office, I asked Joy for guidance. I waited and listened. Silence. Then a string of words appeared in my mind, *Yes... I can... Now...*

I was flabbergasted.

Then I began to laugh.

When Joy was first diagnosed with breast cancer, she wanted to understand the emotional, psychological and even metaphysical significance of her *dis-ease*. She believed that "illness" wasn't entirely a physical phenomenon, but had emotional and even spiritual causes as well. We came across some research which suggested that, from a metaphysical perspective, breast cancer was often the "price of nice."

Women who were inveterate "pleasers" and always saying "Yes" continually fed others emotionally and energetically. The nurturing was one way. Such an imbalance created a weakness in the energy body, which could cause the breast—the symbol of nurture—to be vulnerable to disease.

Joy was constantly in demand—from family, friends, clients. As an astrologer she could help people navigate the stormy seas of life by predicting the potentials of their future. As a counselor she could guide them in negotiating their love lives. If they were depressed and needed a pep talk, she had just the right words to make them feel better. If they needed an apartment, she could effortlessly find them one. Since she was consistently happy, just being in her presence made people feel better. So her phone rang incessantly with requests for her time and attention.

When we learned about the "price of nice," I playfully suggested a remedy to help Joy deal metaphysically with her breast cancer. It was a three-part mantra or declaration. The first part was "No."

Over the years, Joy had observed how her clients unconsciously created illnesses for a variety of reasons: so they wouldn't have to work, so they could control the family dynamics, so they could be taken care of. Since her diagnosis, she wasn't available the way she had been. So I suggested that possibly her breast cancer was helping her say "No" because now she had an excuse to put herself first. In effect, her cancer was saying "No" for her. If she became comfortable saying "No," she might not need the cancer anymore.

The second part of the mantra was "I want." People who have difficulty saying, "No" and always pleasing others lose touch with their own desires. They don't know what *they* want because they're always satisfying everyone else's wants. By regularly stating what she wanted, Joy would reawaken her desire nature. An "I want...." a day might make the emotional payoff from breast cancer go away. "No" and "I want" worked together. You need to know what you want, so you know when to say "No." And you need to be able to say "No" to other people's desires, so you can discover your own.

The third part of the mantra was a simple, declarative "Fuck off!" When someone who's been a pleaser begins to say "No" and "I want," the people in their life don't know how to deal with it. And they usually aren't very happy about it either. Who wants to lose that all-nurturing breast? So being able to forcefully draw boundaries was essential. Being able to say "Fuck off!" when someone objected to Joy's declaration of "No" or "I want" was a crucial part of the regimen.

I suggested that Joy use her new mantra, "No! I want! Fuck off!" once a day, like taking vitamins or medicine. And she took me up on it. She said "No" to all the usual claims and drains on her time and energy without leveraging her illness. She awakened her desire nature by stating daily what she wanted. And, with my help, she even got quite good at saying "Fuck off!" Naturally she practiced on me.

I don't know if the mantra had an effect on her cancer, but I'm certain it enhanced her quality of life. She often said that one of the "gifts" she received from cancer was teaching her to speak up for herself more than ever before, and to put herself first for the first time in her life.

Yes! I can! Now!

Joy was giving *me* a mantra, and I marveled how it mirrored the one I'd given her.

The "Yes" counteracted my instinctive "No" to everything in the wake of her death. If I was going to be reborn, I had to say "Yes" instead of the mourner's automatic "No."

The second part of the mantra, "I can...," was an antidote to my gut feeling about whatever I was confronting, which was an all-purpose "I *can't*." And the third and last part of the mantra was "Now!" because if *No* and *I can't* didn't get me out of something or I didn't want to admit that I was copping out, I could always weasel my way out by declaring, "I'm not ready *yet*."

My unconscious mantra since Joy's passing and the mantra of most mourners is an emphatic *NO! I CAN'T! NOT YET!*—the mantra of inertia, paralysis and death. With this new mantra, Joy was showing me how to change my internal programming from a mourner's life-denying *NO...I CAN'T...NOT YET!* to a life-affirming *YES...I CAN...NOW!*

I'd given Joy a mantra and now she'd given me one. The mantra was a simple yet powerful tool, "training wheels" to help me embrace whatever life was offering me.

ॐ 9 ॐ

Dancing for Joy

>———————————————————————————————<

Almost two months had passed since Joy's transition and I was still receiving a steady stream of condolence cards and letters. One in particular caught my attention. Beyond her condolences, Babette wrote about attending the "12 Steps to Finding Your Soulmate" workshop Joy and I had given over a year ago. During a process I led, in which the participants had to dance their vision, Babette was inspired to create a dance event called "Soul Flow," which she'd been leading on a monthly basis in Pasadena. Besides wishing me well, she invited me to attend whenever I felt up to it. She was leading one that weekend.

Dancing? My last experience dancing had been awful. My gut response to her invitation was *No way—I'm not up to it. Not yet.* You can't dance on Planet Grief. But the fact that I'd inspired this dance event intrigued me. *Maybe in a few months,* I told myself.

As the weekend approached, I kept repeating my mantra, *Yes!...I Can!...Now!* On Saturday evening, despite my profound reluctance, I drove the half hour to Pasadena to honor the mantra Joy had given me and to support the seed we'd planted over a year ago.

Babettte was surprised and delighted to see me. Her Soul Flow event was held at a newly refurbished yoga studio. The wooden floor was pristine, the sound system brand new and a giant brass gong hung in one corner of the studio.

At first Babette had the dozen or so people—more women than men—sit in a circle on the floor and introduce themselves. When it was my turn, I began by saying I'd recently lost my wife. Then I choked up. Babette stepped in and introduced me, telling everyone how I had inspired her to create this dance event.

After introductions she led us in warm-up stretches and then proceeded to facilitate her Soul Flow dance experience. She was a kundalini yoga teacher and wanted to use dance to heal and empower the chakras (the seven energy centers of the body running from the base of the spine to the crown of the head). She'd picked special music for each of the chakras and would guide the dancing with imagery and exercises that facilitated the experience of each chakra.

The first few dances were hard for me. Whether it was the root (first) chakra, the sex (second) chakra or the power (third) chakra at the navel, I wasn't responding to the music. I moved, but my body was leaden. *Have I made a mistake in coming?* My fear had been that I wouldn't be able to dance. *Again*!

For the heart (fourth) chakra, Babette played music that made me want to waltz. Instinctively, I reached out as if to embrace a dance partner. I placed my right hand (which would have been around my partner's back) over my aching heart and extended my left arm as if I were leading. I began the waltz's 1...2...3, 1...2...3.... As I spun around and around, I remembered Joy wanting to go to Vienna to dance the waltz at a formal ball. We never made it. Time ran out.

And then, suddenly, I felt Joy in my arms. I was elated by the sensation. I waltzed her around the studio. Around and around. Faster and faster. Whether it was a fantasy or some supernatural reality didn't matter. If it had been up to me, I would have danced like that forever. But the heart chakra music finally ended and my delight in waltzing with Joy ended with it.

For the rest of the evening I was in such a euphoric state that I danced to every piece of music. The more I danced, the more ecstatic I became. It was like a drug that took away the pain. By the end of the evening, I felt as if I'd found my "dance mojo" again.

On the drive home, I marveled at how a seed Joy and I had planted had taken root and blossomed into this ongoing dance event. And I wondered — *Was it possible that I'd inspired this dance event in the past so that in the future I would be healed by it?*

A week later I was supposed to attend a friend's wedding. I dreaded it. Simply getting dressed for the wedding made me miss Joy. Walking up to the church, I missed the feeling of her on my arm. Sitting in the pew of the small chapel during the ceremony, I ached for her.

At the reception I was seated at a table with friends — all couples. Since we were an odd number, there was an empty seat next to me. It was strange to be the only single at the table. I was very uncomfortable in my new role as "widower."

During the meal the woman seated next to me told me how Joy had saved her life. She whispered to me that she felt as if Joy had spoken to her in the shower a few days after she passed. Other friends came by and sat in the empty seat beside me and told me their Joy stories. With the help of vodka, champagne and all these Joy tributes, I was in a pretty good mood considering how lousy I'd felt when I first sat down. But then the dancing began....

...And I had no partner. At past weddings, Joy and I would have been one of the first couples on the dance floor. Now I sat as one by one couples got up to dance. Until finally, I was the only one left at our table. And my mood took an alcohol-fueled nosedive.

Someone tapped me on the shoulder. It was the bride in her white gown. "Would you like to dance?" she asked. I followed my angel of mercy onto the dance floor.

As we swayed to the music, I felt awkward, even a little embarrassed to have required such an act of kindness. "This is my first big social affair since Joy's passing," I told her.

"I'm glad it's at my wedding," she replied, radiant in her wedding gown.

My grief felt so out of place in the midst of her happiness. "Do you remember how Joy predicted this wedding almost two years ago?" I reminded her.

"I know," she said, beaming. "She gave me a reading at a Sunday of Joy. At the time, I found it hard to believe. But Joy told me to stay open. And here I am."

"Here you are," I echoed, trying to stifle my tears.

The music ended and suddenly the bride was whisked away. Alone on the dance floor, I heard the opening bars of Nat King Cole's "*Unforgettable.*" No! Not *our* song! I wanted to run but froze. This was the worst possible thing that could happen....

"I'll be the proxy!"

My friend Genevieve, appeared from nowhere. She'd left her husband, Marc, on the dance floor and stood before me offering herself as a dance partner. I took her in my arms and we slow danced as I wept. Though tears streamed down my face, I was glad to be dancing with *someone.*

At first I thought it was the alcohol, but I began to feel as if I was dancing with Joy. When the song finally ended, I was so shaken I needed to be helped back to my table. The moment we sat down, Bette Midler's "Wind Beneath My Wings" — Genevieve's Joy-song — began to play and she broke down.

Once Genevieve regained her composure, she marveled at what had happened. "Marc and I were dancing to "*Twist and Shout*" and then I heard "*Unforgettable*" — *your* song. I saw you all alone on the dance floor and you looked like a deer in the headlights. Suddenly I felt as if I was being pushed into your arms. 'Proxy! Proxy!' I said. As we began to slow dance I closed my eyes and asked Joy to dance with you through me. And she answered, 'I already am.' So I just got out of the way. I felt as if I left my body—I felt lighter and danced easily. I didn't step on your toes, did I? I was so happy to give you this moment of Joy. When the next song was Bette Midler's *"Wind Beneath My Wings,"* I started to cry. Joy told me she would communicate to me through songs and I think that was her *thank you* to me for her dance with you on the occasion of your first formal event since her transition. She still loves dancing with you."

What were the odds that, out of a million slow songs, those two songs would be played back to back at somebody's wedding? I wanted to believe that somehow Joy was with me celebrating our friend's wedding. She'd predicted it after all.

Inspired by my recent dance experiences, I wondered if dancing could help heal my grief. I began to dance at home and found that I always felt better after dancing. Even if I began dancing in tears.

I decided to try an experiment. I put together a "Grief Playlist"—music that tugged at my heartstrings, reminded me of Joy and made me cry. I had nearly two hours of music that was guaranteed to open my water works. I intended on playing my grief music to make me cry and then change the music and dance.

Why? When I cried, I felt like I'd never stop. So I tried to avoid it. But to heal my grief, I knew I had to find a way to cry deeply, fully, completely. And to do that, I'd have to find a way to *stop* crying.

I turned on the music and wept...sobbed...bawled... Fifteen minutes? Half an hour? I lost track of time. When I'd had enough, I switched to the dance music and, still sobbing, got up and began to move. At first I danced feebly while I cried. But as I got into the dancing, the crying ebbed and eventually stopped. It *worked*—dancing was the key!

Now I could intentionally cry because I could stop. Maybe I could dance my way out of grief. Maybe there was a fixed amount of tears that came with each great loss, and if I cried the requisite amount, I'd come to the end of my tears and my grieving would be over.

Excited by the possibility that I'd discovered a way to empty my tears, I decided to "cry and dance" every day as part of my healing regimen. I'd found a way to dive into my grief and not drown. Joy had shown me how.

℘ 10 ℘

A Vision of Joy

As I continued my morning yoga practice, I again experienced its many benefits. Paradoxically, I also felt my grief more profoundly. The stretching and breathing of yoga sensitized me to the more subtle nuances of my wound in a way I hadn't experienced before.

I faced a dilemma: stop the yoga, stay partially numb to my pain and perhaps never truly recover, or continue stretching and breathing to experience all the layers of my loss and eventually heal. I'd been told there was no way around grief, the only way out was through it. So I really had no choice.

Yet despite my willingness to embrace deeper and deeper layers of pain, I couldn't seem to perceive Joy in my meditations. I grew despondent and was about to quit my yoga practice when one day during meditation I experienced a fantastic vision. Bedecked and bejeweled like a Hindu deity, I saw a woman with many arms floating before me. I was stunned. In an instant the vision was gone.

Afterwards, the more I replayed the vision in my mind, the more convinced I became that I'd been granted a vision of Joy. But what did it mean?

A few days later my friend Shama called. A friend of hers wanted to film a demonstration of a new massage technique called *tantsu*. Since it sounded like *watsu*, the massage that combined floating in water with shiatsu, I assumed they were related. Shama asked me if I'd like to receive a tantsu. I remembered my mantra and said *Yes*.

The next day Shama, her friend Amber and I were sitting in the shade of a tree at the top of a hill that overlooked the lake near my home. It was one of those glorious Southern California summer days. As Amber spread a blanket on the grass, I remembered previous watsus during which I was floated in water and gently moved in ways that used the resistance of the water to stretch you.

"Tantsu," Amber explained, as if reading my mind, "is a watsu in someone's lap."

I couldn't imagine having a watsu on dry land, let alone in someone's lap.

Shama set up the video camera while Amber made herself comfortable on the blanket. Finally she motioned for me to lie down in her lap.

I'm a slender six feet. Amber was a strapping 5' 9." How was she going to do this? She sat cross-legged and I crawled into in her lap. She positioned me, then told me to close my eyes and relax. And breathe!

As the tantsu began, she rolled me side to side, then back and forth. I relaxed more. She bent me one way, then another. I breathed deeply and surrendered until I felt like dough being kneaded. My body had turned to putty and my mind was in an altered state. As she continued manipulating me—rolling, bending, folding and twisting me—I began to feel as if she had dozens of arms....

Suddenly, my vision of Joy sprang into consciousness and I began to experience the tantsu as if I were being embraced by the many arms of a goddess. As I was passed from one set of arms to the next, each cradling me in a different, loving way, I began to understand what my vision meant. By the time the tantsu demonstration was over, I knew what I had to do next.

The following afternoon I received a visit from an old friend. Marcia had been out of town for several months and this was the first time I'd seen her since Joy's passing. A one-time cabaret singer who'd toured the world, she was currently teaching improvisation to actors and singing to Alzheimer's patients in nursing homes. She was also quite psychic. Last Good Friday, though she hadn't been in L.A., she'd had a "prompting" to call and was shocked to hear that Joy was about to leave this mortal coil.

Since Marcia hadn't been to the memorial service, I played her the DVD that was shown there. Afterwards, we sat on the couch and talked about Joy. I choked up frequently. A longtime body worker, Marcia instinctively began to comfort me by massaging my bare feet. Her touch suddenly reminded me of my vision.

Here was an opportunity to act on my vision, but I was reluctant. Yet I knew that my healing depended on being willing to ask for what I needed. "Marcia," I finally said, "Would you hold me?"

"Sure," she replied, as if it was the most natural thing in the world.

We moved the pillows on the couch aside so we could lie down together. Facing each other, belly to belly, we embraced. I wrapped myself in her arms and our legs entwined, the way Joy and I would lie together every morning.

With Joy, I'd sink into our embrace and we would both begin to breathe deeply. Soon our breathing would synchronize and we'd sigh our exhales so that the sound vibrated through our bodies. Gradually we'd dissolve into each other.

Settling into Marcia's embrace, I imagined lying in Joy's arms. *Oh how I missed being with her like this!* Automatically I began breathing deeply, toning my breath, surrendering to the embrace. Marcia and I began breathing together. Relaxing with each breath, I sank into this subtle cloud of energy that began to envelop us. I felt the soothing relief of her body covering my open wound. I felt the jagged edges of my torn aura dull. As I surrendered to the moment, I left the pain and grief on the storm-tossed surface of my life and dove into the healing pool of Being.

Within a few minutes I was in a deep trance. The thousands of embraces I'd shared with Joy had taught me how to access this state. There was a Pool of Love (some call it Source, others call it God) that everyone is connected to. Being held, Joy and I realized, was a way to dip into that pool.

Marcia and I lay there entwined for five...ten...fifteen minutes. I wondered if I was abusing her kindness, but was too hungry for the healing I was receiving to worry about it.

When we finally separated, I was surprised to experience the rawness of my exposed belly, chest and heart. That feeling of vulnerability, however, was quickly transformed by the warm afterglow that suffused my entire being as a result of this loving embrace.

"I felt Joy's presence," Marcia told me.

I was delighted.

"I saw flickering images of Joy around us," she continued, "as a lion tamer coaxing a lion to jump through a ring of fire."

Was I the lion? I wondered. *And was the ring of fire my grief?*

After Marcia's visit, I marveled at how the universe had brought someone so free and uninhibited to me after I'd been inspired by my vision. Another person might have balked or been uncomfortable with my request to be held, and my hugging journey might have stalled before it had even begun.

If I had any lingering doubts about the meaning of my vision, Marcia's willingness and loving embrace was the best confirmation I could have asked for.

In the same way I'd intuited that *dancing with grief* would help me cry the tears I needed to shed in order to heal, I also sensed I had to obtain a certain number of hugs. How many? I didn't know. But now I was determined to embark on a *Journey of a Thousand Hugs* wherever it would lead.

II

Summer

ℬ 11 ℭ

Journey of a Thousand Hugs

The following Sunday I was presented with a perfect opportunity to take the next step in my *Journey of a Thousand Hugs*. I was invited to a theater weekend at the music center in downtown Los Angeles by Joy's son, Elliot, his wife, Kate, and Joy's best friend, Jackie. On Saturday evening we'd see the light opera *The Merry Widow* and on Sunday a matinee of Gershwin's *Porgy & Bess*. We were staying overnight at the historic Biltmore Hotel, the site of the first Academy Awards.

As I sat in the theater watching *The Merry Widow* I missed Joy sitting beside me—taking her hand, seeing her smile out of the corner of my eye. She would have loved the music, its Viennese period costumes and, of course, the waltzes.

Upon returning to the hotel, Jackie and I went up to the room we were sharing. It was large with two queen-sized beds. As we changed into our pajamas, I realized this was another opportunity to be held. Jackie was a good friend, but I wasn't sure how she'd react to my request, especially in such a provocative setting as a hotel room. I put off asking her until we were sitting on our beds saying goodnight. It was now or never.

Jackie was not your typical business-woman, mother and grandmother. Her most formative experience occurred during a spiritual tour of Egypt with Joy. A life-long sufferer of asthma, the combination of heat, dirt and horses at the Temple of Horus sent Jackie into shock. She was pronounced dead. For nearly half an hour they tried unsuccessfully to revive her. Having always been skeptical about the possibility of life after death, Jackie returned from her "near-death-experience" transformed. She described her NDE as being wrapped in the arms of what she called the Great Spirit and surrounded with love. "Love is all that matters," the Great Spirit had told her. "Love is all there is."

I told her about my vision and the hugging journey I'd embarked on, and asked her if she'd hold me. "Sure," she said, getting out of her bed and climbing onto mine. We laid on top of the covers and embraced for some time. It felt wonderful to have my wounded heart bandaged once again. Yet, I could feel Jackie embracing me with a certain reserve. As the minutes ticked by she relaxed—her body softened, her breath deepened and her energy flowed more freely.

I told her I felt like a newborn just wanting to be held. I hoped that our embrace was healing for her, too, since she was mourning the loss of her best friend. She told me that Joy had always led her into new adventures. She confessed that she was more fearful than Joy, more traditional in her thinking. She told me about the time Joy had dragged her to a workshop where they had to take their clothes off. To Joy—who was comfortable in the nude—that was no big deal. But for Jackie (despite having a terrific figure) nudity was a challenge. Ultimately, she broke through her limitations and was happy she went.

As we embraced, I wondered if Joy was still leading Jackie into new adventures through me.

I continued my *Journey of a Thousand Hugs*, and with each hug I became less tentative and more confident about asking. Of course, a few declined. Others were well-meaning and said Yes, but once I was lying in their arms, I could tell they were uncomfortable. So after a few minutes, I'd thank them and release them from their discomfort. And then sometimes I didn't even have to ask. Sometimes I just shared my story and women friends would offer to hold me.

The biggest obstacle to receiving these healing hugs, I discovered, was me. My pride for one thing. Joy and I had been nicknamed "King & Queen" by our friends. We were a social hub and initiated several ongoing activities like our Wisdom Circle. For many of our friends we were the model of an ideal relationship and counseled many of them through the ups and downs of theirs. I was so used to giving, I felt uncomfortable asking for something. Asking to be held seemed so weak and vulnerable. So unmanly. So "un-kingly." Fortunately, most of our friends were a touchy-feely bunch who appreciated the power of healing touch. And so, despite my pride I had to ask for help. It was time for me to receive.

In a meditation Joy confirmed that I was on the right path, that my willingness to be so vulnerable by asking to be held created the opportunity for her to work through these women.

Even so, it wasn't my friends who were having trouble with the hugs, it was me. Again and again while lying in someone's arms, after the initial euphoria, I would feel uncomfortable about the one-sidedness of it. I'd wonder: Isn't she tired? Isn't it enough? What's she getting out of it? The disquiet I felt threatened to derail my journey.

In meditation, I again asked Joy for guidance. She told me that my truth and my need is my gift. She said that the gift would be revealed to those who become part of my journey. "For each it will be different. Each will receive what they need to further their growth. That's how you become an instrument, not only for your own healing but for others as well."

That evening Marcia, who'd given me my first hug, stopped by. She confided that our previous hug had been healing for her and offered to hold me again. After our embrace, which lasted almost twenty minutes, she told me she'd had another vision of Joy—this time wearing a cape and pouring golden

liquid love like a water bearer over us. I recognized the image—
an uncanny resemblance to Joy's astrological sign, Aquarius.

Days passed and one morning I read in the newspaper about
a man who had suffered a spinal cord injury and described his
sexual paralysis as being "freed from servicing Mr. Penis." His
injury allowed him to explore more nuanced kinds of touch,
more soulful physical connections. I wondered if something
similar was happening to me.

It was as if Joy's death had killed my libido. Despite lying
belly to belly with these women, there was no stirring down
below. Not a glimmer. Just heart-ons. At first I didn't care. It
wasn't sex I was after, just healing embraces. I had no desire to
be with another woman sexually. None at all. Yet I couldn't help
noticing my lack of libido. Under normal circumstances I would
have been concerned. But on Planet Grief, I reassured myself,
there is no libido. Besides, with a libido I couldn't undertake
this *Journey of a Thousand Hugs*. If a friend held me and suddenly
felt my erection poking at her through our clothing, the "sacred
space" of the embrace would change. So I decided to view
my lack of libido as a gift that would return someday, when I
returned from Planet Grief.

I was gradually making my way through a long list of "to
do's," which included returning the many condolence calls
I'd received. I dialed Dana's number and we spoke. She asked
how people were supporting me. I told her about my hugging
journey. To my surprise, she said, "I'd like to sign up."

A few days later Dana arrived at my door bearing a pot of
tasty lamb stew, baked yams and homemade chocolate chip
cookies. We talked about Joy. We talked about Dana's son who
had died a few years earlier. We were both in tears. After dinner,
she asked if I'd like that hug. I said, "Of course."

We lay down on the couch and embraced, and immediately
I sank into the blissful pool of Being. But I could feel from her

shallow breath that Dana wasn't relaxed. She asked me what I was feeling. "It's like disappearing from my personality's grief and becoming my essence," I explained, "pure consciousness, which is a state of bliss beyond the pain."

I sensed her tending me. I told her not to, to just relax into herself. She didn't have to give me anything. I explained that if she relaxed into the infinite Love that abounds, I wouldn't have to be concerned about her because I'd know she was receiving as well. With that, her breathing deepened and synchronized with mine. I could feel her melting.

After a while I murmured, "We're creating an energetic circuit through which Love or Spirit can run."

She seemed to be getting a taste of it. "This could be a therapy," she mused. Since she was a psychotherapist, her remark meant a lot.

"Bereavement groups should have as much holding as talking," I said. "People who've lost a spouse are starved for touch."

"There's a psychological term for what you're referring to," she said, "called skin hunger."

What a perfect description, I thought. These hugs were feeding that hunger.

We lay quietly for a few moments longer, and then sat up. I was beaming. So was she. "Thank you," I said. "I've been lucky to have good friends who aren't afraid to hold me. And that's made all the difference."

I was anticipating Simone's visit for several reasons. Not only was she a close friend and a member of our Wisdom Circle, but she also taught Tantra. Since so much of Tantra is focused on the energetic rather than physical exchange that can be cultivated and harnessed during sex, I felt she'd have some interesting insights into my hugging journey.

Simone arrived at my place around noon. Thin and muscular due to a lifetime of yoga practice, her soft, almost ethereal voice contrasted with the raw physicality she exuded. The moment we sat down in the kitchen she launched into the tale of her disastrous trip to Hawaii with her lover. They had broken up and her devastation was palpable.

Here I was expecting my grief to be cared for, but she was the one who was trembling with grief about her loss. Instinctively, I took her by the hand and suggested we hold each other.

The moment we embraced on the couch, Simone burst into sobs. I felt I had nothing to give and hoped that holding her would be enough. In whispers she tearfully recounted the awful moments in Hawaii, punctuating her tale now and then with the plaintive question, "Why?" She alternated between heartbreak and knowing "It was for the best." Back and forth. We'd breathe and tone together for a few minutes, diving into the depths, and then she'd surface and weep as she shared more of her heartbreak. This went on for over an hour with frequent breaks for tissues. It felt good to be held. It also felt good to help someone else with their grief. Afterwards she said she felt much better. As we hugged goodbye I told her to call if she wanted to talk and to drop by if she wanted to be held.

Alone again, I recalled Joy's recent guidance: "Telling your truth will inspire others to tell theirs. Asking for what you need will inspire others to do the same. Continue on your quest to be held and know that everyone will be blessed."

In this way these women's arms became a sanctuary, a haven, a place of renewal for me. Over and over I experienced the benefits of being cradled like a child, of being embraced with love. Without sex. During one week I was held by four different women. On one occasion, I was held by two in one day. And I began to wonder if, as usual, I was overdoing it?

In meditation one morning I asked Joy for guidance. At first I felt as if I was being enveloped by her presence. Then I heard these words: "I embrace you. Feel my embrace. You're on the right path. It's worth overdoing. Speak your truth. Ask for what you need. You are empty and I will fill you via the arms of my priestesses. You are my King! My Hero! You cared for me so completely! I will embrace you now with my ten thousand arms of love. The faces will change but the love will be the same. In the same way you had the courage to love an older woman, you will have the courage to cross the bridge from Grief to Rebirth into a land of new love and life! Dearest One, your journey is a blessing to all you encounter."

With Joy's encouragement I lived off these hugs for weeks. They were like medicine. I orchestrated them, invited them, manifested them. I didn't know where my Journey of a Thousand Hugs would lead, but I felt certain that the way to heal was to be found in the many arms of the Goddess.

As I made my way from one embrace to another, I felt like I was climbing hand over hand out of a deep, dark emotional pit. Some days I lost my footing and slipped back, but other days I could see, albeit fleetingly, the light up ahead. And along the way, I was learning about grief and its darker, shadow side, its seductions. My grief, I realized, gave me power over other people's sympathy. I saw how it could become a trap, how one could be seduced into playing on people's sympathies and never recover.

I was pondering the pitfalls of indulging in people's sympathy one day when Simone called—she wanted to stop by. She arrived around noon frazzled from visiting her ailing mother at a nursing home. She kept rubbing her knee. I asked her if she'd hurt herself. No, she said, it was just nervous energy. Then she looked up at me. "How about that hug?"

We lay down together on the couch like we had the week before and began to breathe deeply and tone. As we did, her erratic energy calmed and became more harmonious. She began to weep. "What's wrong with me? I want a love like you had with Joy." Through tears she confided that she was grieving never having had a love like that. I told her that Joy didn't have "a love like that" until she was sixty-nine. Simone thanked me for giving her hope that it just wasn't time yet for her great love.

After nearly an hour we got up from our embrace. I felt euphoric. Simone said she felt much better. The gift was mutual. I shared my current fantasy about "hugging stations" around the city where people who were having a rough day could go to get a hug that would make them feel better. We laughed, then said goodbye.

After she left I was struck once again by the fact that someone else had asked for the hug. *She* had initiated it.

A few days later Marcia called—she was going to be in the neighborhood and wanted to visit. She dropped by after lunch and we talked about our last hug. She wanted to try it again. After embracing on my couch for twenty minutes I felt euphoric. For another twenty minutes our embrace became punctuated with intimate pillow talk.

Marcia confided how "vigilant" she usually was. And that she'd begun to realize how her hyper-vigilance, though a survival mechanism, was threatening to choke the life out of her. She saw new encounters as potential problems, not potential opportunities. She expected breakdowns, not breakthroughs. And so that's what she'd been manifesting. She realized she had to make an inner shift before her outer circumstances could change. I held her and listened—that's all she needed from me.

A few days later, my preparations for our monthly Wisdom Circle were interrupted when the phone rang. It was Marcia. She excitedly told me that she'd finally booked a flight back to her hometown in Kansas, a trip she'd wanted to make for several years. She'd also been offered a teaching position at a college in nearby Santa Barbara. She attributed these breakthroughs in her life to our hugs and thanked me.

I was basking in this confirmation of what Joy had told me— that my healing journey would be a gift to everyone—when people began to arrive for the Wisdom Circle.

Each of them greeted me with a warm, loving hug, and asked. "How are you doing?"

Savoring each embrace, I replied, "I'm hugging my way from day to day. I'm hugging my way home."

℘ *12* ℘

Joy's Embrace

My meditations were a great comfort to me. Whether I was imagining these conversations with Joy or actually contacting her spirit ultimately didn't matter. What mattered was feeling that I wasn't alone, that I was still with Joy.

Then one day my meditations with Joy took on a whole new dimension. I *felt* her embrace me. It was the subtlest sensation, as if she'd wrapped angel wings around me. Not actual wings, but energetic ones, as if enfolding me within her aura. Then I felt her *sit* in my lap in *yab yum*[1]. Not for any sexual purpose, but to gaze into my eyes, to blend energies, to merge souls. And I heard her say, *"I will be with you whenever you want, my Beloved."*

I was stunned. Tears spilled down my cheeks. I thought this yab yum meditation with Joy was a special, one-of-a-kind experience. I had no idea it was just the beginning.

A few nights later I had a bizarre dream. I was walking around the lobby of a hotel with Julia Roberts embracing me in yab yum. Though I was dressed, she was naked with her legs wrapped around my waist and her arms around my neck. I was holding her by her hips. We walked around the hotel like that and no one seemed to mind. I loved the sensation of her body

---

1 **Yab-yum** (Tibetan, literally, "father-mother") is a common symbol in Buddhist and Hindu art representing the masculine and feminine deities in sexual union. Often the male is seated in lotus posture while the female sits face to face in his lap, her legs wrapped around him.

pressed against me. There wasn't anything overtly sexual. It was a wonderful feeling. Walking around with my *Shakti*[2].

I began to see how the embrace I experienced with Joy in meditation was a natural evolution of my *Journey of a Thousand Hugs*. I was being embraced both in the outer *and* inner worlds.

For a while these meditations became routine. After yoga I'd sit cross-legged in meditation. After a few minutes Joy would appear and sit in my lap in yab yum. I would experience a wordless, blissful communion. I wondered, *Is this blessed communion the ultimate I could hope to achieve or preparation for something more?*

One day my question was answered. During meditation, I again had the sensation that Joy was standing above me, a shimmering moonlight illuminating the contours of her body. In my mind's eye, she lowered herself onto my lap. She was beaming. I welcomed her. There was nothing sexual about it. Just an energetic flowing as before.

Without realizing it, I began to visualize light flowing between us, entering my third eye, then moving down my spine and out my first chakra into Joy, then up her spine and out her third eye into me. The light seemed to follow the breath—on the inhale into me and on the exhale into Joy. Once the circuit of light that circled between us was firmly established as an egg-shaped oval, delicate filaments of light began to move between us in figure-eight patterns—threading, weaving, interlacing us together, chakra to chakra, until the most beautifully complex web of light had been woven between us.

With my eyes still closed I silently asked what we were doing. But Joy didn't answer. I asked several times, but heard nothing. At last I heard her say, *"No more words"* and I understood—I was supposed to experience this embrace. No talk. *Experience!*

---

2 **Shakti** is the concept or personification of divine feminine creative power. In the Hindu pantheon Shakti is often partnered, often in yab yum, with Shiva, the divine masculine.

When our communion was finally over she told me that this was "preparation." *For what?* I wondered.

The following week I drove out to Pasadena to see a woman healer who worked with the bereaved. After a short debriefing in which I described my life on Planet Grief, she told me to lie down on her massage table face up. She led me through a series of complicated breathing techniques while placing her hands over each of my chakras, one by one, as I followed her instructions, visualizing the color and voicing an affirmation specific to that chakra.

The complicated breath work in combination with whatever else she was doing built up so much energy that I felt I was going to pass out. I wondered if coming to her had been a mistake.

Then she told me to breathe normally. As I regained my senses I realized she was standing behind my head. She began to speak and invoked the image of dolphins. "I see a heart-shaped pod of dolphins surrounding you and they're taking you on a journey."

Dolphins! The hair on my neck stood up. Dolphins had often appeared as an important animal ally in the shamanic journeys I had experienced when I studied the spiritual technique some years earlier. Joy also felt connected to dolphins. We swam with them in Hawaii the day before we were married. In fact, swimming with dolphins had been the impetus for our being in Hawaii in the first place. Even now a brass sculpture of a pair of dolphins at play graces our bedroom.

Had Joy planted the image of dolphins—heart-shaped no less—in this healer's mind to remind me how healing water was for me? In that moment, despite my reluctance to take my first trip alone, I decided to go to Two Bunch Palms, near Palm Springs, and soak in the natural hot springs there.

After my session, the healer suggested I create a *shield* for my heart—an image, an affirmation, anything...perhaps even a picture of Joy and me—and wear it when I napped or lay down—in order to "feed your grieving heart."

The next morning in the shower, thinking about what to use as a "heart shield," I realized I already had one. In my yab yum meditations with Joy, she was shielding and healing my raw underbelly, my severed chords, my torn aura, my broken heart.

Then, during a yab yum meditation, instead of the light energy circling between Joy and I, the radiance concentrated in my chest where it began to pulsate, and, with each breath, expanded until I was completely enveloped by the light.

❧ 13 ❧

Strange Embraces

My *Journey of a Thousand Hugs* took a strange twist. I was so caught up in my hugging obsession that weird things started to happen. For starters, I wound up in other people's dreams.

One day I received a bizarre email from a friend in Sedona. "You came to me in my sleep last night!" she wrote. Her email described a frightening visitation in which I had appeared in her bed spooning with her. I called her the next day to talk about her dream and what it could mean. Since she was a well-known dream expert who'd written a book and often appeared on TV, I was surprised that she was stumped. Though I kidded her about the dream expert having trouble interpreting her own dreams, I wondered if it was possible that my hugging journey had become so intense that I was actually hugging people in their dreams.

I met a woman who had an incredible hugging story of her own. Vinece called her hugging process "a holding," and the inspiration for it came to her in a dream several years earlier. She was so inspired by that dream that she designed a weekend in which she was continuously held. She enrolled friends, organizing them into shifts, so that she would be held day and night (aside from food and bathroom breaks) for forty-eight hours. She described the experience as a kind of rebirthing. It was so powerfully transformative that she's organized "holdings" for other people who, she claims, have also experienced incredible healings.

She was amazed to discover that "holdings" have roots in African tribal culture. As a black woman she felt she'd tapped into the wisdom of her DNA. I mentioned to her that in Bali infants are held for the first six months of their lives—their feet are never allowed to touch the ground. Apparently, the Balinese also have this deep wisdom about the importance of being held.

After meeting Vinece I wondered if I should ask her to create a "holding" for me. Would a solid weekend of being held be the next step in my *Journey of a Thousand Hugs?*

I was told about a man who, after suffering a great loss, began going to malls to hug people. The next day I googled the "hugging man" and read his amazing story.

He'd been living in London when his world turned upside down and was forced to return to his hometown of Sydney, Australia. At the airport no one was there to welcome him home. Watching other passengers being hugged and greeted by friends and family made him yearn for a hug, too. So he made a sign that said, "Free Hugs" and stood outside the busiest mall in the city.

The first person who accepted his offer was a woman whose dog had died that morning, which also happened to be the one-year anniversary of the death of her only daughter in a car accident. The woman told him that what she needed now when she felt most alone in the world was a hug. And so he began an incredible hugging journey of his own, or what he called a "Hugathon" which has turned into a worldwide movement whose stated mission is to "reach out and hug a stranger to brighten up their lives."

On his website he published an *"Illustrated Guide to Free Hugs,"* in which he cited some of the scientific research that substantiates the importance of hugs. Touch, after all, is one of the first senses we humans develop in the womb. Once we're born, one of the first and perhaps primary experiences we have in this world is being held. According to the research, "when people hug, the brain releases a chemical called Oxytocin which decreases fear, increases trust and encourages social bonding. Hugging also reduces blood pressure and lowers the heart rate. Hugs are essential for physical and emotional well-being, providing solace, safety and tenderness, without which we become sad, withdrawn and depressed."

At about this time, someone sent me an email about "The Rescuing Hug," the true story of a set of premature twins. During the first week of their life the twins were kept apart in separate incubators. One was not expected to live. Disobeying hospital rules, a nurse placed the babies together in one incubator. The email included an extraordinary picture of the "rescuing hug" taken when the preemie twins were finally together. They seemed to snuggle against each other with the healthier one's arm over her sister in an embrace. Once together in the "rescuing hug" the frail twin's health began to improve. The caption on the picture read: *Let us not forget to embrace those whom we love.*

Indeed. And never underestimate the power of a hug!

All this information confirmed the healing power of a loving embrace and validated my *Journey of a Thousand Hugs*. In my own way I was also a "hugging man" who was going on his own "hugathon."

• • • •

In my daily meditations, I experienced an extraordinary evolution in my blissful communions with Joy. As we sat in yab yum, she appeared increasingly real in my mind's eye. One time her form became so palpably real I could almost *feel* her.

And then, at the end of our blissful communion, something extraordinary happened—she *kissed* me. It was so "real" I swear I could feel it!

In the moment, I was enraptured by Joy's kiss. But for the rest of the day and the days that followed I realized I'd been shaken by the reality of it. Throughout these encounters, I still wasn't sure whether I was experiencing self-induced hallucinations or an actual spiritual reality. And I was happy to sit on the fence and not question it too closely. But for some reason this kiss provoked me. Was it *really* real?

Then I remembered a story I'd written years earlier, before I ever met Joy. I rummaged through my files until I found it. As I read my heart sank....

"The Fallen" was a mythical fantasy about men who'd been at war for a very long time who, upon finally returning home, discover their beloved women and children gone. It was as if they'd vanished into thin air.

The truth was that the women were there, but the men couldn't see them because they'd been so brutalized by war, they'd fallen in frequency to a lower dimension where their women and children were now invisible to them. The women, however, could see their men and devised a plan to rescue them. The man who'd shown the most mercy in battle and whose soul had been the least brutalized by war would be the Chosen One. His wife would contact him in his dreams. She would teach him how to raise his soul frequency and he would teach the other men. And lead them home.

"And so one night, while the Chosen One slept, his wife appeared to him in a dream." She told him what to do in order to return home. Over the next several months he followed her instructions and his frequency rose. Each time she contacted him, she seemed less and less dream-like, more and more real. Until finally *"...On the very next full moon he not only saw her, he actually felt her hands lovingly stroking his forehead, and soon, the*

rest of his body. All night he made dreamy love to her — the first time since he'd gone off to war so long ago. When at last she kissed him, he realized that he'd finally come home."

Rereading this long forgotten story disturbed me deeply. Was I living out some fantasy I'd created long ago? I became disillusioned. I'd always considered the possibility that these communions with Joy were imaginary, but there was also the possibility that they were real. Now I was certain I'd made the whole thing up — imagined these experiences with Joy to console myself. Though I continued crying, dancing and hugging, I stopped meditating. I couldn't endure another imaginary embrace.

ℬ *14* ℭ

Into the Closet

I went into a tailspin. No longer able to score my drug of choice—my "contact" with Joy—I could no longer numb my pain by imagining that somehow, albeit supernaturally, Joy and I were still together.

I was desolate. I felt like a fool. Like I'd been fooled. I felt pathetic. A fraud. The levees I'd built from my "contacts" with Joy had been breached, and I was drowning in the flood of my unadulterated grief now compounded by scathing self-recrimination.

I was despondent, but I couldn't cry. And that made matters worse. *What's the matter with me that I can't cry?* Something in me had hardened and the tears just didn't flow. Or I'd fallen so far down into a well of sadness that my tears couldn't reach the surface. My voice thickened with unexpressed grief. My eyes stung. But tears didn't flow.

I walked around the lake hoping for some comfort, perhaps even some answers. With its water, trees, and bird life, the lake was a place of renewal, but also a place of painful memories. And I never knew which I would feel. The lake was a barometer of my mood, a Rorschach of my state of mind, which like the surface of the water itself was always changing, never the same.

Thankfully, the lake was also distracting. I'd pass fishermen waiting for that fish to bite, a lone photographer with a big telephoto lens waiting for that snowy egret to take flight. I'd gawk at the men casting their flies. I'd marvel at the childlike-adults sailing radio-powered model boats on the water.

Yet the lake's pastoral beauty also attracted couples young and old. Whether I passed an old couple seated on a bench holding hands watching the world go by or a young couple sprawled on the grass oblivious to the world around them because they were so wrapped up in an embrace, I was reminded of Joy and the thousands of times we had enjoyed ourselves at the lake.

Despite the many opportunities for grief, the lake was like oxygen and blood to me. If I wanted to breathe, I had to be willing to hurt. If I wanted to live, I had to be willing to feel my pain.

The lake was also a place of revelations. One day while wondering whether my *Journey of a Thousand Hugs* was really worth taking, I watched two little girls roll down a hill like logs. First each rolled down the hill alone. Then they *hugged* each other and together rolled farther down the hill. Clearly, embracing someone made everything in life easier.

I often cried at the lake, especially when I listened to certain songs on my iPod. So it was doubly upsetting to walk the lake during my "grief relapse" and listen to my grief music, but *not* be able to cry.

One day the sky above the lake was filled with an unusual cloud formation. It looked like a phalanx of angels—an "angel brigade"—which I hoped was a good omen.

I came home to a surprise: a water main had burst and emergency road work was going on in the street in front of my condominium. Inside my condo the noise was still quite loud, so I closed all the windows and doors to muffle the deafening jackhammers. But the vibrations rattled the windows. My home office faced the street and I couldn't stay in it because of the din. To get away from the racket, I moved from one room to the next, away from the street, until I found myself in the quietest spot of all—inside Joy's walk-in closet.

Joy's closet was the last place I wanted to be. Like everyone who's lost a spouse, I'd been grappling with the issue of what to do with her things. Every time I'd step into the closet, a searing wave of grief would sweep over me and I'd back out as if I'd been physically expelled. Then I'd tell myself that I wasn't ready to go through all of her neatly organized clothes.

So Joy's closet was the last place I expected to find myself. But since the closet was the quietest place I could find, I decided to spend some time just looking at a few things.

I began by smelling her clothes. Then I sniffed her jewelry, which still held the scent of her perfume. I touched her silk blouses and velvet pants, holding them up to my nose and cheek. I soon became intoxicated, and slowly, without realizing it, began going through her clothing. Her blouses, her jackets, her dresses, her shoes, her hats and handbags, her jewelry and belts.

Joy's clothes evoked many sweet memories because I was intimately involved in choosing her wardrobe, probably more so than most husbands. Since she couldn't see to drive or shop for the last six years of her life, we shopped together. I'd scan Nordstrom's, Macy's, even flea markets for clothing that would look good on her. She loved our outings. And luckily, she liked my taste. Since I was the one who had to look at what she was wearing, she graciously tried on everything I brought her. Many times she'd be in the dressing room and I'd bring her yet another armload of clothes to try on. Sometimes she'd sigh, but she had never had a dresser before, so she enjoyed it. I did, too.

Over the next few hours, I touched every piece of clothing in Joy's closet.

In one of her handbags I found butterscotch candy and remembered grabbing them for her whenever we went to the hospital for chemo or radiation. Since she couldn't see, I'd sign in for her and bring her some of the candy the staff had put out in a bowl. She liked the butterscotch.

I began to find tissues in the pockets of her pants and jackets. Lots and lots of tissues. *Why so many tissues?*

Then I remembered that after finishing her meal whenever we dined out, she'd blot her newly applied lipstick with tissues. And I began to whimper. Each pocket held neatly folded unused tissues. A pile began to form on the floor. I began to sob. It was the strangest thing—every pocket's stash of tissues seemed to evoke more tears from me. So I began to wipe my eyes and blow my nose with each new tissue and throw it on top of the growing pile. It was uncanny, as if the tissues needed to be used because I needed to shed tears.

Hours flew by. I emptied dozens and dozens and dozens of pockets of their tissues. And I cried and cried...until I'd emptied every pocket and there were no more tissues and no more tears. Perhaps I was delirious, but the pile of tissues strewn on the floor of the closet now bore an uncanny resemblance to the "angel brigade" of clouds I'd seen earlier in the day.

When I finally emerged from Joy's closet it was dark outside. And quiet. The construction had stopped. I marveled at what a strange day it had been and how the Universe had conspired to provide me a most unexpected and welcome healing.

I called a friend and told him what had happened— that I'd been so depressed I couldn't even cry, and about the angel brigade of clouds that had appeared in the sky, and the emergency road work that drove me into Joy's closet where I found tissues that made me cry and feel better. I wondered aloud if I was being looked after by Joy? Or was it simply my wishful imagination again?

To which my wise friend replied, "Why don't you just accept it as an unexpected gift."

The next day, my morning reading in the book, *Healing After Loss,* had this sage advice:

> "Whether it is our own projection or, in some way,
> the visiting spirit of our loved one, we have no way of

knowing. We would like it to be our loved one—some contact, some assurance of continuing life. But oddly enough, perhaps it doesn't matter a great deal. If we are comforted, let's be grateful for that. And if this easing of the spirit comes from our own imagination—well, the Creator of life gave us our imagination, too."

So it didn't take me long to start "using" again. My withdrawal from the spiritual comfort of "contact" with Joy didn't last long. A few days later, another quote from my morning reading helped me rationalize "falling off the wagon" of sober rationality and skeptical cynicism.

"We who have stood at the doorway of death, watching our loved one pass through, are entitled to all flights of imagination as we contemplate the unknown."

ஐ *15* ೧

Quest for the Ultimate Hug

One day not long after my catharsis in Joy's closet, I received an email announcing the Los Angeles appearance of a woman named Amma, the superstar Indian guru known as the "hugging saint." My *Journey of A Thousand Hugs* appeared to be approaching its culmination as I began my *Quest for the Ultimate Hug.*

I drove out to the airport Hilton where Amma was doing her week-long "hugathon." Though the Hugging Man's Free Hugs campaign had ambitions to be a global movement, Amma hugged on a scale that was truly mind-boggling. She'd personally hugged more than 26 *million* people.

Born to a poor fisherman's family in southern India, by the age of two Amma was singing devotional songs in praise of God and spending most of her time immersed in *samadhi*, union with the Divine. Amma's teaching, or *darshan*, is simply her loving embrace which, according to the email, "allows people to experience true unconditional love."

I'd heard that thousands of devotees showed up, so I knew that I'd have to wait several hours before getting a hug. When I arrived at the hotel around 10:30 a.m., I was given a ticket that read L4. Someone pointed to the signs out in the hall and in the ballroom that continually updated where the line was. When I saw that the sign said C-4, my heart sank. It would be many hours before it would be my turn.

Upon entering the ballroom I was transported by the incense, the live Indian music and the exotic decor—the hall was decked out like an Indian temple. Amma, a large brown-skinned woman, swaddled in white, was seated on a makeshift throne at the foot of the stage hugging one devotee after another. Dozens waited in line while hundreds more—many in meditation—sat on the floor and in chairs, waiting their turn.

Meanwhile, throngs milled about the bazaar that ringed the hall where every kind of Amma merchandise imaginable was displayed for sale: books, CDs, pictures, jewelry, Hindu religious artifacts, clothing, and more. You could buy pictures of Amma to hang on the wall, to wear as pendants, to place on an altar, or to carry as a key ring. Photos of "Amma & Me" were being sold in which you could be photoshopped into the same picture as the guru. All proceeds went to her many charitable activities.

I sat in a chair twenty rows back from the stage and watched. Amma was surrounded by at least four video camera crews. It seemed all the local news outlets were filming segments on her. Answering media questions through a translator didn't stop her from hugging a seemingly endless stream of people.

Dozens of Amma's devotees, both men and women, were dressed in white. For them she was the embodiment of the Divine Mother who bestows unconditional love on her children. What would I experience in the arms of an actual goddess?

I waited. Everyone waited.

Waiting hour after hour added a dimension of anticipation which gathered and increased over time, like thirst in the desert. When the momentous hug finally came, it was like a drink of thirst-quenching, life-giving water. Indescribably refreshing! The wait, I began to see, was part of the hug, the investment of value *we* give it. The longer the wait, the more powerful the hug became because some of the magic lay in us.

I found an adjacent room where people were watching Amma give her hugs (via a closed-circuit feed) on a large flat screen TV. I sat on the floor in front of the TV and watched Amma up close. Her white sari covered and contrasted her brown skin. She was heavy, fleshy, pillowy, maternal. A red scarf draped her shoulders while a red bindi spot on her forehead marked her third eye. She wore a traditional diamond-stud in her nose. Her dark eyes twinkled and she was *always* smiling.

Her hugs lasted between ten and thirty seconds. She hugged men, women, the old, the young, even infants. She hugged couples together, one in each arm. I saw her hug a mother and baby, too. Lots of people brought their children.

As I watched this dark-skinned woman hugging all these white people, I realized that our Judeo-Christian culture was starved for the unconditional love that flows from the Divine Feminine Mother to balance the jealous and vengeful Father God of the bible and his chaste Son. Though Jesus tried to temper the Father's harshness with love, he was still a man. And I don't believe Mary gave many hugs.

Watching this parade of embraces, I became aware of another aspect of the magic—to receive the Divine Mother's love people had to become childlike. To my surprise, I was tearing up. This may have been the result of the lilting Indian music or the carrier wave of love that emanated from Amma as she unceasingly embraced her "children." Whatever the reason, I grew emotional in her presence as I waited my turn for the Ultimate Hug.

F-5. On the bottom of the TV screen the number was continually updated so people would know when it was their turn. As L-4, I'd be here well into the evening. I couldn't stay that long.

Back in the ballroom I scoured the merchandise tables for something to buy as a donation to Amma and her charities. Finally, I chose a blank journal with a beautiful red cover. While waiting to pay for it, I struck up a conversation with a slight, blonde woman wearing black jeans and a hooded sweatshirt. She admired my journal and asked where I'd gotten it. I showed her and, by way of introduction, told her that I'd recently lost my wife. She said I'd come to the perfect place and that Amma's hug would help me with my grief. I confided that I couldn't stay to get a hug because I had to leave. Immediately, she sprang into action. "Don't move," she ordered and disappeared. Puzzled, I waited and in a few minutes she returned with someone who she assured me would get me into the line and make sure I got my hug. It turned out she had been involved with Amma for twenty years and knew everybody.

Like some VIP I was taken to the front of the ballroom. I felt as if Joy had parted the waves for me. I was told to write my message for Amma on a card. "My wife just died," I wrote, "Her name was Joy." I was told to remove my shoes and brought to a waiting area by the side of the stage. After several minutes I was led into one of the two lines. Amma's sweet assistants herd the endless flow of devotees down a chute two by two.

I was about six back (twelve counting the two lines) from Amma, and everyone in front of me was on their knees. I was asked to kneel. I didn't know if it was a sign of submission or just a question of height since Amma was seated in a chair. I was told to remove my eyeglasses, which were put in a basket so they wouldn't be crushed in the hug. Her assistants continually guided people in and out of Amma's brief, enveloping embrace. After the hug people are plucked out of her arms, helped to their feet and led away. Then it's the next person's turn.

As the line became shorter I felt tremors of emotion rippling through me. My eyes began to tear up, then overflow. And then came the moment. I was being ushered into Amma's big, fleshy arms.

I sank into her. She smelled of sandalwood and rubbed my back as she whispered into my ear what sounded to me like, "Ma...Ma...Ma...Ma...Ma." I inhaled her fragrance and felt as if she were infusing me with blasts of some sort of vibratory medicine. She pulled her head away for a moment while an assistant told her what my card said—that my wife had recently died and her name was Joy. Amma doesn't speak English so she asked her translator what my wife died of. They asked me. "Breast cancer," I answered.

Amma then pulled me into a second short hug (a chaser?) and blasted me with rapid-fire *"Ma's."* I felt very emotional—quivering, trembling. Then she opened her arms and handed me a Hershey's chocolate Kiss. And an apple. I was told that she gives the "kiss" to everyone. It's *prasad*, food blessed by the guru. But the apple was special.

Dazed and disoriented, I needed help getting to my feet. Now I understood why the assistants were there—people are stunned. I was.

I was ushered to a holding pen by the side of the stage where they suggest you sit awhile and absorb your experience as well as Amma's continual outpouring of love. I sat on the floor, filled with gratitude that I'd gotten my hug so miraculously.

It must have been fifteen minutes before I regained my bearings. When I did, I was told to eat my "kiss" and especially my blessed apple. As I sat in the audience and savored the sacred chocolate and fruit I'd been given by Amma, I imagined it nurturing my physical body the way her embrace had nurtured my emotional and spiritual body.

It was time to go.

During the hour-long drive home during rush-hour traffic, I was still stunned. After my big day with Amma I should have been ecstatic, but I wasn't. The Hugging Saint's sandalwood-scented embrace had no doubt soothed my grief. But as I drove up the 405 freeway into the San Fernando Valley, my mood soured. By the time I arrived home I was inexplicably depressed. Alone in my condo, the "beloved child" Amma's hug had evoked felt more like an abandoned orphan.

I was confused. I'd just received the ultimate hug from the most famous hugger in the world. And it had required a minor miracle to get that hug. I took solace in the way Joy had miraculously intervened and made the hug possible. With her help I'd experienced the ultimate. As far as hugs go, I'd climbed Everest. So why did I feel bad?

Amma's hug—though lovely, inspiring and heart-opening—didn't rock my world! At least not in any way I was aware of. Maybe that's why I was feeling let down. But what did I expect? And how could anything match my expectations for the "ultimate hug?" Had I reached the end of my *Journey of a Thousand Hugs?* If so, where had I actually arrived?

If anyone embodied my vision of the Many Limbed Goddess it was Amma. She'd hugged more people than anyone in the world. I took comfort in the thought that Joy had sent the vision to inspire me to go on a quest to obtain the hugs I needed to heal my grief. My journey was over. But my grief wasn't.

And I didn't know what to do next.

℘ 16 ℃

A Priestess of Joy

The phone rang, startling me out of my distress. Angelina, a friend who'd offered to give me a massage, was downstairs in the lobby. In all the excitement about Amma, I'd completely forgotten about our meeting. I buzzed her in.

As I waited for her to take the elevator up to my third-floor condo, I realized just what a funk I was in. I should have been looking forward to a massage from a beautiful woman. When she had offered to gift me with a massage a week earlier, it sounded like a great idea. But now I didn't want a massage. I wanted Joy.

The moment Angelina walked in, she gave me a big hug. It felt good to be held.

"How are you doing?" she murmured in my ear.

I held on to her and answered, "Not so good. I'm glad you're here."

We finally separated and she graced me with her dazzling smile. Light brown hair framed her delicately featured face in ringlets that curled gently down to her shoulders. Blue-eyed and dimpled, though pushing sixty she looked closer to forty and had recently begun a second career as a model. I suddenly realized that though I'd seen her several times since Joy's memorial service, she'd never held me. Well, a massage was as good, maybe even better.

Angelina was a longtime friend and a member of our Wisdom Circle. Over the years, Joy and I had counseled her through some challenging love affairs. In return she'd given us the occasional massage, something she felt she had a gift for. Toward the end, she'd been there for Joy in many ways.

We had tea in the kitchen and chatted about the children's book she was writing. I gave her some hard-won advice— "Commit to writing only five minutes a day. First thing. Just show up. Consistency is the key."

She thanked me.

I was happy to give her something—even if only advice—in return for the massage she was about to give me.

She got up and put her cup in the sink. "Why don't we get started."

Joy and I often had massages at home so we had our own massage table. I set up the table in the living room, lit a few candles for ambience, dimmed the lights, put on my favorite massage music, took off my clothes and tossed them on the couch. Angelina and I had shared many hot tubs before and were comfortable with each other's nudity. Dressed, she prepared some creams and oils, then instructed me to lie face down. Naked, I climbed onto the table, where I lay on my stomach. It was a warm evening; no sheet was required.

The moment Angelina placed her palms over the soles of my feet I felt incredible energy pouring into me. But as her hands moved gently over my body I found myself becoming impatient. Her previous massages had been deliberate. Slow. But this was glacially slow. *Too slow!*

I grew increasingly restless and, as she worked on my back, arms, hands, wrists and fingers, my mind raced with judgments: *She's doing too much; her touch is too unfocused; she's in a world by herself and not really feeling ME.* Imagine being irritated while receiving a massage from a beautiful woman! I must have been out of my mind!

Suddenly, I heard a voice in my head. *"Stop trying to control things!"*

Huh?

"You don't know what you need," the Voice continued. *"Just receive. Remember, you're in my hands."*

Was it Joy? Was I talking to myself?

I willed myself to stop judging Angelina's massage and to surrender. Almost immediately I was flooded with a wellspring of appreciation for the loving touch I was receiving. Shifting into an attitude of gratitude, my heart opened. My body relaxed. And I began to relish Angelina's slow, deliberate caresses in a way I hadn't been able to before.

It must have been more than an hour later when she finished the massage. Lying on my back, I opened my eyes and saw her gazing down at me with the most beatific and loving smile.

"Thank you," I whispered, barely able to speak. "That was wonderful!"

"Thank *you!*" she replied, her face glowing.

Feeling utterly vulnerable, I asked, "Would you uh... hold me?"

"Of course," she said with a big smile. She climbed onto the massage table fully clothed and lay down beside me. As I relaxed into her embrace I was hit by a wave of energy that seemed to radiate from her body. For the past hour she'd been touching me with only her hands. Now that she touched me with the length of her body, I was stunned. Our breathing quickly synchronized and I began to spasm involuntarily. She began to undulate along with me. Entwined in each other's arms we were creating a potent energy circuit, and the more we surrendered to it, the more powerfully it ran through us.

She whispered in my ear, "Do you want me to touch you?"

Not quite sure what she meant, I muttered, "Uh...yeah. Sure."

To my surprise she reached between my thighs and took my limp penis into her hand. Waves of energy continued coursing through our bodies. Suddenly, I ejaculated.

I was embarrassed and didn't know what to do. Then I blurted, "Would you like to take a bath?"

"Sure," she replied with a big smile, "That'd be nice."

Somewhat relieved, I hopped off the massage table and handed her a towel. Seeing her wipe her clothes just reinforced my distress at what had just happened. She, on the other hand, seemed unfazed.

In a daze I staggered to the bathroom. Joy and I had often enjoyed our oversized bath built for two. The salts, bath oils and candles were all available, and it took little effort to create an enchanting atmosphere.

Sighing with pleasure, Angelina and I settled into the hot bubbly water. Though we'd shared hot tubs at parties before, I felt strange lying in my bathtub next to a woman who wasn't Joy. I tried not to stare at Angelina's glistening body. I didn't know what to say or do.

When I glanced over at her, Angelina wore a big smile on her face. She looked like the cat who'd eaten the canary. I wasn't sure how to interpret it.

"Wow!" she sighed.

"Wow!" I echoed for lack of something to say. My discomfort was becoming a maddening dislocation.

"I've never experienced anything like that before."

"Uh...me neither," I parroted.

"Initially I asked to be an open channel for healing," she said. "But very soon I felt Joy's presence."

Chills ran through me. "There were moments when I thought I did, too," I admitted.

"At one point I had the distinct impression Joy was directing my hands. So I refined my intention and asked to be a clear channel for Joy to work through. But when I asked Joy to guide my hands I had no idea..." She closed her eyes as if reliving the moment. Then she looked at me. "There was a moment when I looked down and saw *flames* coming from my hands and going into you. Joy told me it was the *Fire of Love.* In all the massages I've given over the years, I've never experienced anything like it."

I was stunned. I closed my eyes to relive the massage, imagining Joy's *Fire of Love* flowing into me.

"I want you to know," Angelina said, interrupting my reverie, "that Joy was the instigator of it all."

I wasn't sure what she was getting at.

"Joy asked me to ask you if you wanted me to touch you."

"Oh that..."

"The first time she asked me to ask you I was hesitant. I said to her, *'You're kidding!'* But she said, *'Go ahead. Ask him!'* So I did. And you said *Yes.*"

"I didn't know what you meant," I muttered. "I hope it was okay."

She smiled warmly. "It all felt very sacred."

I still found it hard to believe what she was saying. Yet hadn't I heard a voice, *Joy's voice,* telling me that I was "in *her* hands?" Could that be why I ejaculated without even an erection? Angelina had barely touched me and I came.

I became aware of Angelina's body in the water slippery against mine. Her breasts glistened and her nipples were hard, yet I felt no desire.

Sensing my discomfort, she joked, "I've never been part of such an extraordinary threesome."

I laughed awkwardly. "Me neither."

After toweling off, she dressed and I put on my bathrobe. It was nearly midnight. As we hugged goodnight at the door, she glanced at the statue of Isis in the foyer and mused, "I guess I'm now a Priestess of Isis."

"And Joy," I added without thinking.

"Yes. A Priestess of Joy."

I couldn't sleep that night, replaying what I'd experienced, but this time, with Joy's participation. Was it possible? Had Joy found a way to communicate her love for me? And had our meditations and my *Journey of a Thousand Hugs* prepared me for this miraculous encounter?

What a day! First I was blessed by the loving embrace of Amma, the embodiment of the Divine Mother, and then by the ecstasy of Joy's loving caresses via the channel of her willing priestess Angelina. Amazing!

I tossed and turned, then got up and paced. I wanted to believe. Yet it was hard to accept. And I had so many questions.

I finally fell asleep hoping the answers would reveal themselves in my dreams. But when I awoke the next morning, dazed from lack of sleep, the extraordinary events of the night before seemed like a dream. In the light of day I had to ask myself—*Was it really possible that Joy had used Angelina as a channel to console, comfort and heal me?*

As I stirred the bubbling cauldron of my mind, one burning question rose to the surface—*What do I do next?*

In meditation I asked Joy for guidance. Her answer came through clearly. *"Don't do anything. Receive...and allow Angelina to lead. Allow her to do whatever she's guided to do. Give up control. Surrender. Your surrender is part of your healing as well as your 'gift' to her. She's my priestess. I will guide her."*

℘ 17 ℘

Doubts & Confirmations

What had seemed so vividly real in a candlelit living room decorated like an Egyptian palace began to fade in the bright sunlit days filled with mundane chores like shopping, washing dishes and paying bills. As the days wore on I found it harder to accept the idea that Joy had found a way to heal my grief, even though this "miracle" was corroborated by a third party. The experience felt more and more like a dream and my belief faltered.

Then something happened that made me question my disbelief.

I'd been taking little Natalie to gymnastics almost every week. This time Terri joined us so she could see her daughter jumping on the trampoline, doing a headstand and swinging on the rope. Afterwards, we went to lunch. Throughout the meal I had a strong sense that Joy was sitting in the fourth empty chair enjoying the family being together. Then again, I could have been imagining it.

"I haven't been dreaming of Joy," I said.

Neither had Terri. "Natalie says she hears *Nana* in her head sometimes," Terri said in frustration, "but she won't tell me what she hears."

After lunch I went home and took a nap. When I woke up, I realized I'd dreamt of Joy. She appeared in a dream almost immediately after I told someone I hadn't been dreaming of her, as if letting me know that she'd been present at our lunch.

This dream also assuaged those nagging doubts about my miraculous encounter with Joy via Angelina. And if my dream of Joy wasn't proof enough, another strange incident drove the point home.

The following Sunday I had brunch with some friends whom I hadn't seen since the memorial service. Over coffee, Mark told me he had a confession to make. He claimed that throughout our brunch Joy had been prodding him to reveal what had happened on the day of her memorial.

On that day he'd received a message from Joy (he's quite psychic and does readings for people) instructing him to bring me something. He apologized for not fulfilling her request and wanted to get together as soon as possible so he could finally give me what he was supposed to have given me three months ago. We arranged to get together the following week.

When Mark came over he presented me with a pink, heart-shaped crystal the size of large plum that he claimed Joy had wanted him to give me at the memorial service.

"To be honest," he admitted, "I wasn't too thrilled to be told to give away one of my prized possessions."

On the way to the memorial service, he realized he'd forgotten to bring it, and Joy insisted he go back and get it. "Which I did. After the service I tried to get your attention, but you were surrounded by people. I couldn't stay for the reception, so I left. And Joy was very upset with me for not delivering her message to you." It had taken him three months to finally fulfill her request.

I held the crystal in my hand and studied it. Pink was one of Joy's favorite colors. The heart shape was the symbol of love. And crystal reminded me of Joy's essence. I was astounded by how wonderfully this object communicated Joy.

I was touched, but also a little angry and annoyed. Joy had been so insistent back then because she knew how much it would have meant for me to receive such a "sign" on the day of her memorial. I could only wonder how different my grief would have been.

And yet, despite the three-month delay, I was grateful to receive this sign now. Since her passing, I'd had many signs and yet no matter how many I received or how incredible they were, I still had doubts. So in a way, the timing was perfect—as if Joy knew Mark would procrastinate for three months and then deliver this sign to me exactly when I needed it.

Receiving these confirmations of Joy's presence in my life— in a dream and with this crystal—in the space of a few days, renewed my belief in our communication. Naturally, I couldn't wait to see if Angelina would also be inspired to once again play her new role as a Priestess of Joy.

☙ 18 ❧

Temple of Isis

>—————————————————————<

The following week I received an email from Angelina and was thrilled to read the subject line: "Your Next Massage." She'd received a message from Joy that it was time for another encounter. "Joy also told me what she wants me to add to your massage," she wrote, "which I think you'll enjoy."

As if a champagne bottle uncorked inside me, a bubbling anticipation coursed through my fingers as I wrote back that I was available at her convenience, and that "this morning Joy told me how happy she is that I'm *yessing* my way into a new life. *Yes*, to our unfolding!"

When the day finally arrived, I was full of questions. Would Joy communicate with me? How would Joy, through Angelina, comfort me? To be honest, I also wondered if I was losing my mind.

As I showered and got ready, I felt as if I was going out on a date. With Joy. I wore one of her favorite shirts even though I'd eventually be naked. As I primped in front of the mirror, my eye caught a framed picture of us, wearing black bowler hats and white gloves, in a dance pose with "jazz hands." Joy resembled Ginger Rogers and I, a bearded Fred Astaire. I blew her image a kiss and prepared for Angelina's arrival.

As I was setting up the massage table in the living room for the evening's strange encounter, I wondered if this was the strangest, most bizarre experience I'd ever had.

Suddenly, I flashbacked to a memory that I hadn't thought about in over a quarter century. In fact, the memory was so freakish and disturbing, I'd tried to banish it from my mind. It was the mid '80's and I was licking my wounds after my first marriage fell apart. I'd returned to Israel after seven years in Manhattan—this time not to the holy city of Jerusalem, but to the "fleshpots" of swinging Tel Aviv.

My first wife and I had been together since our twenties, and eventually birthed a book instead of a child. We lived in New York and labored on our "baby" for several years until it was finally published by Simon & Schuster to critical acclaim. *The Washington Post* hailed it as "an important contribution." Phil Donahue (the Oprah of the time) devoted an entire show to our book, but our publisher dropped the ball and there were no books in the stores. Our "baby" was aborted and it took a tremendous toll on our marriage. Heartbroken, after twelve years together, my wife and I went our separate ways.

So there I was, living in Tel Aviv and performing in a revue based on the stories of Sholem Aleichem, the Jewish Mark Twain, upon which *Fiddler on the Roof* was based. I also acted in the occasional movie, like *Delta Force* with Chuck Norris and Lee Marvin. But most important, I was having a torrid and tempestuous affair with a beautiful British actress.

During sweltering summer evenings, Tel Avivians flock to the beach to picnic and swim in the warm Mediterranean. On one of those evenings, I was standing in about four feet of gently lapping water. The protective jetties created a lagoon-like calm. Since it was low tide, I could stand several hundred feet from shore. With my British lover wrapped around me and veiled in darkness, we made love in the warm silky water. Our skin slick with the sea, we slid effortlessly against each other. As our passion grew, I became blind to everything but the feel of her body against mine.

Suddenly, something bumped into me. Caught up in our sexual frenzy, I tried to ignore it. It bumped against me again. I looked down—a dead body was bobbing in the water.

While my lover screamed, I pulled the bloated, bluish-grey corpse of a young man who appeared to be in his early twenties toward the shore and dragged it onto the beach. A crowd immediately gathered; a doctor stepped forward. The man had drowned and had been dead for several hours.

For weeks I was haunted by this bizzare incident. I had been touched by death! While having sex! What did it mean? Why had Death been drawn to our lovemaking? Why had Death reached out and actually *touched* me?

At the time, it had disturbed me so much that I'd tried to erase the image from my mind. And I had succeeded until this moment. Many years ago I'd been touched by Death. Now I was about to be touched by the Afterlife.

As I continued to prepare for Angelina's arrival, I decided to treat this miraculous encounter with the reverence it deserved. So I placed two votive candles beneath the wings of the Isis statue that stood on its three-foot black marble pedestal in the foyer. In *Love Ever After*, Joy wrote about this statue of Isis, the great goddess of ancient Egypt. "When I returned from Egypt, I kept getting a message in my meditations to purchase a statue or a picture depicting Isis." Joy found what she was looking for. "Suddenly there was Isis in all her glory—15 inches high with a 20 inch wingspan. Her wings, in the richest hues of blue, red and gold, seemed to be inviting the whole world into her arms."

I stood in front of the statue, closed my eyes and tried to prepare myself for the sacred encounter that I hoped was about to take place. Another memory from long ago sprang to mind—a grainy image from a black and white movie in which a drunken young man kisses a statue of the goddess Venus and she comes to life.

As a ten year old I was fascinated with the movie, *One Touch of Venus*, about a goddess, played by Ava Gardner (the Angelina Jolie of the time) who falls in love with a mortal. This was unusual for me since most of the movies I loved as a child were war movies. In the late '50's there was something on TV called the *Million Dollar Movie* that played one movie three times a day for an entire week. I tried to see every showing of this movie that was based on a Broadway musical and eventually remade into the '80's movie, *Mannequin*.

Was my childhood fascination with this movie about the goddess Venus coming to life a premonition of the miraculous encounter about to unfold?

I greeted Angelina at the door and we hugged for a long moment—a new tenderness between us now that we were joined in a great adventure. She wore a blue, form-fitting top that accentuated her sky blue eyes and revealed her shapely figure. I led her into the living room, where we sat together on the couch. I was dying to know what Joy had told her to "add" to the massage, but I didn't ask. Following Joy's instructions, I wanted to "allow the unfolding." We chatted a while, until at last Angelina took my hand and informed me that Joy wanted her to add "toning" to the massage.

Toning?! I was disappointed. Humming during the massage was certainly not the great next step I'd anticipated. But I held my judgments in check. I wanted to put myself in Joy's hands. If she wanted Angelina to tone during the massage, so be it.

To honor the significance of what Angelina and I were about to do, I suggested we light the votive candles I'd prepared to invoke Joy's spirit and create the sacred space of the Temple of Isis. Angelina suggested that we also set our intentions for the evening. Lighting one of the candles, she declared her intention to be a clear channel for Joy's love and healing. I lit my candle and declared my intention to receive as much love and healing as possible. The moment we completed our invocation,

I felt the energy shift. Angelina and I looked at each other in recognition—something extraordinary was about to happen.

Face down on the massage table I was much more relaxed than last time. Angelina's touch was as slow and deliberate as before, but I experienced none of the restlessness I had during the previous massage.

Yet as Angelina's fingers gently kneaded my flesh, a new frustration was brewing. I was hoping to communicate with Joy—to experience some kind of contact, even conversation. But as much as I tried, I got nothing. I definitely felt Joy's presence, especially in Angelina's touch, but I heard no words. I spoke to Joy in my mind. *Are you there?* I asked.

Nothing.

I was growing increasingly frustrated by my inability to make contact, when in the depths of my mind I heard a commanding voice that wasn't my own say, *"Experience!"* At that moment I understood—my healing wasn't about *talking* to Joy the way she'd talked to Bob. *My* healing was about experiencing something beyond words. My challenge was to surrender without expectation.

How can one describe an experience beyond words? I experienced all the varieties of loving touch: the patient, nurturing ministrations of a mother for a child, the sensual and healing caresses of a priestess for a wounded warrior, the etheric embrace of a Guardian Angel for their beloved embodied human. I felt this extraordinary touch grounding me in my body and healing me in ways beyond my comprehension.

At times there was also something strangely alien or *non-human* about it, as if a spirit (Joy's?) was working on me from another dimension. I'd never experienced anything like it.

As she worked my neck and shoulders, Angelina whispered in my ear, "I see golden energy around my hands and around your body." Later she added, "Joy is standing beside me reaching into my hands as if I were a portal!"

103

No wonder this massage felt so *out of this world*! I surrendered to the ecstasy of Joy's love flowing from the Afterlife through Angelina into me. I pictured Joy reaching through time and space, through life and death, loving me eternally. And I wept.

The moment Angelina began toning I understood why Joy wanted to add sound to the massage. The vibration of Angelina's voice amplified her touch, adding a whole new dimension to the experience. She lowered her face close to my body and toned up and down my torso, focusing on each chakra.

At a certain point her now supercharged touch became sexually arousing, yet it was so much more than sex. I was trembling, undulating, spasming in an orgasmic state for nearly an hour. Afterwards I discovered that I'd ejaculated sometime during my *out of this world* hour-long orgasm, but that had no effect on the ecstasy. The toning had aroused my energy body, which wasn't limited by the climaxing of my physical body. In such an ecstatic state, my ejaculation seemed inconsequential, like a firecracker next to the roar of a shuttle lift-off. To have experienced—and the operative word is "experience"—such ecstasy in the midst of my grief was a miracle.

When Angelina finished the massage she suggested a bath. I smiled—it was becoming part of our ritual. Since we were both hungry I grabbed some snacks from the kitchen.

We sank into the hot, bubbly water with sighs, then we nibbled on grapes and cheese. We'd been silenced by the magnitude of the experience. As we relaxed we began to express our awe at what had happened.

Angelina was astounded at the way Joy used her as a portal. "I feel so honored to be in service in this sacred way," she said, her eyes filling with tears. "I'd asked Joy to be my spirit guide. But I had no idea anything like this would or *could* happen!"

"I know. It's unbelievable! And yet...." I hesitated to put what we'd just experienced into words. It was beyond words, even beyond belief. Describing it required judging it. And I just wanted to bask in the afterglow of the experience. Apparently

Angelina did, too, but after a few minutes of silence she murmured, "God, she *loves* you!"

Normally, hearing such a sentiment would have brought me to tears. But I was in such an exalted state that instead I found it inspiring. "Loving touch must be the best medicine for grief," I said, "because the healing is cellular *and* energetic."

At one point I complimented Angelina on her wonderful toning. "Wasn't it tiring?" I asked, since she'd toned through most of the massage.

"No," she said, "because I'm not really there. It's not really me who is giving you the massage. I step aside and allow Joy to use me. *I* don't get tired."

I was astounded by what she was saying. And yet it made perfect sense.

"It was amazing how Joy was guiding me, amplifying my energy and using my body as a conduit for her love."

I admitted that I felt a little uncomfortable receiving so much without reciprocating.

She popped a grape into her mouth and then put one in mine. "Don't worry," she reassured me. "I felt Joy's pleasure at loving you. I felt Joy's incredible love for you. And then I felt Joy feeling your pleasure moving back through me. It was like a figure-eight between Joy and you, and I was the midpoint through which everything flowed. Around and around and in and out through *me*. It was…amazing!"

Once again I noticed that cat-who'd-eaten-the-canary smile on her face. Then I realized I had a similar smile on *my* face. Incredible as it seemed, was I really being made love to by my late wife?

After Angelina left I lay in bed unable to sleep. Tonight's experience was more intentional than the first time and consequently more profound. This strange adventure, which I began to think of as the "Rites of Joy," was just beginning. Where, I wondered, would it lead?

℘ *19* ℘

Orgy of Grief

To mark our July 3rd wedding anniversary I decided to spend the day with Joy. I gathered all of our photo albums as well as letters and cards we'd given each other over the years for birthdays, Valentine's Day and anniversaries. I wanted to bask (maybe "wallow" is more accurate) in all the expressions of love we'd shared. I wanted to remember.

I spread everything out on the carpet of our bedroom, sat down on the floor and waded in. I began at the beginning...a letter Joy wrote me to celebrate our "falling in love."

> *My Darling,*
> *I love you because I see so much good in you*
> *I see so much good in you because I love you*
> *I delight in your body, mind and spirit*
> *I drink you as a tonic*
> *I devour you as nourishment for my soul*
>
> *These are just a few of the things I love about you:*
> *The creativity, imagination and depth of your mind*
> *Your curiosity and concern for people, animals and nature*
> *Your need to learn and know about everything that*
> *   interests you*
> *Your openness to all possibilities*
> *The way you question and analyze everything*

The way you express yourself verbally and in writing
Your thoughtfulness and respect for all living things
Your honesty and willingness to expose your inner feelings
Your desire for adventure and new experiences
All the ways you let me know how you feel about me
Your constant concern for my comfort, happiness and
pleasure
Your independence and courage to be yourself
Your sense of humor and willingness to laugh at yourself
Your playfulness
Your generosity
Your love for your family
Your sensitivity
Your love of music and dancing
Your passion for spiritual subjects and your openness to
all of it
Your search for self discovery and understanding the
mysteries of life
Your ability and willingness to listen
Your trust in me
Your sensuality and enjoyment of pleasure
The way you make me feel like a Goddess
Your skill and heart as a lover (the best I've ever had)
The way you touch me, hold me, kiss me, look at me, and
lead me into ecstasy
The strength and gentleness of your arms and hands
Your staying power
Your gorgeous body
Your incredible, edible cock
The love, honesty and intensity I see in your eyes
Your respect for me and my ideas
The way I feel about myself when I'm with you
Joy

Tears streamed down my cheeks. A portal into the past had been opened and the memories came flooding back. Like an appetizer, this letter made me hungry for *us*. I devoured the next letter in which Joy celebrated our first anniversary together. At the top she'd written, *"Memories of You"* and catalogued her favorite memories which included our climb up a Mayan pyramid and collecting seashells on the beach of a Mexican fishing village; her dressing up for Halloween as Howard Stern while I dressed as Princess Di; and, of course, "dancing, dancing, dancing." Her list of favorite memories concluded with—

> *Most Memorable Love-Making Experiences*
> * *In a hammock by moonlight on the beach at Puerto Morales*
> * *At Bodhi's tantra workshop*
> * *On swinging beds in Cancun and Sutter Creek*
> * *In the hammock on the patio*
> * *In front of the fire, on the chaise, the sectional and the floor*
> * *Making love for six hours straight*
> * *Holding you, hugging you, kissing you, touching you, stroking you, smelling you, tasting you, talking to you, playing with you, making love to you*
> *   I love you with all my heart and soul,*
> *   Your Joy*

I reveled in Joy's love. I crawled over the photo albums and, like a starving man at a buffet, devoured the images of us, posed and candid, that illustrated her letters.

I found an envelop which read "For Jerry—the love of my life on our second anniversary." As I opened the two-page typewritten letter, I was so grateful that Joy's way of commemorating our love and life was by savoring the memories. But as I read, I cried realizing how many I'd forgotten.

Like an archeologist of love, I sifted through the artifacts of our lost civilization of romance, and came upon a folder marked "Wedding" in which I found our post-wedding announcement.

> *Aloha!*
>
> *We are delighted to announce our marriage on July 3rd on the beach in beautiful Hawaii. The wedding was held at sunset at a sacred Hawaiian site, The Place of Refuge, just south of*

Kona on the Big Island. A black lava beach ringed with caves, pools and palm trees provided a picture-postcard setting and a powerful energy of "new beginnings."

The intimate ceremony was performed by Joy's daughter-in-law, Kate, and a local metaphysical minister, Chris, who was also our dolphin guide. After Chris invoked the local Hawaiian spirits and led us in a traditional exchange of flower leis, Kate performed a moving service written by Joy who is also a minister. The highlight was the letters we read to each other expressing the depth of our love and commitment. The ceremony concluded with Joy's daughter Terri singing the romantic "Hawaiian Wedding Song." As champagne flowed and we posed for pictures, a breathtaking sunset crowned our magical moment.

We spent the week in a beautiful house on the ocean in Kona and had a great time creating many unforgettable memories: para-sailing 800 ft. above the ocean; snorkeling and kayaking; Fourth of July fireworks; a Hawaiian luau; Lomi Lomi massages and swimming with the amazing and gentle Dolphins off a boat in the middle of the blue Pacific.

Even though the wedding was very small, we carried all of you in our hearts as part of our Circle of Love. And we look forward to celebrating our new adventure with you.

With all our love,

Joy & Jerry

I re-read my vows, which I'd shared with Joy on that black lava beach in Hawaii. They began with words I'd written when we first fell in love:

MY BEST ASSET IS MY CAPACITY FOR JOY...
BEING WITH YOU IS LIKE RETURNING HOME....
IT DOESN'T MATTER...THE BIG, THE SMALL
THE PROFOUND, THE CASUAL...
THE WAY WE CROSS A STREET TOGETHER,
OPEN A DOOR, MAKE LOVE, SHARE SILENCE OR

SNACK WHILE WATCHING TV....
WHATEVER WE DO IS A HOLOGRAM OF LOVE...

My vows concluded with an acknowledgement of the health challenges we faced due to Joy's recently diagnosed breast cancer.

Our love has been like the blooming of a rose. Now we've been pricked by Love's thorn. And amazingly it's still wonderful!

You're so courageous, fearless, lacking in self-pity. How do you do it?

Thank you...for giving me the opportunity to take care of you and to learn a greater love that can only be experienced when you are impaled on Love's thorn.

Thank you for letting me be your "Guardian Angel" for a change.

Thank you for all the gifts...even those that hurt.

You are my Joy, in sickness and in health. Your ever-unfolding grace and beauty astounds and inspires me. Know that despite all we've gone through and all we're going to go through, I feel I'm the luckiest man in the world.

Now we are about to come together even more...and it will be an even greater adventure than before.

I adore you...you are the treasure of my life.

You take my breath away!

I wiped away the tears streaming down my face and caught my breath as I rummaged through the file looking for Joy's vows. I found them—two pages that were written in large bold

24 point type

—a painful reminder that she was already losing her sight.

110

I had prayed for someone like you to love...but you have surpassed my wildest dreams. You are the best friend I've ever had...you are the most supportive partner and romantic lover I could ever wish for...you are my hero, my soul mate and the love of my life.

I can't even imagine my life without you by my side. You nourish my soul with the strength and constancy of your devotion. And after 5 years together, you continue to fill my days and nights with your loving words and thoughtful deeds.

I thank you with all my heart for coming into my life. Thank you for a thousand glorious yesterdays and the promise of thousands of beautiful tomorrows.

I know we have loved before in other lifetimes, but never like this. So take my hand and walk with me to the end of this earthly journey and I will cherish you all the days of my life.

Joy

Stretched out on the carpet I surrendered to another paroxysm of grief. When the storm finally passed I looked up and saw a handwritten anniversary letter from Joy. Though it bore no date, I could see from the way Joy's once immaculate handwriting had deteriorated that she'd lost most of her sight due to macular degeneration. What an effort it must have been for her to write this letter. As I read her scrawl, I was seized by another round of weeping for the blindness that she—that *we*—endured. And yet it didn't lessen our love. In many ways it deepened it.

Throughout this day-long *orgy of grief* I tried to make contact with Joy but got nothing. I sniffed the air for some telltale scent of gardenia. *Nothing.* I listened for the whisper of her voice... *Nothing!* Only when I was exhausted from weeping and the summer sun had set did I suddenly hear her say—*"Put it away!"* I understood—I'd grieved enough.

I put the letters and photos away. I thought about journaling but was too exhausted. In the morning I sat down and wrote—

Spent the day reading all the expressions of our love and life together. A delirium of memories...an orgy of grief. I couldn't stop. I didn't want to stop. I wanted to remember...and cry forever.

I wept a lot. *Hours.* Until my chest got sore. I may have pulled something! On our Wedding Anniversary I mainlined us. Got high on us! It hurt...but it was so beautiful! And I'm so grateful! I'm filled with such gratitude for the love I experienced with Joy.

Loss is healed by Gratitude.
Tears of Loss...become Tears of Gratitude....
A thunderstorm. A waterfall...of tears
I'm left with an aching heart! Literally!
I've taken a beating. I put myself through a ringer. Why?
To *FEEL* it...!

The next day I was dumbstruck to receive an email from a friend who claimed to have received a message for me from Joy on our anniversary.

It's good that you've been ACTIVELY grieving and releasing your loss. Thank you for spending this day together with me. It was wonderful! My experience here is heavenly—you'll see. Enjoy every moment—it all "counts." I love you, Joy

My friend didn't know how I had spent our wedding anniversary. And yet the "message" implied that Joy had been with me all day. Why hadn't I experienced her?

The following day in meditation I received this answer: I was so busy experiencing our old relationship, Joy couldn't communicate with me in our new one. I was in the past so much, I couldn't be in the present. I was so sad and sorrowful that it lowered my frequency. Wallowing in my grief put me out of reach.

೫ 20 ೕ

A Rite of Joy

)————————————————————————————(

A few days after my orgy of grief I was still reeling. Maybe metaphorically "slitting my wrists" on our anniversary wasn't such a good idea. Perhaps my blues were also due to completing the first season of my grief. It was now three months since Joy's passing. Whatever the reason, I was in such a funk I wasn't even excited about Angelina coming over in the evening for a Rite of Joy.

A few days before my orgy of grief I was delighted to receive an email from Angelina. It had been several weeks since our last encounter.

> *Hello Dear "King" Jerry....*
> *Last night in dance class during a quieter, "inner movement" part*
> *of the class, I asked Joy to tell me or show me what she would like*
> *me to add to your next massage. Well, she did show AND tell me,*
> *so now you get to be in the Joy-ous anticipation :-)*

I was "in Joy-ous anticipation" until my orgy of grief. In comparison to the great love I relived on our anniversary, these supernatural encounters with Angelina seemed a poor substitute for my life with Joy.

When Angelina arrived, I confided to her that I was feeling blue. To my surprise, she knew—Joy had told her. Wasting no time, she informed me that, "Joy wants me to kiss you all over your body."

Great," I said, trying to sound excited. I should have been thrilled, but was too depressed to feel much of anything.

As we had the last time, we lit the two votive candles in front of the Isis statue and set our intentions for the evening. Again, Angelina wanted to be a clear and loving a channel for Joy's love. I wanted Joy's love to heal me from the depletion and depression I'd slipped into since our wedding anniversary when I'd indulged in my orgy of grief.

As before, the living room was illuminated by candlelight and instrumental music played in the background. Unlike before, I was unmoved by it. I disrobed, climbed up on the massage table and lay face down. As I breathed deeply waiting for the massage to begin, I realized that I felt like a block of stone.

Angelina's hands and fingers began to collaborate in ceaseless combinations of loving touch. Very soon, the stone that seemed to encase me dissolved. My gloom was no match for such exquisite sensual delight. I began to feel Joy's presence in the utter care and devotion with which I was caressed.

Suddenly Angelina's lips grazed my back. Incredibly, I felt eruptions of energy explode in the wake of her tender kisses. These kisses—Joy's kisses—sent me into full-bodied spasms. When she resumed massaging me with her hands, my trembling subsided. The moment her lips touched my flesh, I convulsed.

She, or should I say they, kissed every part of me—my back, arms, hands, palms, wrists, fingertips, waist, hips, buttocks, thighs, the back of my knees, my calves, ankles and feet...they even sucked my toes!

If I had any lingering doubts that Joy was working through Angelina, they were banished by this overwhelming act of love. And then I heard Joy's voice—"Have you ever been so loved, my darling?"

Never!

A wave of profound gratitude swept over me. Joy's love was leading me out of the underworld of grief and back to life.

Angelina instructed me to turn over on my back. I was parched. I sat up and she handed me a glass of water.

While I drank, she marveled, "Joy has been standing next to me. She was putting her hands through mine. When I looked down at my hands, I saw Joy's bejeweled hands and the sleeves of her gown. She was wearing this beautiful Egyptian fabric that only royalty or a goddess like Isis would wear. It's amazing!"

I was in too altered a state to speak, but my heart overflowed and my eyes filled with tears. I handed her the glass and laid back down again on the massage table, this time facing up. Angelina positioned herself behind my head and began working on my neck and chest.

"When I was kissing you," she whispered in my ear, "I could see Joy next to me kissing you. Her lips were somehow merged with mine." She paused to let the miracle of what she was describing sink in. "And while she was kissing you, I could hear her whispering *'I love you...I love you...I love you...'* with each kiss."

Now I understood why those kisses sent me into paroxysms of pleasure. Even though I didn't actually hear the "I love you's," I *felt* them.

Angelina bent over me as she began working on my chest. Her fingers kneaded my heart area, opening another layer of vulnerability. I became aware of the rawness around my chest. I reached up and pulled her down over me to cover my aching heart. It was a hug, albeit an upside-down one.

Her face wound up near my groin, and mine was pressed against her breasts. It felt very comforting. Then she toned—*Ommm!* The powerful vibration, so near my genitals, sent a current up my spine. I began to writhe beneath her. Her toning grew stronger and I began to tremble as the vibrations traveled through my body. I gasped when I felt her kissing my penis. And not sexually. She was kissing me in the same way she had kissed every other part of my body. This wasn't stimulation, this was *adoration*. And it propelled me into a mind-blowing ecstasy!

She resumed toning "Ommm" with my limp penis still in her mouth, and from deep within, I heard these words—*Ecstasy, darling, is the antidote to grief*. With that, I was catapulted into an astounding vision.

A brilliant light suddenly dawned in my mind's eye as the most magnificent multifaceted crystal began to emerge, then transformed into the splendor of a woman wearing a jewel-encrusted blue gown. To my frustration, her sparkling, bejeweled-headdress was so blinding, it was impossible to see her face.

The blinding brilliance dimmed to darkness and the silhouette of a nude woman gradually appeared as if illuminated by moonlight. Her face was obscured by shadows, but her body glowed as if her flesh was made of mother-of-pearl, its iridescence reflecting her aura. She was luminous, luscious and voluptuous—breathtakingly beautiful and irresistibly desirable.

The rainbow of living light surrounding her began to pulsate, and then move like wings. She seemed to be flying, or rather floating, in space. Her movements, at first slow and deliberate, became more expressive until I realized she was dancing. Again I tried to make out her face, but couldn't. As she danced, her face was a blur of motion. Then I realized she was dancing with ME….

Suddenly I was standing on the edge of a wind-swept cliff looking into a fog-enshrouded abyss. I felt Joy behind me but was afraid to turn around. For some reason, I didn't want to see her face for fear that I wouldn't recognize her soul in its non-human form. I sensed her wanting me to jump, urging me to take a leap of faith into the unknown. But I was afraid.

"Trust," she said.

So I jumped….

...AHHH!!! My fall was ecstatic! Down and down...then I felt her, like a parachute above me, slowing my fall. Like an autumn leaf falling from a tree, we gently spiraled down, round and round....

Next thing I knew I was lying beneath an ancient oak tree on a summer day, my head resting in a woman's lap. She wore a checkered summer dress and was stroking my forehead. Who was she? I wondered. Was it Joy? I looked up and she slowly turned her face towards me. But suddenly, I was overcome with a profound drowsiness and, despite fighting it, my eyes closed....

I woke up on the massage table with a blanket thrown over me. Alone. Angelina had left. Only a few candles were still burning. Nat King Cole's song, "There Is No Greater Love" was playing. Disoriented, I got off the table, wrapped myself in a robe and blew out the candles. In the kitchen I found a note from Angelina—"Sweet Dreams" was all it said.

• • • •

Three months earlier, on the day of Joy's death, I'd danced my goodbye beside her lifeless body. Since then I'd been plagued by an unconscious guilt that had been festering inside me until it erupted during my anniversary orgy of grief. Looking at so many photographs of Joy and I dancing together reminded me of our Last Dance and I was suddenly mortified at the way I said goodbye.

Though Joy had passed at noon, the family put off the mortuary all day because we couldn't bear to have her body taken away. Not until evening. First we wanted to say our goodbyes. One by one, the family took turns going into the bedroom alone to have a final private moment. I went in last.

I stood by the hospital bed on which Joy had slept for the last three nights and looked at her lifeless body. Only hours earlier I'd held her in my arms and pressed my cheek against hers so I could share her last breath.

Goodbye? What could I possibly say? My feelings were beyond words. The time for tears stretched before me, but in that moment I wanted to mirror Joy's grace-filled exit. My grief wouldn't help her in this sacred moment of transition. I'd have time for tears later.

I suddenly knew how I would say goodbye—I wanted one last dance. Dancing was the perfect expression of our love and how we danced through life together. I played Michael Frank's, "Let Me Count the Ways," which had been my "dancing Valentine" to her less than two months earlier when I'd danced and lip-synched the words, reminding her of the countless ways I loved her.

Beside her deathbed I danced again to the music. Though her body lay before me, I looked up at the ceiling and imagined her spirit watching me dance my love for her. I danced because, at that moment, she inspired my highest, most sublime self. I danced because she deserved a send-off worthy of her glorious passing. I danced because I wanted to celebrate her soul's journey back to Spirit.

As I danced, I imagined Joy watching me celebrate her "graduation." That's what she would have wanted. No tears. Just one last dance.

Now, several months into mourning the greatest loss of my life, I was no longer in that state of exaltation which had inspired me to dance my goodbye. Wallowing in my grief on our anniversary, the memory of my "last dance" horrified me. *How could I?* I kept asking myself. *And why didn't I cry? Why didn't I climb into that hospital bed with her and wail, tear my clothes, gnash my teeth?...like any normal man who'd lost the love of his life?* I was appalled at my behavior.

During this last Rite of Joy, my vision of Joy dancing was a gift of grace. It showed me that she'd been dancing with me then, now and always. And it absolved me of any lingering guilt or regret. By dancing for me, Joy had shown me that my Last Dance was a perfect way to say goodbye.

• • • •

The next day, as if Joy wanted to be certain I got the message, she orchestrated another incredible synchronicity. I received an email from her daughter-in-law, Kate, who was vacationing in Europe. While visiting the Grand Opera House in Paris—which had impressed Joy when we were there—Kate (who is psychic) was instructed by Joy to buy a postcard and send it to me.

A few days later I received the postcard from Paris postmarked July 6—the same day as the Rite of Joy during which I had my vision. Kate wrote, "Jerry, Joy wanted you to see her dance. This is the postcard she had me buy." The postcard depicted a female dancer whose white dress billowed around her as she leapt into the air—seeming to fly—with her face turned away....

℘ 21 ℘

Blessing of the Palms

>—————————————————————————————<

If love and ecstasy are the antidote to grief, then these Rites of Joy were a supremely healing gift. Like a wind beneath my wings, they literally lightened me, lifting my frequency, at least temporarily, so that I became more receptive to communications from Joy. And, on a more mundane and practical level, they gave me the courage to take the next step in my journey—that trip to Two Bunch Palms.

Back in May, a month after Joy's transition, when I first began *taking care of business*, I realized to my dismay that, in January, Joy had booked a reservation for us at Two Bunch Palms, our favorite desert spa. The Monday-Friday reservation was for the beginning of June—then only a few weeks away. *I didn't want to go!* The thought of spending five days alone at a resort was less than appealing, and the idea of eating alone in a dining room where Joy and I had enjoyed many fabulous meals was something I dreaded. However, the fact that Joy had booked the trip gave me pause and I hesitated canceling. Her booking seemed like a dying wish I felt obligated to honor.

As the June date approached I was still feeling ambivalent about going on this first Joy-less trip. I knew I had to go, that it would be good for me, that Joy would have wanted me to go. But I wasn't ready. (I hadn't received my mantra yet.) So I postponed my reservation in the hopes that by the end of July I'd be ready to venture out into the world on my first solo trip.

It was late July and the sun was high in the summer sky as I drove to my five-day retreat at the spa that touted itself as "an almost mystical sanctuary." After a two-hour drive through the desert I arrived at Two Bunch Palms. I stepped out of my air-conditioned SUV into what felt like a sauna and got slammed by the mid-afternoon 107º heat of Desert Hot Springs.

Two Bunch Palms was dedicated to the "Art of Letting Go" where one could "Embrace the spirit of serenity." The desert spa was an oasis of quiet where people came to get away from the hubbub of their daily lives. The spa invited guests to "enjoy the freedom of simply being" and reminded them, "You are ruled by everything until you understand the power in doing nothing."

The local Native American tribes believed the hot mineral spring waters that created this desert oasis to be sacred ground. The spa became a legendary Hollywood hideaway where people who could afford to go anywhere, came for a unique experience money couldn't buy. Celebrities donned robes, floated in the healing waters of the Grotto pool (rich in mood-elevating lithium), and abided by the spa's invitation to "quiet the noise in your life and allow the silence. It may be your soul talking to you."

I was glad to be back.

Hot and hungry, I headed for the small air-conditioned dining room. The place was empty so late in the afternoon, and it was off-season. The hostess greeted me. "Sit anywhere," she said, gesturing toward the twelve linen-covered tables.

I froze for a moment—Joy and I had eaten at *all* of these tables. Finally, I sat down at a table near the large wrap-around picture-window overlooking the patio, the bougainvillea and a view of the mountains. I hadn't realized how quickly and easily memories would be triggered. I hadn't expected to be the only diner.

A waitress brought me a limited after-lunch menu. The cold gazpacho soup with chunks of avocado would be perfect for a sweltering summer day. After taking my order, she put bread sticks on the table and left.

I was completely alone. Absentmindedly, I bit into a bread stick and was suddenly flooded with memories of sitting with Joy at this very table. And I wept.

• • • •

Over the years Joy and I had visited Two Bunch Palms many times. We enjoyed the informality—everyone walking around in robes, even in the dining room—and the spa offered an eclectic menu of massage treatments, from Ayurvedic to Thai. Our last visit had been the previous January when we treated ourselves to a birthday celebration since both of our birthdays were that month.

On that last visit, Joy was still feeling side effects from her radiation treatments in November, so she didn't spend much time in the Grotto pool. The hot water took too much out of her. The winter weather was quite cold, below freezing at night. During the day I pulled the couch over to the sliding glass door that opened onto our private backyard (with a jacuzzi and a grapefruit tree) so she could take advantage of the southern exposure. While I soaked in the steaming waters of the Grotto, she spent many hours lying naked on the couch sunbathing and listening to one of her books on tape. We had massages in the morning and afternoon, and in the evening we enjoyed delicious meals in the dining room. After dinner we sat around the crackling fireplace, sipping wine and getting to know the other guests.

Last January's visit had been very different than our previous visits primarily because Joy wasn't with me in the pools. I missed her and yet sensed that this was preparation for the time when I'd be living without her. She didn't know it yet, but I knew she was terminal.

Once, while floating in the Grotto back in January, I opened my eyes and looked up at the sky. The palm trees encircling the Grotto swayed in the breeze. They seemed alive...*conscious!* Instinctively, I asked to be blessed and received what I now realized was a premonition—Two Bunch would play an important role in healing my grief, and I would return and renew myself here.

• • • •

Refreshed after the gazpacho soup, I went to my room— #6—the room Joy and I had chosen for our next visit before we left last January. It was ideally located—a minute's walk across a lush green lawn from the pools.

I unpacked and discovered I'd forgotten to bring my phone charger and the natural sweetener for my coffee. Traveling with Joy, between us, we always had everything covered. I'd have to learn how to travel solo.

I put on a bathing suit and walked barefoot across the lawn to the Grotto. Over the years I'd seen people read books and magazines while soaking. I couldn't do that. The moment I sank into the hot water, I dropped my adult persona and donned my inner child. I positioned three foam "noodles" underneath me—one under each knee and another behind my neck—so I could float with maximum freedom of movement. Slowly, meditatively, I moved my body in as many ways as possible... stretching, twisting...a kind of aqua yoga. *Woga!* Then I began to *dance* in the water...until I felt I was *flying!*

That's when I heard Joy say, *"I made the booking for YOU!"*

I was startled! Then I remembered....

A few days after we'd returned from our trip in January, Joy came into my office and said, "Honey, Two Bunch was so great—why don't we book another trip in the beginning of the summer?" I knew she wouldn't feel well enough to come back, but I smiled and said, "Sure, sweetheart. Let's do that." I knew she wouldn't make the trip, but I didn't realize she'd be gone.

And I certainly didn't expect to be here alone. Yet somehow she knew. Back in January Joy booked this trip for *me*.

Floating weightless in the water and staring up at the circle of blue sky ringed by swaying palms fronds, I was overcome with gratitude. Again I felt the *Blessing of the Palms*.

A little before 5:00 p.m., I got out of the pool, wrapped myself in a robe and walked the fifty feet to the spa for my scheduled massage. After the brilliant sunlight, it took my eyes a few moments to adjust to the spa's dim lighting. I inhaled the refreshingly cool air scented with lavender and vanilla while gentle strains of soft, ambient New Age music played in the background.

After soaking in the hot mineral water my muscles were soft, my skin pliable and my pores wide open. I was like putty in the hands of the masseuse, who was both firm and gentle as she worked on me.

And then a remarkable thing happened. While being massaged, a montage of Joy's last months, weeks and days unspooled in my mind. Like a home movie entitled, "Care-giving," I saw how I did everything I could to make Joy's life easier, how I worked to keep her spirits up, to hide my fear, my grief, my sorrow. I saw myself crying every morning in the shower that last year. I saw how her six years of blindness had demanded love, devotion and care-giving in a 1001 ways. And that, though I loved it all, the burden had taken its toll.

Whenever the masseuse touched my chest I choked up. As soon as the massage ended and I was alone in the treatment room, I sobbed.

Wrapped again in my robe and dazed by the blinding desert sunlight, I headed to the Grotto, which was thankfully in shade. With a sigh I sank into the hot water. After such a profound emotional release, I was soon in a state of bliss.

After awhile, an instinctive inner alarm went off inside me: *I should check in with Joy to see if she needs anything.* No! I could float like this for as long as I like. All night if I want! There was no one I had to take care of. For the first time since her transition, I felt pleasure in my aloneness. *It's good to be on my own, not taking care of anyone else but me.*

Incredible! During the massage I'd experienced the *burden* of care-giving, and now, floating in the water, I was experiencing my *freedom* from care-giving. What a truly powerful healing Two Bunch was turning out to be. I hadn't even been here a day.

I soaked until nearly 9 p.m. Wearing a robe over my wet bathing suit, I went from the pool to the dining room. It was late, so there were only a few diners. Still, I felt awkward being seated alone, ordering alone, waiting for the meal to be served. As a couple, I could interact with people at other tables—ask them where they were from, what they were eating, how long they were staying? As a single man, I had to be careful where I looked. If I caught another diner's eye, they might think I was staring. I'd have to relearn the art of dining out alone.

I must have been desperately ill at ease because I suddenly imagined Joy sitting opposite me. Embracing this fantasy, I leaned forward as if to take her hand as I'd done countless times when we were out to dinner. I reached across the table... then caught myself—*What the hell am I doing?!* I berated myself for resorting to an "imaginary friend" and slumped back in my chair feeling sorry for myself.

Suddenly the music on the sound system changed. A saxophone began playing a familiar melody, a Kenny G-like rendition of the *Hawaiian Wedding Song*! Was it a coincidence? Was Joy communicating with me? Whatever the truth, for the moment I was elated.

My dinner—grilled salmon on a bed of salad—arrived and I dove in. I don't know if I ate with such relish because I was famished or because it gave me something to do.

After the meal, I sat there in my robe—the last diner in the restaurant—reliving the peace, pleasure and fulfillment Joy and I had experienced at Two Bunch Palms. And so I had my first dinner there alone…but also with Joy.

I wrote in my journal every day—

> **TUESDAY**: 1st night without sleeping pill…in almost half a year. They were Joy's but she rarely used them. I started in Jan-Feb as Joy's situation deteriorated. I wanted to be able to get up at night with her and go back to sleep. It worked. I've weaned myself this past month to half a pill. I intend to quit here at Two Bunch. Last night I slept lightly in 2 hour blocks and woke at 5:30 AM. I'm hoping tonight will be better.
>
> I ate breakfast outside on the shaded patio of the dining room. After several trips to the buffet I sat sipping coffee, gazing at the mountains and listening to bird song. Wearing shorts I feel the gentle wind against my skin. Delicious. Sensual. I'm soaking in the breeze…like the hot spring.
>
> I seem to be the only one at breakfast paying attention to Nature. Other guests talk to each other or read newspapers.
>
> *The Gift of Being can only be opened when you pay attention to the Present. Is this the Gift of Being Alone?*
>
> Called Terri and sang "Happy Birthday" to her. She's been feeling sad and depressed. Especially on her first birthday without her Mom. She told me she got *a birthday card from Joy!* Kate channeled the card, waking up in the middle of the night to take dictation from Joy. This birthday card from Joy lifted Terri's spirits.
>
> > *To Terri.*
> > *On her first birthday*
> > *To heal let go of anger*
> > To love let go of judgment
> > To laugh let go of pride
> > To succeed helps others succeed
> > I Love You,
> > *Mom*

During my morning soak in the Grotto, I tried to communicate with Joy but wasn't getting anywhere. Finally I quit…and had a revelation. Joy wasn't communicating with me because she wanted me to experience *myself*, not *our relationship*. She was communicating with me through my *enJOYment*. In the breeze that caressed my skin, in the palm fronds I heard rustling in the wind, in the water in which I blissfully floated, in the delicious food I savored and in the sensual massages I received. In *everything* I enJOYed!

I ate dinner late again, delaying my arrival in the dining room until nearly nine, when the room would be almost empty. My anxiety wasn't as bad as the first time. I ordered the same meal as the night before, but was disappointed—it didn't taste as good. Then I realized why—*I* was different. *Don't try to repeat experiences!* I could hear Joy admonish me. *She's right*, I thought. *The river is always moving and I am the river!*

> **WEDNESDAY:** Slept til 6:30…solid! *Without* a sleeping pill.
>
> After breakfast I read my journal. I brought the nearly 150 pages with me. I thought Two Bunch would be a good place to read what I've been through these last three months. If I understand where I've been, perhaps I'll understand where I'm going.
>
> Lola is coming for lunch. I'm looking forward to her visit….

• • • •

When I announced my plans to go to Two Bunch, a friend suggested I call a woman she knew who lived in nearby Palm Springs. My friend thought it would be good for me to meet Lola since she's an exceptional healer. The more I thought about it, the less I wanted to set up a "date" with a woman I didn't know. And yet the idea of four days alone made me reconsider. Perhaps a visit toward the end of my stay might be okay. After all, if the Universe—through a friend—brought this woman into my life, I should say, "Yes…I Can…Now!"

I called Lola a week before my trip. She was warm, friendly and excited about visiting me at Two Bunch. As she spoke, I realized we had a lot in common—she'd taken care of her late husband who died of cancer—and felt she was meant to be part of my Two Bunch initiation.

Lola arrived in the afternoon. She was pretty but I wasn't attracted to her, which was both a relief and a disappointment. Though I might have fantasized some romantic scenario, the truth was I was incapable of anything but company.

We went down to the Grotto and found a cozy spot to soak and talk. She'd been raised a southern belle from Dallas, Texas who rode horses as a child and competed in "Barrel Races" in the rodeo. As a teen she was a debutante who liked to ride motorcycles. In the aftermath of her husband's death, her grief journey took the form of a road trip and vision quest through the Southwest desert. She'd studied Native American ritual and had received an Indian spirit name and been given an Eagle feather, which was a great honor. I told her about Joy's guidance and "hugging my way home." She understood—touch had gotten her through her grief, too. But she wasn't held. She claimed that the touch she gave others as a body worker helped heal her.

She stayed for dinner and I was grateful not to have to dine alone. It was so much easier to relate to the other diners as a couple. One couple even asked us about *our* stay.

After dinner we enjoyed the balmy night, reclining on lounges by the swimming pool. Lola had polished off a bottle of wine at dinner and became talkative. As the full moon's reflection shimmered on the surface of the water, she described her adventures traveling in Bali, hostessing in Japan, and trekking the Himalayas. Though her stories were interesting, I found myself growing restless. I wanted to be alone.

Hoping to end our "date," I told her I didn't feel well and that perhaps I'd spent too much time in the water. We returned to my room so she could get her things and be on her way. But instead of packing up, she unpacked feathers and healing crystals, and offered to do some healing work on me.

I wasn't pleased but decided to "allow." As I lay on the bed, she burned some dried sage and placed crystals on various parts of my body. With her eagle feather she "cleared" my aura and chakras. She confirmed what I'd been feeling—my aura was torn like an open wound at my heart and belly. And my immune system, she informed me, was weak.

I was touched by the healing Lola lavished upon me and asked her if she'd hold me. "Of course," she said. We embraced on the bed and she began to tone and breathe with me while moving her hands up and down my spine. Within a short time, I felt rejuvenated. And profoundly grateful.

As I walked Lola to her car, I thanked her for sharing so much of herself. She kissed me on the cheek, got in her car and drove off into the desert night. Walking back to my room by moonlight, I looked up at the stars and gave thanks. Lola's presence had dulled the ache of being alone. Indeed, her visit had been another kind of baptism—into dating.

· · · ·

THURSDAY: Woke at 7:30 am. Slept all night.

No pills! Hurray!

Wound up spending 2 hours over a long breakfast on the shaded patio reading my journal. As I read I'm struck by the sense of Joy guiding me, sending me on a journey—a *Joyride*.

On Friday I packed to leave, then ate a leisurely breakfast on the patio. Incredibly, my iPod shuffled to three Joy-songs in a row! Alone on the patio, I wept for ten minutes, sipping dregs of coffee.... And loving Joy!

As I loaded the car, I could see how my trip had been a kind of "baptism" into a new life and traveling solo wasn't as bad as I'd feared. At times I had felt like a war-weary soldier on R&R. I'd been more carefree these past few days than I could remember. I hadn't let down like that in years. I'd even enjoyed myself! Maybe enjoyment was the cure for what ails me.

℘ 22 ☙

Complications

>———<

It had been several weeks since the last Rite of Joy and I began to wonder if there would ever be another. Then one day I received an email from Angelina—"I had a conversation with Joy tonight about your next massage."

I wanted to show Angelina my appreciation for all she was doing for me and for Joy, so when she arrived for our next Rite of Joy, I surprised her with a gift—a small reproduction of the Sphinx.

"Consider this an offering to the Priestess of Joy," I said.

"I love it!" Her blue eyes teared up. Then she glanced at the Isis statue. "She loves it, too,"

Once we made ourselves comfortable on a couch in the living room, Angelina got right down to business. "Along with the toning and kisses," she announced, "Joy wants me to use my entire body to massage you."

"Sounds like fun," I said, trying not to sound too excited. Incredibly, the "path of enjoyment" Joy had shown me at Two Bunch Palms seemed to be the goal of this evening's Rite.

We lit the votive candles, as before, and declared our intentions. I disrobed and climbed naked onto the massage table. As I lay face down waiting for the Rite to begin, I couldn't help wondering how Angelina was going to use her body to massage me, and how I could possibly experience greater pleasure than I already had. And most importantly, how would Joy communicate with me?

Angelina began to massage my back. After kneading my muscles for a while, I felt as if she were tenderizing me. Then, like the last time, she added her lips to the mix. The moment Angelina's lips touched my skin those eruptions of energy happened again. Her tender kisses propelled me into full-bodied spasms. Wherever her lips touched my flesh, I convulsed. This was Joy! As she kissed me all over, I heard Joy's voice whispering again and again, *"I love you..."* At one point I heard, *"Love is Vitamin L and it's the most important ingredient in your healing. In your life."*

Indeed, Angelina's Joy-inspired loving and adoration were like essential medicine to me, absolutely necessary to sustain my life. Perhaps because I'd fallen into such a deep and desperate emotional pit of grief, the life-saving rope of her loving touch seemed all the more precious. I couldn't have asked for more, couldn't have *imagined* more! I was flooded with gratitude. To Joy for her guidance, inspiration and, most of all, her love. To Angelina for her willingness, selflessness, and capacity to be a channel for Joy's love.

Then I heard Joy say, *"Angelina doesn't have expectations of a relationship so she can experience being a channel of love without complications."* Who knew I would be the one to experience "complications."

Angelina asked me to turn over on my back. Lying face up on the table, I opened my eyes and saw that, following Joy's instructions, Angelina had removed her clothes. She stood behind my head and began massaging my neck. As she worked her way down to my chest and heart area, I began to feel incredibly vulnerable. Melting in gratitude for her generous and selfless touch, I reached up to embrace her and gently pulled her down into an upside-down hug. She began kissing and toning her way down my abdomen. The current coursing through my body grew stronger, making me undulate beneath her. Meanwhile her tender kisses on my belly and inner thighs continued to trigger involuntary spasms.

For the first time, we were both naked, and she was using her entire body to massage me—as Joy had suggested. With the suddenness of an earthquake, the energy became more sexual. Without realizing it, I found myself instinctively stroking her thighs and caressing her hips. The dynamic of the Rite had shifted. From the moment I'd reached up to embrace her, I'd stopped being totally receptive. This was a slippery slope. Part of me wanted to stop, but the sexual impulse was overpowering.

I decided to slow things down. "I'm thirsty," I muttered. "I need a drink of water."

Angelina hopped off the table. I sat up and she handed me a glass. We both drank. By taking a break to drink water I was hoping to quench not only my thirst but to douse the sexual fire that had raged moments ago.

I invited Angelina to lie in my arms, face to face, heart to heart. I wanted to brake the runaway sexual train. As we embraced on the table, we began to breathe together. We were still simmering, our embers so hot it took little to fan the flames into a sexual blaze.

Nuzzling, we breathed into each other's mouths. I was reluctant to kiss her—it seemed too intimate—but our lips touched, tentatively, over and over. Each time they did, I spasmed. I felt the urge to devour her mouth but restrained myself. After waging an internal battle, I finally succumbed, telling myself that this storm of kisses was an exploration. Who was the *kisser*? Who the *kissee*? As I explored these nuances— monitoring whether I was *giving* or *receiving*—our kissing escalated. Each time our tongues touched a current jumped between us. We writhed. In this mad dance of lips and tongues I searched for Joy.

I couldn't find her.

Though it was getting late, we couldn't pull ourselves apart. Every time we tried to separate, we found another excuse to embrace.

Finally, Angelina said she had an early morning meeting and quickly dressed and left. Now that I was alone — the candles extinguished, the music turned off — all the troubling thoughts that had been gathering on the horizon of my consciousness rushed in. Being made love to was turning out to be harder than I ever imagined.

After this surprising turn of events, I wasn't sure what was going on in Angelina's mind, but I immediately journaled some of the thoughts that were racing through mine.

> Joy wanted Angelina to use her entire body in this massage. She did and it became very sexual...and *confusing*! In this Rite I confronted how difficult it is for me to just receive.
>
> It became complicated when I pulled her down over me so that I could be closer to her. That's when I became *active* and no longer passive. But being active..."making love"...doesn't feel right. I can't! Not now. Not yet.
>
> I can *receive* Joy's love. But I can't pretend I'm "making love" to Joy. The lips I'm kissing aren't Joy's, they're Angelina's. The body I'm caressing isn't Joy's, it's Angelina's. I can receive from Joy but I can't give to Joy. I can be loved by Joy but I can't make love to Joy. When I try, I lose Joy.
>
> *Only in receiving do I experience Joy.*

I couldn't sleep so I drew a bath. It had become a tradition after a Rite of Joy. Only this time I was alone. As I soaked I found myself wondering why, of all the people in our circle of friends, Joy had chosen Angelina for these precious Rites of Joy? Then I remembered that at one point during the Rite I heard Joy say, *"Here's my Priestess Angelina. I've given you the most beautiful woman of them all* [among our circle of friends]. *I had to give you the best in order to heal you from the worst."* Yes, she was beautiful. But there had to be more....

I began to recall a thread of connection between Joy and Angelina in the last months of Joy's life. I remembered the pictures that had been taken at Joy's last Wisdom Circle in March. I got out of the bath, wrapped myself in a towel, and found them. Incredibly, most of photos were of Joy and Angelina sitting on the couch deep in conversation. I checked Joy's desk calendar and noticed that Angelina had massaged her twice in the final weeks. In fact, it was Angelina who gave Joy her last massage on this earth.

And then there were Joy's last pictures. On the day of Joy's transition people had flocked to our home. Everyone who saw Joy was astonished by how beautiful she looked. Even in death. Several people suggested a picture be taken. I couldn't bring myself to do it. It was Angelina who offered and, with my camera, took those last pictures of Joy.

What was their connection? Angelina had told me that at that last Wisdom Circle she'd asked Joy to be her spirit guide. Perhaps Angelina's request had opened the door for Joy to use her as a channel for these Rites.

I tried to sleep, but tossed and turned, plagued by concerns. Had I crossed some line that had somehow tainted or even perverted the sacredness of these Rites? Would Joy be upset with me? Would she continue to inspire Angelina? And, where was Angelina in all this? Was I beginning to desire her and masking it with a desire to experience Joy? So many complications!

I remembered what Joy had said and wondered if Angelina, unlike me, was still without complications.

The next day I sent Angelina an email. I focused on the positive, thanking her for "Joy-ing me back to life." I was very relieved by her reply which put things into perspective.

As I was massaging you and toning and kissing you and moving my body across yours, Joy whispered in my ear that she was right by my side in every moment, even as she moved her loving energy through me. I could feel her face next to mine as I was kissing your body, and I could feel her kissing you through my lips. At other times, I saw her watching us "playing" with each other and smiling happily. Words don't express the profoundness and sacredness of these special moments with you and Joy. We are Joy-fully nurturing you back to life.

With love and more love, Angelina, Priestess of Joy

Though I hadn't directly received any guidance from Joy, my confusion about "giving and receiving" didn't appear to be a problem for her. Of course. Joy had no judgments about what happened. And now I realized that we couldn't do these Rites wrong. "Play" was healing, too. It was only to be expected that each Rite would be different and present new challenges. I could only wonder what they would be.

❧ 23 ❧

Signs in Sedona

By mid-August I was ready for another trip. This one would be farther and longer than my trip to Two Bunch. I was going to Sedona, Arizona.

Joy and I had been there several times over the years and loved the otherworldly vistas and red rock formations for which Sedona was famous. Our visits had been to New Age conferences since we didn't know anyone who lived there. Now, however, I had friends living there—Judy, who had moved to Sedona from Los Angeles more than a year earlier, and Cynthia, another L.A. transplant, took turns inviting me to visit, assuring me the enchanted red rock country of Sedona would be a great place for healing.

Driving east through the desert toward Phoenix I was filled with great expectations. My Two Bunch baptism had been a touchstone and I was expecting something marvelous, magical, even miraculous to happen on this trip. As I sped past giant Saguaro cactus, their arms outstretched as if in welcome, I hoped Joy would communicate with me the way she had in the Grotto at Two Bunch. And I couldn't help wonder what part Cynthia might play in all this.

Cynthia was a relatively new acquaintance. Several years earlier, she'd been recommended to Joy as a possible editor for a book she was planning. The only time I'd actually met her was at

Joy's memorial service. Since then I'd noticed signs indicating Cynthia's potential significance in my new life. Her condolence card, for instance, had depicted a moonlit beach so familiar I felt as I'd visited it in one of my dreams. Our occasional phone conversations elicited other resonances: not only had she taken care of her then-husband after he became ill, but their wedding anniversary was the same as Joy's and mine. She'd written a book about dream interpretation; I'd written a story entitled "DreaMaster." And, finally, there was that bizarre dream she'd had in which I'd embraced her in her sleep. I asked Joy in meditation for guidance and was told, *"All will be revealed in Sedona."*

As I turned north by-passing Phoenix and heading for the high desert of northwest Arizona, I recalled my last trip to Sedona with Joy. After the New Age conference, we stayed on for several days and took tours to the vortexes for which Sedona is famous. The monumental red rock formations that have made Sedona the spectacular setting for many Technicolor westerns were the result of great iron deposits that, exposed to the air over millennia, rust and turn the soil red. The iron also functioned like a magnet, supposedly creating vortexes of energy that sensitive people can feel.

The high point of our trip had been our unforgettable daylong vision quest at Cathedral Rock. All day we hiked up the majestic red rock buttes topped by twin spires that are known as the "cathedral of the gods." We returned from our vision-filled sojourn just as the setting sun cast Cathedral Rock in a glorious apocalyptic twilight at the same time a full moon rose in the east above the enchanted, purple-hued landscape.

The gray desert whizzing past my car window grew increasingly infused with color, as if a black and white movie was gradually being saturated with a vivid palette. Green plants, especially the cactus, took on an otherworldly bluish tint beside the red earth. The scenery seemed psychedelic. I was back in Sedona, this time without Joy. I could hardly wait to discover what surprises this New Age mecca had in store.

My friend Judy was out of town and due back the next evening, so it was Cynthia I saw first. She met me at my hotel in the morning and we had breakfast. She was more attractive than I'd remembered—blonde and statuesque. During Joy's memorial service, I wasn't in any state to appreciate her beauty. Over pancakes she told me about her media career, authoring a book on dreams, and writing a regular dream column for the *Los Angeles Times*. I could see why she was regularly flown to both coasts as a "dream expert" on shows like "Entertainment Tonight" and "Today." Even more than her physical beauty, I was attracted to her upbeat personality. Like Joy, she seemed to always look on the bright side of life.

As I downed my scrambled eggs and sipped my coffee, I wondered if all the correspondences between Cynthia and myself—care-taking her spouse, our identical wedding anniversaries, the dream she had about me—were signs that there might be some romantic connection between us.

As if she could read my mind, Cynthia told me about her latest love interest, which made me question the "signs" I thought I'd been given. But then she pointed out some uncanny parallels between this man and me. His wife had also died in April, of brain cancer. According to Cynthia, he described his wife as a "high being" who had taught him how to love. He was on a grief journey, too. How curious that Cynthia was playing the role of the new woman in *his* life. What role, I wondered, would she play in mine?

After breakfast Cynthia announced that she had a surprise for me. *Great!* I thought. Perhaps this is what Joy was referring to when she told me that "all will be revealed in Sedona."

I climbed into Cynthia's car and asked, "Where are we going?"

"To a labyrinth," she said, a knowing smile on her face. As she drove, she informed me that we were going to one of the largest outdoor labyrinths in the country.

In five minutes we'd arrived. The labyrinth was located on the grounds of a 50-year old estate that had been turned into a charming bed & breakfast. It was almost hidden, but in a clearing surrounded by trees we found the labyrinth. "It's constructed entirely from local riverbed rocks," Cynthia told me.

I recognized the design the hundreds of rocks made on the ground—the curling involutions of its paths reminded me of a human brain.

"It's a classical seven-path labyrinth," Cynthia explained, "a type often found in many indigenous cultures throughout the world. The seven rings symbolize the seven planets, the seven days of the week, and even the seven chakras of the body."

A palpable peace emanated from the labyrinth. I took a deep breath.

"I often come to the labyrinth when I'm looking for guidance," she said. "All you have to do is walk the labyrinth with a question in your mind and, by the time you finish, you'll receive some kind of answer."

I knew labyrinths were ancient symbols of wholeness and had long been used as meditation and prayer tools. Walking a labyrinth represented a journey to the center of one's deepest self and back out into the world, a symbolic form of pilgrimage.

Cynthia reminded me that a labyrinth was not a *maze* with twists, turns, blind alleys and dead ends, like a puzzle that has to be solved. "You can get lost in a maze. But you can't get lost in a labyrinth because it has only one path. The way in is the way out. When you walk a labyrinth, you trust the path will lead you where you need to be, and you open to the possibility of gaining new insights about who and where you are in your life's journey."

I stood at the entrance to the labyrinth, looked out over the concentric circles of rocks that formed the winding paths and asked for guidance. With a deep breath and an open heart, I stepped into the labyrinth and walked slowly, meditatively, holding one question in my mind—*What is the next step in my healing journey?*

As I walked, a thought began to form in my mind, growing stronger and clearer with each step. Five minutes later, when I emerged from the labyrinth, I'd received the guidance I was looking for: my experience, my life, our love story and my grief journey was as important to share as anything else I have ever wanted to write about.

After my walk, I joined Cynthia who was sitting on a nearby bench. We sat in silence while I absorbed my labyrinth experience. Then she took me to meet some friends of hers, "The Twins."

These were the Doublemint Twins who, years earlier as young women, had promoted Wrigley's chewing gum with the jingle, "Double your pleasure, double your fun, with Doublemint, Doublemint, Doublemint gum." Older, grayer and heavier, the Twins were still a lot of fun.

Besides finishing each other's sentences and laughing at each other's jokes, the Twins insisted on taking me on a guided tour of Sedona, which meant all the scenic places from which you could view their landmark house that had once been owned by Lucille Ball. The Twins were funny and creative and had lots of stories about Hollywood. They'd written a bestseller entitled, *You'll Never Make Love In This Town Again*, and had just completed a joint memoir called, *Kiss, Kiss...Tell, Tell*. That's how they'd met Cynthia—attending her memoir writing class. They raved about the class and how much Cynthia had inspired them. Cynthia invited me to sit in on her next class the day after tomorrow.

My friend Judy arrived back in town and we spent the next day together. In the morning we drove out to 700-year-old Indian ruins and in the afternoon took a Jeep tour of the magnificent red rock country that combined scenic vistas with off-road thrills.

I first met Judy when Joy went to her for lymphatic massage after her mastectomy to reduce the pain and swelling that occurs after the removal of lymph nodes. Judy was so passionate about the importance of the lymphatic system to one's overall health that I'd dubbed her "a lymphomaniac." It stuck and she used it in her massage practice ever since.

Judy had also been a member of our Wisdom Circle and we'd become close over the years. Since I hadn't seen her since Joy's memorial service, I felt this was an opportunity to grieve with her. That evening after dinner at her house I asked her to hold me. She was glad to.

I played my Grief CD (which I'd brought with me) and cried in her arms. She cried, too. Afterwards, we pillow-talked about loss and love and Joy. Then I played my Dance CD (which I'd also brought along) and we danced until we were out of breath and drenched in sweat. Crying, dancing…what a great evening.

The next morning I found myself sitting around a large table with eight members of Cynthia's memoir writing class—all senior citizens. As we sipped coffee everyone took turns reading what they'd written in the past week. Though the quality of the writing varied, the lives described were fascinating. There was terrible marital abuse and staggering wartime traumas, and all of it, however painful, needed to be expressed and witnessed. The meeting seemed as much a therapy session as a writing class, and I marveled at what Cynthia was doing. With great compassion and skill, she provided a tremendous gift—helping these people write the stories of their lives. She was facilitating their immortality.

After the class I took Cynthia to a nearby Thai restaurant for lunch. She asked if I was considering writing about Joy and myself. "Your love story has the makings of a great memoir." I told her about the guidance I'd received at the labyrinth, and that it could be interpreted as a prompting to do a memoir. "I guess it's no accident that I was in your class today."

Later that afternoon I met Judy for an afternoon hike up Coffee Pot Rock. This red rock, shaped like a giant coffee pot, was one of Sedona's most famous. The moment we began the climb and entered this enchanted world—the sky above a cobalt blue and the plants below a psychedelic purple against the ochre rock and earth—I felt as if I'd entered a dream.

After a half-hour climb, we sat down on an outcropping and looked out over the valley. Judy told me how moving to Sedona had rejuvenated her.

"Maybe it's because you're willing to risk in pursuit of your dreams," I suggested. "That's the opposite of what most people do as they age. When people get older, they usually choose security above all else. Taking risks and having dreams is what's keeping you young."

Our conversation was interrupted by a hiker. Judy invited him to join us with an aside to me that Sedona was like this— people show up and synchronicities abound. Tobias introduced himself and was soon telling us about his recent journey to the Amazon. An enthusiastic hiker, he pointed out some great hikes in the area. Since he knew all the trails on Coffee Pot, he offered to lead us down in the dark so we could watch the glorious sunset from our red rock perch.

As the clouds and sky turned gold, orange, red and then purple, Tobias mused about how Nature responds to appreciation—"When we appreciate Nature it reveals more of itself."

I commented, "The more we appreciate, the more we get to appreciate." Judy added, "Appreciation begins with oneself."

With the candor of a lifetime seeker, Tobias confessed that appreciating himself was still his greatest challenge. Our conversation was silenced by the magnificence of the sunset.

At dusk we followed Tobias down the now darkened trails. When we arrived at the trailhead, he told us about leading a "swimming with dolphins" tour in Kona, Hawaii. He said, "Joy and I were at the Place of Refuge—"

"Joy?" I gasped, interrupting him. His girlfriend's name, it turned out, was Joy. I choked up as I shared the recent loss of my wife and that we'd been married at the Place of Refuge in Kona.

After the guidance I'd been given at the Labyrinth and the inspiration I'd received in Cynthia's class that morning, I felt certain that, here at the foot of Coffee Pot Rock, beneath clouds shimmering with the last light of the setting sun, the Universe had given me a sign, by way of this gentle stranger, that our love story had to be told. I decided then and there that I would write a memoir. And at just that moment, I looked up and saw a shooting star streak across the darkening sky.

The next day Judy and I picnicked near a rushing stream where we saw *eight* small waterfalls. After we ate, we made our way into the creek and sat on boulders so we could be in the middle of the rushing water. Surrounded by nature I immediately felt myself uplifted. I laid down on the warm boulder, dropped one bare foot into the cool creek, and let the stream's energy wash over me. I was soon in a trance. Then I heard Joy's voice. *"I'm always with you. Whenever you pay attention. Whenever you call. I'm the joy within...that's where we can meet."*

A major meteor shower was expected on my last night in Sedona. Cynthia invited me and Judy over to her house to open a bottle of wine, lie out in her backyard and watch the fireworks display of shooting stars. Under the breathtaking Sedona night sky—since it's a "blackout" town with no street lights, the night sky is literally *filled* with stars—we shared stories, toasted dreams and laughed about love. Our conversation was punctuated by shooting stars like divine exclamation points! "There's one! D'ya see it?" We each saw *dozens*.

As I sipped my wine flanked by my two Sedona angels, I looked up at the sparkling stars and remembered Joy's words— *"All will be revealed in Sedona."* My intention to write a memoir— the fruit of my Sedona sojourn—seemed to be celebrated in the heavens and across the universe.

℘ 24 ℃

A Blessing in Disguise

On my way out of Sedona heading back to Los Angeles, the clouds above Bell Rock were breathtaking—heavenly, Hollywoody—the best since I'd been there! I suddenly wished Joy was with me so she could experience this incredible sight. Then I heard myself say to her: "But you wouldn't be able to see it." I heard her reply, "I know. That's why I set you free." And I wept.

After six hours on the road, I pulled into a rest stop near Palm Springs and was so tired and delirious from the long drive, I mistakenly used the *women's* bathroom (to the horror of some female travelers).

Exiting the freeway in L.A. two hours later, I was starving. I had nothing to eat at home and was too tired to shop. I needed to grab some food, so I drove to the Coral Tree Café. It was nearly nine o'clock. The eight hour drive had been a grueling ordeal. As I sat in a stupor, waiting for my order to be brought to the table, I had an unexpected epiphany.

The Coral Tree Cafe had replaced Joy's and my favorite restaurant—a wonderful Caribbean-themed place called Cha Cha's, housed in a barn-like building, with walls covered in brightly colored tropical paintings and a twenty-foot wrought-iron angel hanging from the A-framed ceiling.

After each monthly Sunday of Joy (during which Joy gave physic readings), we invited everyone to join us for brunch at Cha Cha's. These monthly brunches became as important to people as the inspiration they received from Joy. She provided the guidance, but the brunches created the community.

One day the owner informed us they were closing. Naturally, we were upset. We'd grown attached to the place. Coincidentally, Joy had decided to stop doing the Sunday of Joy due to her diminished energy, the toll her cancer was taking. Our last post-Sunday of Joy brunch coincided with Cha Cha's final day. Our group of fifteen was the last table served at Cha Cha's before closing its doors forever.

For me, the fact that Cha Cha's and our Sunday of Joy closed on the same day cemented the identification between them. For months, the building remained empty, and every time I drove by, I mentally cursed whoever was going to take over the lease. Somehow Joy's cancer and the new tenants had assumed one identity in my mind—the enemy.

Half a year passed. One day some friends told us the Coral Tree Cafe was opening in Cha Cha's old building. Weeks later they invited us to join them there for lunch. Joy, who didn't hold grudges, agreed to go. I couldn't say No to her so we went. The moment we walked in, I noticed every change in the remodel of the place. Everything they'd done was wrong! I felt like a traitor. I couldn't eat there and walked out.

Fast-forward another half a year. Joy is gone. I'm alone. I'm not eating that well. I prepare some meals at home, but sometimes I want to be fed. But I don't want to go out to eat since dining alone stirs up my grief. Desperate for a place that's easy for a single to eat out, I find myself at the Coral Tree. There are no hosts, no waiters. You go up to the counter and order off the menu. They give you a number and the food is brought to your table. Informal. Lots of single people eating with their laptops for company. The food was good, healthy. Dining out wasn't so bad. So I went back for an occasional lunch, even a dinner now and then. Gradually, the Coral Tree Cafe became my go-to place for a meal. My home away from home.

As I sat there famished and frazzled from my eight hour drive, waiting for my Chicken Panini, I was overcome with gratitude for the Coral Tree Cafe. I realized that my beloved Cha Cha's wouldn't have been a comfortable place to come to tonight in my condition with its hostess, waiters, linen-covered tables and romantic couples dining everywhere. Coral Tree's informality suited my needs now in a way Cha Cha's couldn't.

I don't know if it was the ordeal of the drive or my extreme hunger, but I was suddenly transported into a state of bliss. *Everything changes!*

What I'd resisted so fiercely and perceived as a curse in my life—the loss of Cha Cha's and its replacement by the Coral Tree Cafe—had turned out to be a blessing in disguise!

Would I feel this way about Joy? Was it possible that the curse of her loss would ultimately be transformed into a blessing?

❧ 25 ❧

The Antidote to Grief

›————————————————————————‹

When I returned from Sedona I realized I wasn't ready to write a memoir. Not yet. Perhaps in time, but first I had to heal. It had been several weeks since the last Rite of Joy and I was beginning to wonder if, after what had happened, there would ever be another one. In the heat of August, my fevered imaginings included the possibility that Joy—as far as the Rites went—had abandoned me.

To my great relief, I received an email from Angelina wanting to schedule another Rite of Joy. She'd felt my ambivalence at the last Rite and wanted to know if I had any guidance for her. "I really want to be in sync with you and Joy," she wrote.

I meditated on Angelina's question and realized that, as the Rites unfolded, Joy continually clarified what we were doing. Her most recent clarification was: *"To fully receive my healing, you have to be totally receptive."*

When I responded to Angelina's loving touch, to her beauty, to her desirability—first by touching her and then by kissing her—I was no longer *receiving* which was the most powerfully healing energy.

I was discovering that one of the main purposes of these Rites was for me to learn to completely receive, to experience the healing of being totally loved. I wrote Angelina an email sharing this realization and concluded with this request—

> *So...in our next session I will <u>not</u> touch you and I'm asking for your help because you are sooooo delicious.* **Do not allow** *me to reciprocate in any way. These Rites are about filling the hole in my heart...about my being* **FILLED** *with Joy's love. When Joy was in physical form, she taught me* **how much I could love.** *Now she's teaching me—through you, Angelina—**how much I can be loved.***

Since it had been weeks since we'd seen each other, when Angelina arrived we caught up over tea. I shared some dispatches from my grief front, she shared the trials of moving into her new home. Hearing about the ordeal she'd been through, I thought to myself—*she needs a massage more than I do.* But when I offered to give her one, she declined and insisted on giving me mine.

Once again I saw how easily I stepped out of the receiving role—six years of care-giving created habits that were hard to break.

"Why don't you go out onto the patio and swing in the hammock," I suggested, "while I get things ready." Though it was dusk, it was still a balmy evening. Angelina liked the idea. Once she got into the hammock, I gave her a gentle push to start the swinging and left her to set everything up—the massage table, candles and music.

I hadn't given much thought to which music I wanted to play for this Rite, but I was suddenly curious to try my Grief Playlist.

When I finally got Angelina, she was beaming. "Are you ready?" she asked me. I was.

Together, we lit the votive candles and Angelina declared her intention to be a "pure channel for Joy's love." This time I wanted to receive fully and exclusively without needing to give anything back in return. "And I also want to experience Joy as much as possible," I added, choking up.

As Angelina's hands worked their magic, the music

triggered a flood of emotion. Overcome with grief, I wept. It was awful *and* sublime. Opening to my grief in this way made me feel Joy's presence like nothing else. I trembled as tears ran down my cheeks. This music was like the soundtrack of our life together. Laughing. Loving. Playing. Inspiring. Supporting. Understanding. All the shades and colors of our love. As Nat King Cole sang, "… *the Rockies may crumble/ Gibraltar may tumble/ They're only made of clay/ But our love is here to stay,*" I sobbed. Throughout it all, Angelina, with the utmost compassion and tenderness, massaged every inch of me.

The stark contrast between my emotional heartache and my physical pleasure created an almost unbearable contradiction within me. To be loved so much and to grieve so deeply *simultaneously!* To feel so awful *and* wonderful at the same time! I didn't think I could bear it.

Angelina kissed my hands...and I cried.

She kissed each finger...and I cried.

She rained kisses down my back...and I cried.

She kissed me everywhere...and I cried.

I was struck by the terrible irony that to experience being loved so much, I had to lose the love of my life.

With every kiss Joy's presence grew. No one but her could love me so much. And then, as if she wanted to give me confirmation, the *"Hawaiian Wedding Song"* began to play. *Our* wedding song! As Andy Williams sang, "*I will love you longer than forever,*" I felt Joy bending over me and kissing the tears from my cheeks, and fell apart.

And then came an ecstatic revelation—Love (like ecstasy) is the antidote to grief. Being made love to while grieving the loss of love can transmute grief. All love comes with the seed of grief within it. That's why love requires courage. Loss and grief are inevitable. Love and grief are two sides of the same coin. Life and death. Love and loss. Inhale. Exhale.

I had reached a transcendent place in which agony and ecstasy were one and the same—simply emotions. It was beautiful. And brutal. Liberating and so healing.

The Grief Playlist ended.

Angelina told me it was time to turn over onto my back. She handed me tissues and water. I could see that she was aglow, in some other world.

"Joy was showering me with her energy," she said quietly, "which I feel as bliss from my feet up through my body and out my hands and mouth wherever they touch you."

I nodded, unable to speak. We were both in ecstatic states.

As I lay face up on the table—eyes swollen, cheeks wet, nose still running—I felt unusually receptive to Angelina's loving ministrations. Such deep grieving had opened my heart, tenderized me, heightened my vulnerability. I could receive more, and more deeply.

I was much more sensitive to her touch. No longer actively grieving, I relished every sensation. I was euphoric, drunk on the sensual delight she and Joy were providing. My body began to undulate and moans erupted from my throat. I surrendered to the joy flowing through me. I felt the quickening of an orgasmic wave that broke over me and lifted me off the table. I convulsed involuntarily until the orgasm faded away and Joy was gone....

Afterwards, Angelina and I shared a bath and snacked on strawberries and sliced mango. Between mouthfuls I kissed her hands and thanked her for channeling such an incredible, "out of this world" love. "It's truly sacred to love so selflessly," I told her. "I want you to know that *you* are the key to these healing Rites of Joy."

She thanked me and Joy for giving her this once-in-a-lifetime experience.

We continued showering each other with gratitude until I finally admitted that "there were times during the massage when I felt such profound gratitude well up in me, I had to fight the impulse to embrace you."

She laughed. "You're learning your lesson well."

After Angelina left I thought about all that had happened during this Rite of Joy. I was surprised by the immense grief I'd experienced, though, in hindsight, I shouldn't have been—the music, a soundtrack to stir the emotions, had been like pouring salt on a wound.

But the greatest revelation of this Rite had been to experience being *witnessed* in my grief. Losing a spouse leaves one feeling so alone. Where before there was a "together," now there's only an "alone." I'd even coined a term for it—I was suffering from *SAS—Sudden Aloneness Shock/Syndrome*. Tonight's Rite inspired me to have my grief witnessed. I didn't know what form it would take, but I was sure it would reveal itself. And I was certain that this was the next step on my journey of healing.

I. J. Weinstock

III

Fall

ℬ 26 ℭ

A Grief Witnessed

A few days later, I shared my revelation with some friends about the importance of having my grief witnessed. Before I knew it a "Jerry Camp" had been organized. About a dozen people were coming to my home the following Saturday to make themselves available all day for whatever I needed. Deeply touched, I wanted to make the most of my friends' gift of time and attention, so I set about creating the best healing ritual I could.

What's helped heal my grief? I asked myself. The answer was simple—crying, being held and dancing. And, of course, the Rites of Joy.

But I was reluctant to share these otherworldly sexual encounters with others. At least for now. The Rites were too intimate, too magical and I didn't want to expose them or myself to judgment. I'd also promised to protect Angelina's privacy. But most of all I wanted to protect myself. These Rites were too important and too sacred to be spoken about. For the time being they had to remain secret. For Jerry Camp I wanted to cry, hug and dance...for Joy...with my friends.

On Saturday friends started arriving around 10 a.m. By 11:00 a.m. everyone was there. Many were members of our Wisdom Circle but Angelina was absent. With the dozen or so friends joining me, I lit the candles by the Isis statue to create a "sacred space" for healing. We then gathered in a circle in the living room and made ourselves comfortable. I sat on the floor.

I began by going around the circle and thanking each of these dear friends for the unique gifts they'd given me during this dark passage in my life. The hugs, the love, the meals, the support, the time, the phone calls, the checking up, the dropping by, the invitations, the myriad forms of love...taking time out from their busy lives to save me.

I passed around a dozen 8x10 pictures of Joy and the two of us together, which I'd printed especially for the occasion. I spoke in depth about my grief journey—about crying and dancing, and about my vision of Joy that inspired my *Journey of a Thousand Hugs*. And finally I revealed the guidance I'd received about needing to be witnessed in my grief.

I played the Grief Playlist, talked about Joy and cried. My grief triggered other people's grief and they cried, too. I wept, and spoke, and shared stories. Some friends offered to hold me while the grief music played. After a couple of hours, the Grief Playlist ended and I put on my Dance Playlist and invited everyone to dance with me. We danced for several hours until that Playlist ended. We talked as we danced. I was the only one who danced all the time while my friends took turns dancing with me and each other. After a day of crying, dancing and being held by my friends, a sense of peace descended upon me.

It was dark by the time everyone left. I thanked Joy (and her priestess Angelina) for inspiring this healing day. And from the bottom of my grieving heart to the tip of my dancing toes, I thanked my wonderfully generous friends for helping me experience such a healing catharsis. I felt incredibly blessed!

When I went to bed that night I found something on my pillow—a golden flower with a jigsaw piece cut out into which a silver butterfly fit like a puzzle. The flower and butterfly were attached by an elastic string and were meant to be used as a

bookmark. A note from one of my friends said, "Joy told me to leave it for you." Looking more closely at the golden flower, I saw that it was inscribed with the word *Believe*.

The next week I followed up on a suggestion someone at the Jerry Camp had made, that I meet with a woman named Samantha who lived in Malibu. Currently married, Samantha had been widowed a couple of times and my friend thought she might have some advice for me.

At a restaurant on the beach near her home, Samantha and I ate with the sun on our faces and our feet in the sand. I talked about my grief journey. "I feel as if I've died and am in the process of being reborn," I told her.

She suggested a journaling exercise she'd done several times in her life called *Emptying the Vessel*. It involved writing for four continuous hours (no breaks except for the bathroom and to drink water) for three consecutive days. "It has to be done by hand and every thought has to be written down. The pen can't leave the page." She paused for a moment as if remembering her own process, then added, "It's remarkable what comes up."

"Sounds interesting," I said

"Since you're beginning a new life, it might be helpful to empty *your* vessel to prepare yourself for what's to come."

I felt as if I was already doing a version of this by journaling. It wasn't as extreme or as intense as her exercise, but it was sustained over a much longer period of time. Over coffee I told her about having my grief witnessed at Jerry Camp. She thought that was wonderful and suggested I seek out a bereavement group. She had met her current husband that way and encouraged me to try one.

Immediately after Joy passed, Hospice had offered me information about bereavement groups. At the time I wasn't interested. But I told myself that one day I'd check it out. Now nearly half a year later I was interested, but I still had concerns.

The fact that I believed my wife was guiding me from the Other Side was something I hesitated to share with strangers, especially people who had just lost *their* loved ones. Still, the time had come for me to have my grief witnessed by those who had experienced a similar loss. Though I was blessed with loving friends and family, I'd come to realize that only people who had lost their spouse could truly understand my loss.

As I drove to my first meeting, I wondered why it had taken me so long? I wanted privacy so I could experience my grief undiluted by the experience of others, I reasoned. I also didn't want to be concerned about other people's judgments. Now I had to stop judging myself for taking nearly six months to grieve alone before being willing to be witnessed by strangers.

The bereavement group met at the weSPARK Cancer Support Center in a cozy room furnished with couches and a rocking chair. The group was small—nine people, more women than men. Their ages varied from a woman in her early forties to a man in his seventies. They had been on this grief journey together for some time.

The facilitator, a psychologist who'd lost her husband twelve years earlier and had since remarried, welcomed me. "A broken heart is an open heart," she said. The woman I sat down next to extended her hand in greeting and said, "It's awfully shitty to meet you." I understood what she meant. Everyone expressed how important the group was to them—"like family."

They introduced themselves. One woman had married her husband two days before he died. They'd been together for eight years but he'd never wanted to marry. A songwriter who'd lost his wife of thirty-five years (former college sweethearts) spoke movingly about trying to play the songs he'd written for his wife after she'd passed but couldn't finish one without bursting into tears. Only when he brought his guitar to the group and sang for them was he able to finish a song. One of the women described herself as "stuck" and unable to function since her husband's death. Another widow's stepchildren were fighting her for the money their father had left her. The older man confessed that he had to take down the collage of pictures of his wife that had been made for her memorial service after only a month because it was too painful for him to look at.

At last, it was my turn. I introduced myself, choking up often as I spoke. I explained that I was keeping a journal to help me track my progress. I told them Joy wasn't afraid of dying and how she'd planned her memorial service up until the end. I described my conflicting feelings of wanting to run away — somewhere, anywhere across the world — and also wanting to never leave our home so I could dwell on my memories. I told them how I had wallowed in grief on our wedding anniversary: how I discovered that I needed to cry and had found a way to turn on my tears with music; how I danced alone at home to stop crying so I would be free to cry whenever I wanted; how important touch was and how I'd been hugged by friends. I didn't tell them about the Rites of Joy. When I finished speaking, I passed around pictures of Joy so they could see how beautiful she was.

There were many memorable moments at that first meeting. The songwriter shared how he and his wife loved the Big Sur coast. He had recently taken her ashes to beaches they'd been to there and at the water's edge made a handprint in the wet sand, poured some of her ashes into it, and waited for the waves to wash her ashes away. In this way, he traveled up the coast to all the different beaches they'd been to until her ashes were gone.

I related to much of what had been shared and felt hopeful that the group was a good match for me and that I'd learn from other people's struggle with grief.

After the meeting I drove over the hill to Dance Home in Santa Monica, where I danced for two hours. This was part of the commitment I'd made to myself: I would cry at the bereavement group, then dance. Fortuitously, the group met early Tuesday evening, the same evening as Dance Home. Every Tuesday evening I looked forward to my cry-and-dance therapy.

Week after week I found myself gradually being embraced by these kindred spirits and began to experience the healing power of such a group. On the most basic level, my grief was being witnessed. And I was witnessing other people's grief. In this most natural way we were healing each other. We cried in front of each other. We bared our deepest wounds to each other. We understood one another in a way neither family nor friends could.

We were a battered bunch, wandering in a daze, lost on our own private Planet Griefs. Some prayed not to wake up in the morning, others drank so much they'd pass out at night. In a drunken stupor one of the men had walked through a sliding glass door, cutting himself badly. One of the women talked about wanting to commit suicide. She confessed she'd squirreled away enough of the morphine patches that hospice had provided her dying husband to do the job. She claimed that having an "exit strategy" kept her going.

Listening to this litany of pain and anguish reminded me of a widower I knew, who confessed to me that after losing his wife, he sat in front of the TV day and night, like a zombie, contemplating murdering his stepfamily in revenge for the wrongs he felt they had done him. In hindsight, he admitted that what he had really wanted was to be caught, convicted and executed so he'd be put out of his misery. Was there such a thing as the "grief defense?"

Those of us who had lost our loved ones *were* temporarily insane in some way. We were bereaved survivors, sleepwalking through the rubble and ruin of what had once been our worlds. Our lives were in tatters and we were barely hanging on. Most admitted to medicating themselves with antidepressants or sleeping pills. At our weekly meetings we shared war stories. Some felt "numb and dead," some felt "worse," but there was always someone who confided that they were feeling "a little better." And, like the warming rays of the sun after the ravages of a storm, "a little better" gave everyone hope.

That isn't to say that all we did was cry together. On the contrary. We laughed a lot, too. A special brand of gallows humor seemed to flow after such an intimate brush with death. I organized a bowling outing for the group—thinking laughter and play would be good medicine—and while taking pictures I got everyone to smile by instructing, "Say *grief!*" They all laughed.

One day a bunch of us went to a Dim Sum restaurant in Chinatown that had been a favorite of the songwriter and his late wife. We were seated around a table sampling the delicious food rolled by on carts when one of the women popped a dumpling into her mouth and asked, "Is anybody masturbating?" We burst out laughing and immediately got into a hilarious discussion about sex. Widow sex. Grief sex. Solo sex. The women talked about vibrators and the men admitted they didn't have much of a libido these days.

For many of us Tuesday evenings was the high point of our week. We could talk about our loved ones, about their dying, about our love and loss, about the unbearable pain and inconsolable grief.

I soon discovered that I wasn't the only one in the group who believed in life after death, nor was I the only one receiving guidance from the Other Side. One of the men, while cooking a lasagna dish his wife had often prepared, couldn't remember an important ingredient. No matter what he did, it just didn't taste the way she made it. Suddenly, he felt "guided" to look in a drawer in an unmarked container where he found the missing ingredient—nutmeg.

I shared dreams about Joy, and it turned out that other people had dreamt about their spouses, too. One of the men said he'd dreamt that he was driving in a car with his wife and she seemed troubled. He asked what was wrong and she told him she wanted a party. When he woke up, he decided to throw a party for her to mark the one-year anniversary of her passing.

I soon felt comfortable enough to share Joy's memoir with the group and gave everyone a copy. Over the years I'd seen how it had helped people deal with their grief and the loss of a loved one. The very next week one of the women excitedly told the group that the book had helped her make contact with her husband. I was thrilled that Joy was still helping people, especially these new sisters and brothers of my bereavement group family.

Once a week my grief was witnessed by the only people who could really understand my loss, my pain, my fears and tears, my hopes and dreams. I cried. I laughed. And I remembered Joy. Gradually my terrible dislocation and disorientation normalized. Every week the bonds of my new family were strengthened. Week after week I felt less and less alone.

The group became a buoy, a life preserver that I clung to in order to keep from drowning in the stormy seas of grief and despair. The group gave me hope as I witnessed others further along reaching dry land. We cheered as we watched each other take the first tentative steps onto the shores of a new life. The group became a mirror where I was witnessed, a sacred container where my grief was honored, and a womb where I was ultimately reborn.

Every Tuesday night I gathered with these new friends and warmed by the campfire of our memories, we'd tell stories of love and death, loss and new life, and give thanks that we were traveling this difficult, dangerous, desperate journey together. And that we were no longer alone.

Then I'd go dancing.

℘ 27 ℚ

The Ultimate Gift

)———————————————————————————————(

Angelina arrived for another Rite of Joy just as a mid-September sun was setting. We sat for a while and caught up. I told her about my bereavement group and she shared her new modeling adventures. As the golden light of sunset illuminated her face, I was struck once again by her delicate beauty. I asked if she'd received any guidance about tonight's Rite.

"Joy wants us to do everything we've been doing," she replied, "and to remain open for the new."

My guidance had been similar. I didn't want to repeat the last experience either, so I combined my Massage and Grief Playlists, put the iPod on shuffle, to allow chance (or what I preferred to think of as Spirit) choose the soundtrack for tonight's Rite.

I was delighted that Angelina and I seemed to have been given similar guidance—remain open to "new possibilities"—and wondered what this new combination of music would inspire?

Joy never wanted to repeat experiences, no matter how wonderful. She believed that it couldn't be done, that it was a prescription for disappointment and a way to get stuck and inhibit growth. No matter how wonderful any experience might be, trying to repeat it wasn't something Joy would have encouraged. Staying open to new possibilities seemed to me like pure Joy.

Once again, Angelina's massage was extraordinary. Beyond her loving touch and adoring kisses, I was overwhelmed by the sublime grace of being loved so completely. And with absolutely *nothing* expected of me. What a gift! Such an ultimate act of love may be the greatest gift one human being can give another. This was Joy's gift—inspiring Angelina to love so selflessly.

In the midst of being loved so completely I experienced Joy's presence—no one else could love and adore me so thoroughly, so absolutely. Being loved in this way allowed me to experience my own *loveableness.* In that moment, I realized I was not only being healed, I was being challenged: *Could I accept being so loveable?* Every touch, every kiss, each and every adoration was proof! How could any part of me deny such overwhelming evidence? Yet, the irony was that receiving so much triggered old, unconscious programs that questioned my own worthiness. Do I deserve so much love? Angelina is treating me like a king! What is she getting in return? I'm receiving so much by being so loved. What is *she* receiving by being so loving?

As I pondered these questions I became aware that I no longer felt Joy's presence. I called on her—*Where are you?* Her answer was more of an idea than specific words. Joy had stepped back during this Rite because she wanted me to engage with what *is*, not with what *was.* She wanted me to *let go* of the past (her), so I could embrace the present. She was employing a kind of tough love, so I wouldn't create a dependency on her. She was weaning me from her for my own good.

She also communicated to me that it was my choice whether to interpret the lack of her presence as a negative or a positive—a negative "forgetting" or a positive "healing." It's always my choice whether I interpret my experience as positive or negative. I appreciated this wisdom and also took comfort in feeling her renewed presence since these ideas were so Joy!

In meditation the next morning I wanted to understand what Angelina was getting out of these Rites of Joy. Joy explained, *"I've brought her into your life so you can both be healed. If you're healed, she becomes a healer. It's a dance. There's no better role. I needed to get sick to appreciate and learn how important receiving is. Illness was my great teacher. Love can be yours."*

As I reflected on Joy's words, I realized she was not only healing me now, but, if I learned to fully receive, her healing would enhance the rest of my life.

Later in the day I sent Angelina an email thanking her. "To love so completely is the ultimate gift one can give another," I wrote. I explained that being loved so completely made me wonder what she was getting out of being so loving? "How are you being healed?" I asked her.

Angelina wrote back, "When my loving energy is being received and appreciated, it's like a loop of energy that feeds me, too. So when I'm giving, I have this immense, life-giving and life-inspiring energy (Joy's in this case, in combination with mine) running through me to share. Also Joy has been helping me to remember my 'temple' days in Egypt as a Priestess. This remembering is also healing since I'm being shown my power and the gifts I hold within me."

In my email, I'd also written that being loved so much had triggered questions about my own worthiness. To which she replied, "Know that you are worthy of all the love Joy and I share with you :-) After all, she needs a channel—an instrument of love in a body (like me)—to be able to send her love to you at this physical level. Evidently I made a soul agreement with Joy to be doing this. And it does feel right and good to me, too."

I let Angelina's words sink in, hoping to put to rest any lingering doubts. As I read the rest of her email, my excitement grew.

> *My experience of our encounters is that of "feeling like a Love Goddess" and being a clear channel for Joy's sacred love and*

> *adoration of you. By your openness to receive Joy's love through me, I feel loved and honored by you and Joy. I continue to hold a huge space of deep love and sacred connection with you without any attachments. I have not felt any pressure or obligation. It just IS.*
>
> *With my love and adoration and blessings,*
> *Angelina, Priestess of Joy / Isis*

It was just as Joy had communicated to me in meditation. Apparently, the more completely I can receive and appreciate Angelina's loving, the more empowered she feels. Amen!

Angelina had a question for me, as well. "Just as it's important for you to know how I'm benefiting from these Rites of Joy," she wrote, "it's equally important for me to know what your experience is. How are these Rites of Joy healing you?"

Before responding, I gave her question a lot of thought, grateful for the opportunity to list the gifts and express gratitude for each of them.

How are these Rites of Joy healing me?

The first and most obvious way these Rites are healing me is that *love and pleasure are the greatest antidotes to grief!* It's not possible to contain such polar opposite emotions simultaneously. So every moment of pleasure is a moment of respite from grief.

A *pleasure instead of pain connection to Joy.* These Rites keep me connected to Joy in the most beautiful and pleasurable way. In large part, because of these Rites, Joy is no longer primarily a source of pain, but rather of pleasure, too.

Fighting depression! My frequency or life energy is lowered by grief, and I continually struggle against the dreaded D's. These Rites raise my frequency and help fight off depression. I've noticed that when several weeks pass between Rites, the storm clouds start to gather on my horizon. All the damn D's—despair, doubt, doldrums, depression—show up like unwanted visitors.

The Rites keep me healthy! Not only am I receiving the proven benefit that loving touch strengthens the immune system, I am also receiving a profound spiritual re-balancing. Joy came to realize that her cancer and blindness were necessary to teach her how to receive. The Rites are teaching me to receive through *love* so I don't have to learn to receive through *illness*. They are also re-balancing me in another way. I am completely out of balance from doing so much care-giving for the past six years. There is no better remedy for the burnout of care-giving than care-receiving. These Rites are *medicine for burnout!*

Something to live for. When you've lost so much, you feel such desolation and despair. As I surveyed the ruins of my life, it was hard to find a reason to go on. Why bother? These Rites have been something to look forward to, and that has made all the difference.

Heal any unworthiness by demonstrating my lovability. These Rites are healing any residue of feelings of unworthiness. To receive so completely has been a great challenge. I don't know if it's typical for most men, but I've discovered it isn't easy to totally receive. Deep programming demands that I *do, give, act* in order to be loved. These Rites have shown me—by requiring me to *experience* my lovability—that I deserve to be loved for who I am, not what I do.

As I shared all these "gifts" in my email to Angelina, I felt overcome with gratitude. These Rites have challenged me in ways I could have never imagined. And so were healing in ways I couldn't imagine. And I couldn't help but wonder what the next step in our adventure would be and where it would lead.

℘ 28 ℃

New Possibilities

Lately, whenever I thought about the Rites of Joy, a nagging question surfaced which transformed my joyful reveries into an unsettling dilemma. I suppose it was inevitable. I began wondering about Angelina...as a *woman*. After repeatedly experiencing such incredible "out of this world" ecstasies at her hands, it was only a matter of time before I'd start to wonder if I should explore the possibility—indeed, the *new possibility*—of a romantic relationship.

Joy may have been the inspiration for the Rites, but Angelina was the vehicle. If she was capable of this kind of loving, of transmitting this ecstatic sensuality, could Joy be leading me to a new love? Didn't Joy tell me to "let go of the past" and "embrace the present." Maybe I should take her literally and embrace Angelina. But—and here was the rub—how would a relationship with Angelina impact the Rites of Joy?

In my journal I wrestled with this dilemma—

> What are we outside of the Rites? There's a part of me that wants to get closer to her. After all, we've shared such intimacy, such ecstasy. Yet I feel myself holding back. I'm afraid that if I begin a relationship with Angelina, I'll lose the Rites of Joy.

Since Angelina and I moved in the same social circles, we ran into each other frequently at events and parties. Once we began the Rites of Joy, we greeted each other with a long embrace charged with the special intimacy that exists between people who have a secret. After that, I'd keep my distance. I didn't want to do anything that might tamper with, dilute, or somehow hex the magic of our Rites.

But since our last Rite of Joy I began to wonder—Was I *letting go of the past* and *embracing the present?* Was I truly open to new possibilities? I felt as if Joy were posing these questions, prodding me forward.

Since Angelina had recently moved, I seized the opportunity—I bought her a housewarming gift and asked her out to dinner to celebrate her new home. It would be tricky socializing—this was like a *date*—but it was time to explore "new possibilities."

I drove to Angelina's home in the Hollywood Hills and, after she showed me around, we walked to an Italian restaurant. After toasting Joy over a glass of Merlot, we talked. Or should I say *she* talked. In her defense, I asked lots of questions. I was curious about this creature who'd been ministering to me in such a profound and intimate way.

Though raised Catholic, by first grade Angelina had decided that the punishing God the nuns worshipped wasn't for her. She was so outspoken as a child that her mother called her "Sassy" and often washed her mouth out with soap. She confided that she'd had several mystical experiences, including two painless childbirths during which she'd heard voices guiding her, telling her what to do.

Back at her apartment after our meal, I gave Angelina the housewarming present—a small version of the winged-Isis statue. She was moved to tears. I told her how grateful I was for all she'd done for me. We embraced. I thanked her for saving my life. She thanked me for sharing the great love that Joy and I had with her. Our grateful embrace overflowed into tender kisses....

I was immediately aware of the chemistry—or rather the *lack* of it. No sparks flew between our lips. No ecstatic energy surged between our bodies. No trembling, no shuddering. Not a hint of an orgasmic wave on the horizon. And I understood why. Without Joy there was no magic. Outside of the Rites, Angelina and I didn't have any chemistry. We were good friends, very good friends, but we would never be lovers.

I pulled away from our embrace as gently as I could. "So where do think you'll put the Isis statue?" I asked, looking around.

If Angelina felt any awkwardness, she hid it. She picked up the statue and tried it out in several locations. Finally, I pleaded fatigue and left.

On the drive home I wasn't sure whether to be relieved or disappointed. But more importantly, I wondered if resolving my dilemma would have unintended consequences. The more I thought about it, the more concerned I became—was it possible that we'd had our last Rite of Joy.

As the days turned into weeks, my concerns only grew. When I finally received an email from Angelina with the subject heading: *Your Next Massage*, I was greatly relieved. But my relief was short-lived because once the arrangements were made, I was flooded with new concerns. Had I crossed some line and ruined the magic? Would Joy be present like before? Would she inspire a profound healing in this next Rite of Joy like she had in previous ones?

Angelina arrived around 8:00 in the evening. It had been more than a month since she'd walked through my front door, so I felt a bit awkward as we sat and chatted. Finally, unable to contain myself any longer, I asked what we were going to do tonight.

"Joy told me to use a feather," she announced.

I was stunned by the synchronicity. I'd spent a good part of the day reading over the shamanic journeys I'd undergone over ten years ago, particularly one in which Joy had appeared, transforming magically from an eagle. Having just recently met Joy, I interpreted her appearance in my journey as a sign that she might play a significant role in my life. Months later, when I came to her condo for the first time to have my horoscope read, the winged Isis statue in her foyer seemed to corroborate this. So Joy's instruction to "use a feather" for today's Rite was confirmation that I was in alignment with her.

Standing before the Isis statue, Angelina wore a beautiful blue hip veil and nothing more, the very image of an Egyptian Temple Priestess. We lit the votive candles and declared our intentions. For music, I selected the combined Massage-Grief Playlist I had used at the last Rite. I chose it partly as a "control" to see if anything had changed because of our "date."

With the living room aglow in candlelight, I lay down on the table and waited for the massage to begin. But I couldn't relax. I kept wondering—*Will Angelina's massage be different? Will Joy appear to either of us?*

I received my answer almost immediately. This Playlist contained 125 songs—a little over twelve hours. The majority of it was instrumental massage music. What was the probability that the first three randomly chosen songs would invoke Joy?

The first song, a bluesy version of "Over the Rainbow," was one of Joy's favorites. The second song was a Bobby McFarrin number from his *Circlesong* album. But it was the third song that blew me away: "Lullaby in Ragtime," from the 1959 movie, *The Five Pennies,* starring Danny Kaye, Louis Armstrong and Barbara Bel Geddes. The song—which Joy sang with her children when they were young—is composed of three distinct melodies sung together in a round. When Terri was four years old, her father recorded her singing the child's part. For Terri's fortieth birthday, her brother Elliot surprised her with a mix of the song in which both he and Joy sang the Danny Kaye and Barbara Bel Geddes parts mixed with Terri's long ago pitch-perfect recording.

171

So here I was being massaged as Joy sang, *"…in spite of any sorrow / There's a brand new day on its way tomorrow."*

As the massage progressed the iPod randomly shuffled to many of the songs from the Grief Playlist portion, all of them sure-fire tearjerkers. Yet, to my surprise, I didn't get emotional hearing them. Didn't choke up. Didn't even tear up. And I didn't know what to make of it. On one hand I was pleased at what could be interpreted as a sign of healing. On the other hand I was saddened, even disappointed, that I no longer felt so much grief.

All this time Angelina had been using her hands to work her magic on my body and I was reveling in her loving touch. When she began using the feather, my response was immediate. The feather, a much subtler sensation, activated my energy body. I trembled and writhed, I shook, rattled and rolled. So much so that when Angelina finally placed her hands over my chakras, especially my heart chakra (without actually touching me), I spasmed in full-body orgasms for a long, long time.

When the Rite was over, I felt disappointed. Though such sublime pleasure from these Joy-inspired, feather-induced ecstasies was wonderfully healing, I wasn't *experiencing* Joy. I wasn't feeling her presence. I consoled myself with the thought that the only way I could experience such profound and powerful ecstasies was because Joy was working through Angelina, channeling her love into me. Our "date" had been proof of that. Nevertheless, I missed feeling Joy's presence the way I had during past Rites.

The next morning in meditation Joy told me that I shouldn't feel bad that I didn't cry. I should bless the lack of tears, the lack of sadness. It was a good thing. After the meditation I wrote in my journal—

> Last night's Rite was a milestone for me because it was the first time I didn't get emotional hearing the "grief music." Ironically, I'm glad and also sad that I'm not feeling my grief as much. Yet it demonstrates how much I've healed. I don't need

> *grief* to have a relationship with Joy. Grief is temporary. It's not the default emotion of our relationship. That's *Love!*
>
> Yet I'm left with a nagging feeling of failure that I didn't have visions of Joy during the Rite. I experienced visions of Joy earlier in the Rites cause that's what I needed. I don't need that now.

In my "thank you" email to Angelina, I pointed out how the feather Joy suggested she use was another reminder of her connection to Isis, the winged Goddess of ancient Egypt. I explained how Isis could also have been called the *Goddess of Grief* since she was possibly the greatest griever in ancient myth. When her lover, the god Osiris, was murdered and his body torn to pieces and scattered throughout Egypt, a grief-stricken Isis searched everywhere until she'd gathered all the dismembered pieces and, by *re-membering* him, magically brought him back to life.

I ended my email to Angelina with these words: "Thank you for being the beautiful being, a Priestess of Isis, who serves and surrenders in love. I'm so grateful to you for raising me from the dead."

℘ 29 ℃

Enjoying My Grief

When I came down with a cold on October 6th, the six-month anniversary of Joy's passing, I didn't feel sorry for myself. It was another hopeful sign that my grief was passing and that I was healing.

There were other indications that perhaps I was over the worst of my grief. I walked around the lake listening to my Grief Playlist on my iPod and didn't even tear up. To my surprise, I experienced a radiant sweetness. At the supermarket checkout line, when asked, "How're you doing?" I responded truthfully, "Good." I remembered how hard it had been to answer that question in those first weeks after Joy's death. When Judy from Sedona called and asked how I was, I said, "Great." She was surprised. So was I. Maybe I wasn't really "great," but I was "good" and that felt great.

I attributed my healing to the grief work I'd been doing, especially the Rites of Joy. Yet, strangely, a part of me was sad that I wasn't grieving as much. Sure, I was glad I was healing, but I was sad that I was losing the feeling that had so powerfully connected me to Joy.

• • • •

I was invited to a Vision Board Party at the home of a friend. A vision board is a collage of images and words that represent your hopes and dreams for the future, and is supposed to help you create the life you want.

I didn't want to go. I made excuses, but the truth was that I wasn't that anxious to create a new future which, like a swift-moving current, took me further and further away from Joy.

At about this time, my friend Marcia gave me a special gift. She'd been the first to hold me on my *Journey of a Thousand Hugs,* and had credited our hugs with helping her make the emotional shift that enabled her to finally revisit her hometown in Kansas. Before leaving on her trip, she came by to gift me with a psychic reading.

She sat on a stool by the bar, closed her eyes, and breathed deeply several times to enter a trance state. I listened intently as she spoke in a stilted, formal way, unlike her usual speech. She (or her guides) explained that my grief journey was one of the major purposes of my relationship with Joy. "To lose your great love in order to go through the pain to transform yourself. Only in that way can you obtain your knowingness of what pain and suffering and grief is for the work that you have remaining for you to do that may be the greatest work you have done in this life."

To hear that my grief passage had a purpose beyond my understanding was a comfort. That it was one of the key reasons Joy and I came together was more difficult to comprehend. But there was more. Marcia's reading also contained a warning—I was told to be careful about using my grief as a "crutch." "Joy won't be a crutch," Marcia said. "She will help you stand. She will help you take a stand. She will help you know you have a leg to stand on. But your memory of her, your grieving process— like a drug—can be a crutch. Be careful about wallowing or the getting trapped in the sorrow, and the stories about loss..."

I swallowed hard. Was the memoir I planned to write and its "stories about loss" a "crutch?" I had to admit it was a way to hold on and not let go. But a "crutch?" Thankfully, the rest of Marcia's reading eased my concerns. "Joy says she's capable of being a taskmaster, of not allowing you to get stuck there. And she says she knows you have a good sense about that. Indulging your grief with as much awareness as you can will bring the grace and blessing of Joy. Indulging it out of fear, out of feeling scared to do anything else, or overindulging will simply weaken you. But not for long."

After Marcia's reading and Joy's warning not to use her as a crutch, I decided to take my foot off the brake and go to the Vision Board Party. At a friend's home, a dozen of us sat on the living room floor, surrounded by 2'x3' poster board, piles of magazines, scissors, glue sticks and Scotch tape. We were instructed to search through the magazines looking for words and images that called to us with which we would create a vision board to help us manifest a new future. The idea being that when you surround yourself with images of what you want in your life, you'll attract it.

I chose words like "Appreciate"...Imagine"..."Marvel"... "Delight"... "Celebrate!"...and "Trust." I found nature images of the four seasons that included sayings such as, *The world of reality has its limits, the world of imagination is boundless"* and *"Miracles are impossible things that happen anyway."* I inserted a picture of myself in Hawaii with a lei around my neck, as well as one of me being hugged by a woman's arms (Joy's) to illustrate my being in a loving relationship once again with someone whose identity was still unknown. Someone found the words, *"Anything worth doing is worth overdoing"* in a magazine and insisted it was for me. I included it in my vision board.

To my surprise, the collage of words and images that represented my future dreams turned out to be quite beautiful. I had envisioned a new future, thanks to Joy, and I was excited by the possibilities.

• • • •

The earth's turning on its axis is inexorable. Spring. Summer. Fall. Winter. The endless turning of the seasonal wheel. Before the dreaded holidays were upon me, I arrived at November 6 — an important day in the year's cycle.

Not only was it the seven-month anniversary of Joy's passing, but, more important, it was our "Love Anniversary" — the day we fell in love. That was our anniversary until we got married. Even after, we celebrated November 6th every year. I wanted to mark the day in some special way but had learned my lesson from July's wedding anniversary. I wrote the following entry in my journal for November 6th.

> In the afternoon I looked at some photo albums... Didn't cry! Just wanted to see Joy. Wished I could blow up the pictures of her...so big I could get inside them. She looked so beautiful. Pictures of when we first got together. She lay naked on a bed with a bouquet of balloons tethered to a ribbon she clasped between her knees...
>
> A very different experience than the July 3rd Wedding Anniversary immersion. The feelings are much less painful.

At my weekly bereavement group I shared that I'd been sick all week and that I was surprised I hadn't experienced any self-pity. I also shared how therapeutic it had been to celebrate our Love Anniversary by reliving the wonderful romantic memories instead of the more recent illness-dying ones. The facilitator thought it was a great exercise for everyone. It was amazing to witness the grief-induced anguish in everyone's face melt away as they relived the happiness of first meeting and then falling in love with their spouse.

At our monthly Wisdom Circle I talked about how my task now was to love everything in my life the way I loved Joy — the sky, the birds, the trees...even myself. I shared that one of the great lessons of losing Joy was learning to appreciate myself, care for myself and love myself as well as I loved, appreciated and took care of Joy. To survive my grief I'd had to take care of myself in ways I never had before. "Joy's illness gave her an excuse to practice self-love in a way she never had before. Joy's death gave me the excuse to love myself as never before. Healing my grief has required all the self-love I'm capable of. Don't wait for illness or the death of a loved one to love yourself."

At one point during the evening someone acknowledged me for "enjoying my grief."

I was stunned.

Enjoying grief was an oxymoron, a contradiction in terms, an impossibility. How could someone *enjoy* their grief?

The person explained that by feeling my grief to the fullest and then using it to expand and grow—in other words, making the most of it—I was *enjoying* my grief.

I could understand that. And I was sure Joy would have approved.

∞ 30 ∞

Falling Into the Holidays

In mid-November I reviewed my journal for October and it was clear that the theme for that month was *healing*..."no tears." The worst seemed to be over.

How wrong I was!

Fall comes later in Los Angeles than most other parts of the country. There's no real sense of autumn until after Halloween. As the temperature grew colder and the days shorter, I found myself experiencing an emotional "fall." My grief, which had seemed to be diminishing, suddenly intensified. There was something so visceral about the dark, the cold. The Fall is the dying, Winter is the death. My first Joy-less holidays were fast approaching and there was no way to avoid them.

As usual I celebrated Thanksgiving with Joy's son and daughter-in-law since my family lived back East. An unspoken gloom hovered over the cheerful gathering. There was good food on the table and lots of diversity seated around it— almost every continent, three major religions, and many ethnic backgrounds. I gave thanks for the love and miracles I'd been experiencing. And I appreciated my family and friends more than ever. Though I enjoyed the evening and counted my blessings, I teared up on several occasions and felt a persistent heaviness in my chest, as if the air had been sucked out of room. I couldn't take a deep breath.

The rest of Thanksgiving weekend was a blur. I kept moving in hopes that I could outrun my grief. I attended two other parties—a "beastly feast" of leftovers and an evening of Indian food hosted by friends who'd just returned from a trip to the subcontinent.

At the "beastly feast" I surprised myself by playing the "ringmaster"—providing music, getting people to dance, and initiating Joy's "Trading Secrets" game.[3] Whenever people played her game, I felt her presence.

The following evening was no different—I was the proverbial "life of the party," leading the discussion around the dinner table and later "interviewing" the hosts to help them present the slide show of their month-long trip to India.

As I drove home, I was troubled by my behavior. I'd been almost manic in my need to engage socially. Like a starving man at the social buffet, I was desperate to interact, to fill up on life, to laugh, joke, talk, relate—until the next opportunity, whenever that would be. With Joy I experienced fulfillment. Now I was a "hungry ghost" who had to gorge on social life whenever I had the opportunity in order to see me through the famine of aloneness that could last days, possibly weeks. Perhaps forever.

Seeing myself as "a starving man" sent me into a tailspin. As though looking into a mirror for the first time after a harrowing illness, I didn't recognize myself.

In my bereavement group everyone dreaded the holidays. I shared my Thanksgiving mania—how starved I was and how hard I worked—and compared it to the fulfillment of my life before when I had Joy on tap 24/7.

Driving home from the meeting, I had a realization about the dangers of grieving. Grief was a downward spiral of negativity because it was always reminding you what was *missing*—your

---

3 Joy created *Trading Secrets* to help people get to know each other and stimulate conversation. The card deck of intriguing questions came in a beautiful gift bag out of which you pulled a question. It was a great date or party game.

loved one and the life you shared. You became used to focusing on the glass being half empty. Since what you put your attention on grows, that kind of thinking was a prescription for depression.

With this in mind, I tried to reinterpret my Thanksgiving mania in a more positive light. It was a cry: *"Here I Am!"* A lion's roar that *I'm alive!* Being "the life of the party" was a way to give myself a pep talk—a morale booster—to show myself I could function. I could even put the *fun* in "function." I also realized it was self-medicating.

Laughing, joking, sharing, relating and, of course, dancing, changes the chemistry of my body in a positive, healthy way so that the stress-induced chemistry of grief is diluted and even transformed. Beyond that, I could see that walking the love of my life to the brink of death had been like a near-death experience which had imprinted in my very cells how precious life really is. And so I wanted to make the most of Thanksgiving. Carpe diem! *Seize the day!*

The next morning I received an email request from a member of the Wisdom Circle asking us all to share our *"10 Keys to Life."* I sat down and without much thought came up with mine.

10 Keys to Life

1. Don't Take Yourself Too Seriously & Laugh As Much As You Can—it's great exercise.

2. An Attitude of Gratitude.

3. Stay Away From "Shit Hounds"—people who are always sniffing out trouble (shit) in life and leading you to it.

4. Follow Your Bliss & Fill Your Life with Joy.

5. Embrace Your Uniqueness in Totality with Both its Light & Dark.

6. Always Think a Better Thought.

7. Smell Good.

8. See the Glass as Half Full & Accentuate the Positive.

9. Life is a Placebo—the more MAGICAL you believe it to be, the more MAGICAL it will be.

10. Wonder is Where It's At If You Want To Live A Wonder-Ful Life.

11. Sell All Your Cleverness to Buy Amazement.

12. If It's Worth Doing, It's Worth Overdoing.

By the time I finished compiling (and *overdoing!*) these *10 Keys To Life*, I felt much better about life in general and about my life in particular. I was inspired to use this Thanksgiving season to really give thanks for all the gifts I still had...and, most especially, for the gift of having loved Joy.

℘ *31* ℭ

To Date Or Not To Date

⊢————————————————————⊣

Sooner or later the issue of dating was bound to come up. On December 1st I wrote these entries in my journal—

> My life is empty. I'm getting by...barely. In comparison to my life with Joy, my life is so empty. I want to love again.
>
> I looked at myself in the mirror today in a new way—as if through a woman's eyes. I hadn't really looked at myself that way in years. Pictures of myself seven years earlier show a much fuller head of brown wavy hair and a copper-tinged beard without any gray. Now my hair is thin on top and my beard is frosted. Does looking at myself in this new way mean I'm ready to date?
>
> People in my bereavement group are starting to date and have ambivalent feelings. Some feel guilty and feel they're betraying their loved one. One of the men made a date with someone he'd met online. "The first time I go out on a date in thirty-five years, I get stood up." So he went home and drank himself into a stupor.

Initially, my *Journey of a Thousand Hugs* took care of my need to be held and touched. Without realizing it, I'd substituted "hugging" for dating so I could get affection without complication. My low libido took away any urgency to have sex. And I didn't have any desire to touch a woman who wasn't Joy. Everyone grieves differently. There are people who, after

183

losing their spouse, take comfort in sex. That's *not* how I reacted. One factor may have been that once the Rites of Joy began, I was experiencing ecstatic, sensual touch and didn't want to do anything sexual that might interfere with those encounters.

Mostly I wanted companionship and intimacy. Anything more was too much—too provocative, too distracting from my memories and my grief. I wanted to spend time with women as friends. My grief was like a "get out of jail free" card. I was freed from commitments and yet had a pass to intimacy.

The truth was I really didn't want to get involved because getting close was painful. Even depressing. I needed playmates now, not another soulmate. Not yet. I wasn't looking for that special someone. No one was going to take Joy's place, not for a very long time, if ever. Clearly, I was in no place to fall in love or embark on a relationship. I had neither the desire nor the emotional capacity. Some women knew it and didn't want to waste their time. Who could blame them? Some women were attracted to me *because* of my love story. Having been Joy's beloved was the best PR a man could have. Perhaps my vulnerability appealed to some women. In my journal I wrote— "this grief journey makes me the poem of myself."

What I wanted were friends to spend time with, to soothe my loneliness during this terrible grief passage. And without obligation, complication or commitment. Since I'd been held and was now being loved, pleasured and even adored in the Rites of Joy, the main thing I missed was dancing.

So I began to tell women I met that I'd lost my wife and that dancing helped relieve my grief. If the woman said she loved to dance, I'd invite her to my home. To *dance*. At that time a dance evening was better than sex. I'd serve finger food and wine, play Trading Secrets as a way to get to know her, talk about Joy, dance again, talk about life. Dance some more. During these "play dates" I shared about my hugging journey and that might inspire a hug. Occasionally there were foot massages, even playful kissing. But the wild in me seemed dead — I hoped only dormant and hibernating through grief's winter.

Though custom-designed, these "play dates" were provocative since I never knew when they would stir up my grief. Meeting someone new seemed safest because it was as far from comparison with Joy as possible. But if I liked someone enough to see them a second and possibly even a third time, I'd feel the "couple" energy emerge, and that reminded me of Joy and stoked my grief. So I'd back away. This yoyo-ing dance became familiar. And since the yoyo-ing reared itself with the women I liked, it depressed me.

Though dating could be depressing, it dulled the excruciating loneliness. And though dating could exacerbate my grief, being alone, especially on weekends, made me miserable.

A journal entry about my Labor Day weekend summed up my dilemma.

> I went to a party and though it had the most wonderful elements—friends, great music, warm pool—I'm not with Joy. I go out with a woman and, though she's attractive, she's not Joy. And if I stay home alone, it's awful because I'm not with Joy. So no matter what I do, I can't escape the fact that I'm no longer with Joy. How was my holiday weekend? *Three different kinds of miserable!*

I was starved for the intimacy I'd shared with Joy, and yet intimacy with a new woman was a painful reminder of all I'd lost. I was discovering that my grief was like wearing an "emotional condom." One woman I'd seen several times asked me point blank — what was my "level of interest?" I replied that I was as interested as I could be, but that probably wasn't going to be nearly enough for her.

My tentative explorations into dating hit rock bottom on a Sunday in early December when I woke up in a terrible funk. I was depressed and couldn't understand why. I'd spent

Friday *and* Saturday evening on dates with two attractive and interesting women. And I had a good time. I was mystified.

When I shared my bewildering experience with a friend, she said she understood completely—"It's like having all the ingredients but no cake."

The more I thought about her comment, the more I realized why a "romantic evening" without the romance could be depressing. Even with all the "ingredients" present, there wasn't the feeling, the trust, the bond, the knowing, the understanding, the acceptance, the *love*.

I was in a quandary. Had I stayed home alone and watched TV, I would have been less depressed. I guess this depression was just something that accompanied these initial forays into dating. If I'd learned anything, it was that I'd have to say *Yes* and embrace the comparison, the potential depression, possibly even despair...and move through it. The alternative was to stay home...and that wasn't an option.

℘ 32 ℭ

Tantric Quest

}————————————————————————————{

In the dead of winter my body ached to be warmed by the flesh of another human being. I hadn't heard from Angelina in awhile and it felt like ages since I'd been held, so I was pleased to receive an invitation to a reunion of Tantra students who'd studied with Bodhi Avinasha, author of *Jewel In The Lotus*. Just what the doctor ordered, I thought, as I imagined the many opportunities for loving touch that such a gathering would provide. As the day of the reunion approached, however, I found myself coming up with all sorts of excuses not to go.

There were many reasons for my reluctance. It was at Bodhi's beginner's Tantra workshop where I first experienced Joy's youthful essence and the veil of our age difference began to dissolve. At Bodhi's advanced weeklong workshop in Cancun several months later, we celebrated our birthdays and our "honeymoon" where—employing tantric techniques such as Cobra Breath in swinging beds—our lovemaking transported us to transcendent states of bliss.

What had brought me to Bodhi's tantra workshops in the first place? A dream about sex. Not a wet dream, but more like a biblical "burning bush." In this visionary dream I witnessed a sacred sexual rite taking place in another dimension with beings more angelic than human and where the sex was actually worship. This dream haunted me for years until, in the midst of depositions in a lawsuit, that still soft voice within asked me what I would regret on my deathbed. The answer to that question and my vow to write about that dream changed the course of my life.

I researched Tantra, the yoga of sex. I studied with several teachers and took numerous workshops. I learned how to cultivate arousal and pleasure through breath, and to harness those energies for spiritual purposes. I explored Hindu, Tibetan Buddhist, Taoist, even Native American sacred sexuality, and discovered that at the core of each tradition lies the secret and often suppressed knowledge that our lovemaking has the potential to transport us to transcendent states. Sexual communion, refined like an art, harnessed like a yoga, is the most powerful form of prayer — a direct way to access the divine.

My "deal with God" to write about my dream vision seemed to have been blessed by the gods because it brought Joy into my life. After several false starts, my vision ultimately took the form of a novel entitled, "The Secret Sex Life of Angels." In this book I was going to share the secrets I'd learned and hoped to create a vision of sex as a "gateway to Heaven." I wanted to inspire a new sexual evolution. (A lofty ambition, I know.) Yet Joy was inspired, too, and devoted herself to editing the book.

In her memoir, Joy described her late husband, Bob, telling her from the Afterlife that my book was "the primary reason you were attracted to each other. The reason you're enjoying your involvement so much is that it touches a deep part of your soul." He also told her that there was a greater purpose to our relationship, and that our mission was "shining a new light on two of the most misunderstood areas of our lives — sex and death."

Joy's interest in sex went beyond the personal. Though a widely respected astrologer, the title of her first book says it all — *DAYS AND NIGHTS FOR MAKING LOVE: Sexual Timing With Astrology.*

When I first met Joy, she was driving a blue Lincoln Continental that she called "Desiree" with a license plate that read *JOYOUS 6*. Indeed. *Joyous sex* was such an important part of our life that Joy wrote an essay about it entitled, "Sexy at Seventy." Though Joy was free and uninhibited sexually, our tantra studies and practice made a great impact on her. She wrote about it in her essay. "The truly remarkable part of our relationship is our sex life, which is on a whole different level than anything I've ever experienced. From Jerry's Tantra training, he's taught me how to prolong sensual pleasure so that the journey becomes even more important and memorable than the destination."

Joy was freer sexually than people realized. On the outside she appeared as wholesome as Doris Day, but on the inside she was as wild as Madonna. She was game for anything and everything. Even I didn't realize to what degree until the day I asked her to write a sex fantasy.

I was working on my novel, which was full of fantastic sexual rites and initiations, and was curious what fantasies Joy might come up with. She loved the idea of writing a sex fantasy and immediately sat down at the computer. A few hours later she handed me a sex fantasy entitled, "Isis' Pleasure Palace." According to Joy, "this fantasy takes place somewhere in the Middle East at least 3,000 years ago, before religion made sex shameful." Described in graphic detail, Joy's "Love Festival" was an opulent and erotic monthly celebration involving hundreds of people. Since it was an orgy fit for a king, it was "considered a great honor to be invited and participants vied for the privilege."

I was amazed by Joy's lack of inhibition, her imagination and her joyful embracing of sexuality in all its wonderful variety. But that was the least of it. She confessed that this exotic orgy was only partly fantasy. It was also, she claimed, partly memory.

As she wrote it, she began recalling the Love Festivals we celebrated (which she organized) during our past life together. In Joy's words:

"I've experienced several spontaneous past lives. One of them was a few months after falling in love with Jerry. While we were making love one night, an entire lifetime came through. This life involved the two of us about 3,000 years ago when Jerry was king of a small province in the Middle East near Egypt. Although the king was married, that relationship was political for the purpose of additional land holdings and treaties, so it didn't mean much to him or his wife. He had his own lovers and the queen had hers. I worked in the palace as a handmaiden to one of the royals and after my husband was killed, the king invited me to his chambers. I fell madly in love with him and became his favorite mistress. However, since he was totally spoiled and got whatever he wanted without any emotional investment, he didn't know much about love.

Once after making love, Jerry looked at me with a mischievous twinkle in his eye and said, "You know, you're really good. I think you're a keeper." Instantly I remembered hearing similar words from him in that other lifetime and vowing to myself that one day I would make him fall in love with me. Well, it took about 3,000 years, but I finally did.

Our relationship was very satisfying to me then, even though he had many other women at his beck and call. I danced for him in sexy outfits with beautiful veils and helped organize fantastic orgies, which his wife didn't attend. During these festivities I got to be the queen bee.

Several months after remembering that past life, I went to an exhibit at LACMA (Los Angeles Country Museum of Art) featuring artifacts from this particular time and place. As I studied a map of the territory, a specific state seemed to jump out at me. I also found a gold plate engraved with a picture of one of the kings, which I felt was Jerry back then. Actually, he didn't look much different than he does now."

Joy's revelation that her sex fantasy was a memory of our past life together made me wonder if my magnificent obsession to write about my visionary dream was also fueled by that past life.

There were signs of that past life everywhere. The condo in which we lived was decorated like an ancient Egyptian palace. I was affectionately called "King" by our friends, yet had never asked for or invited such a grandiose nickname. As hard as it was to believe, it seemed as if we'd been re-creating and working with themes from that past life thousands of years ago.

Despite our plans for my novel about sacred sexuality, life intervened and we became increasingly preoccupied with Joy's six year bout with cancer and blindness. Faced with these life-threatening challenges, my book seemed unimportant. Even so, I continued writing whenever I could and Joy continued editing my book. Even when she could no longer see, she asked me to read new pages to her line by line. It was painfully slow going, but she loved doing it.

Knowing that our time together was limited, I didn't have the heart to isolate myself to write, but instead dedicated myself to making her life as fulfilling as possible. And I never finished my novel. Joy regretted the fact that her health challenges had consumed so much of my time and energy. A week or so before she passed, she implored me to "finish the book." One of her last wishes was that I complete our "mission."

I could see that there were lots of reasons for my reluctance to attend the Tantra Reunion. But now that I understood the depth of my feelings, I knew I had no choice but to face them.

ஜ 33 ஐ

Eyes Wide Open

)——————————————————————————————————————(

Despite my reluctance, I used my mantra (*Yes! I can! Now!*) and drove forty-five minutes north along the coast to Santa Barbara, then fifteen minutes inland to Ojai. This picturesque town — a haven for artists, musicians and health enthusiasts — was where the Tantra Reunion was to be held.

I hadn't seen Bodhi in nearly ten years. She remembered me and Joy, especially from our time in Cancun, and told me we radiated a powerful and palpable presence she could still recall.

Throughout the afternoon, I had wonderful conversations with people I knew and people I'd just met. Everyone was sympathetic about my loss and expressed it with wonderful "melting hugs." Someone started drumming and dancing broke out. I wound up having a terrific dance with a woman wearing a belly dance outfit. It was a great warm-up for the evening's *puja*.

At tantra events a puja, which literally means "ritual" or "worship" in Sanskrit, refers to a group exercise in which an equal number of men and women form two concentric circles facing each other. Everyone is paired. The leader of the puja guides the "couples" in brief exercises that are heart-opening and intended to honor the "god and goddess within." After each exercise the circles rotate so that everyone has a new partner.

Over the years, I'd participated in dozens of pujas. When Joy's eyesight became so poor she couldn't see her partners, we stopped attending. I hadn't been to a puja in seven years.

There were about two dozen of us gathered that evening in a large candlelit room. We formed two circles, the men on the outside facing in and the women on the inside facing out. Everyone wore flowing, comfortable clothing. My first partner was a strikingly attractive woman, which I took to be a good omen. We were instructed to ask our partner what part of their body they wanted touched. She wanted a sacrum massage to awaken her kundalini. I obliged and tapped the base of her spine then stroked the energy up her back. *I* wanted my neck nuzzled. There's a spot that's ticklish, yet arousing. She obliged and I convulsed with pleasure. The puja was off to a great start.

We rotated and my next partner was the belly dancer. In this exercise we were going to work on our third chakra — our power center. We were shown a martial arts kick and simultaneous opposite hand thrust, and told to also make a sound that expressed our power. We kicked, thrust and growled at each other, not to overpower the other, but to equalize and *balance* with each other. Again and again we kicked, thrust and growled until we calibrated ourselves to each other. Then we were instructed to sit across from each other and take turns asking, "What change do you want to make in your life?" I answered, "I want to love again."

With my next partner I explored the heart chakra. We were to tell each other what we loved. I rattled off a list of things: ice cream cones, my granddaughter, memories of Joy, dancing, creating, hot showers, laughing.

My next partner and I were instructed to talk gibberish as a way to activate the throat chakra. In gibberish we had to tell each other what we admired about the other. I jabbered about how much I admired her ability to have fun, to let her hair down and play the fool. Her gibberish to me was breathily seductive and, although I didn't know what she said, I felt incredibly admired. To complete the exercise we were instructed to embrace each other with our necks as if our throats could kiss. What an unusual sensation!

My next partner was a freckled redhead with whom I was instructed to share a "tantric kiss" by formally bowing, eye gazing and then lowering my forehead to hers so our third eyes gently touched.

Finally, I returned to my original partner to explore the crown chakra at the top of the head. We were told to sit in yab yum. Without any hesitation she climbed into my lap and wrapped her legs around me. Then we were instructed to tone the mantras (*Vam... Lam... Ram...*) for each of the seven chakras, starting with the root (at the base of the spine) and moving up to the crown chakra. As we did this, she moved her head beside mine, so that her ear covered mine. With one hand she closed my other ear, and with her other hand guided my hand over her other ear. As we toned the mantras, I could hear them resonating both in her head and in mine.

In the afterglow of the puja, I was glad I'd forced myself to attend the reunion. I felt as if I'd reawakened parts of myself, and hoped that reconnecting with my tantric quest might rekindle my libido. Ironically, in the days that followed, I experienced a malaise, even despair...as if I'd reawakened my grief.

A week later, as I prepared for Angelina's arrival—lighting candles, stoking the fireplace, selecting the music—I was surprised at how much it felt like a chore. If another Rite of Joy couldn't excite me, I was in big trouble.

It was a windy and wintry night, and when Angelina arrived she wanted to warm up. So we danced to some reggae music and then sat in front of the fireplace.

"Tell me about the tantra reunion," she said, her face now flushed from the heat of the fire and her eyes wide with curiosity. As I related the exercises we did for each chakra, she climbed into my lap so I could demonstrate. I began talking gibberish to her—the way we had at the reunion—and she immediately jabbered back at me until we broke up laughing.

When the laughter subsided we found ourselves overcome by the palpable beauty of embracing each other in yab yum in front of the fire. In silence we basked in each other's presence and swayed in circles as the energy coiled around us. Instinctively we began toning and I moved my ear against hers and showed her how to block her other ear so that she could feel the vibrations. We instinctively completed this merging with a "tantric kiss," bowing our heads so that our third eyes touched. Our impromptu puja took us out of our minds and into our hearts and bodies. My doldrums were gone.

Warm now, Angelina stood and removed her street clothes, trading them for one of her priestess outfits. She'd begun to play her role by wearing revealing costumes that might be worn by a belly dancer.

I asked if she'd received any guidance from Joy. "We're in transition," she said. "And should allow it to unfold."

I climbed onto the massage table, wondering where this "transition" would lead. As Angelina's fingers caressed my scalp, a stream of energy poured from her hands into the top of my head through my crown chakra, and I felt my mind turn off.

Guided by Joy, Angelina's hands touched me tenderly and deeply. Whenever her lips touched my skin, I convulsed. One by one, she sucked my fingers while toning, and the vibration seemed to move along the energy meridians of each finger into the depths of my being. Once again, I felt utterly adored! Such adoration seemed to be the ultimate expression of love.

Overwhelmed that I could be "loved" so completely, I opened my eyes to see for myself. For the first time, I *watched* Angelina adore me. I'd never looked before because seeing another woman would have interfered with my experience of

Joy. But now I took pleasure in watching this beautiful woman touching, caressing, kissing and adoring me. It was breathtaking!

As the Rite continued, I realized that I'd never experienced such ultimate adoration when Joy was alive. We pleased each other often. And there were times when she made love to me. But this depth and degree of adoration was new. Of course, I hadn't been suffering from a devastating grief. And so I'd never allowed myself to receive like this.

While ecstatic, orgasmic shudders swept through my body, I wept at the price I'd paid to experience such profound love and adoration—*losing* Joy.

After Angelina left, I sat alone by the fire and thought about the evening's Rite. I hadn't sensed Joy's presence much. Maybe that was why I was able to watch Angelina adore me. And though I knew Joy was the inspiration for these Rites, I missed experiencing her.

The next day I wrote Angelina a "thank you" email, but her email response provoked me. She seemed to be experiencing Joy so much more than me and, I had to admit, I envied her.

In my morning meditation I asked Joy for help. This is the guidance I received. *"It isn't as important for you to experience me. In fact, it would retard your healing from grief if you experienced me making love to you. What's important is that you experience being adored in a way you never have before. Know that I'm inspiring Angelina and that she's channeling my Love and Adoration for you. That's the best medicine right now. So don't question your experience. Don't go to disappointment. Don't compare your experience to Angelina's. She is experiencing what she needs. You are receiving exactly what you need. I love you more than you can possibly imagine. Receive my love without question or doubt. Revel in it. You deserve it."*

IV

Winter

℘ 34 ℘

Joy-less To The World

)————————————————————(

Like a thief in the night, the holiday blues crept up on me and picked my pocket of any well being I'd managed to accumulate. The holidays are the hardest for those who've suffered a loss, especially the first time around. With so many memories of celebrations in years past and the world preparing to celebrate once again, the loss of a loved one becomes unbearable. Is it any wonder that I cringed at even the thought of the holidays?

As a Jew born of Holocaust survivors I never celebrated Christmas as a child. During the years I lived in Israel as an adult, Christmas was no big deal. I celebrated my first real Christmas with Joy. She made Christmas magical. As that first Joy-filled Christmas approached, I watched in amazement as day after day exquisitely wrapped gifts began appearing beneath the tree in the living room. The abundance was breathtaking.

Joy wasn't Christian, but believed that Jesus was an enlightened teacher—one among many. What Joy celebrated about Christmas was the love that could be expressed and shared during the holiday season.

Christmas seemed effortless for her. Shopping? She bought gifts throughout the year. For Joy, Christmas wasn't the time to shop for gifts, but rather the time to *give* them.

As this dreaded Christmas approached, I felt tortured and tormented. Christmas music was piped in everywhere 24/7. I was bombarded with ads proclaiming "Joy to the World" and cards wishing me a "Joyous Holiday Season." Surrounded by all of these *Joy*-filled sentiments, I was constantly being reminded (more like shoving my nose in the fact) that I was Joy-*less* this Christmas. I had been feeling a little better, but the holidays insisted I miss Joy!

Medical science has proven that after a serious loss, people are more prone to injury and disease. The chemistry of grief lowers our immune system. And holidays compound the problem. Was I at risk?

On December 16th I came down with a bad cold. Being so sick accentuated how vulnerable I was living alone. It was scary and depressing. I stayed in bed, napped and read a memoir about Internet dating. How ironic that I tried to distract myself from my grief and illness by reading about a thirty-seven-year-old man who was "a tiny bit desperate to meet the woman of his dreams," while I, on the other hand, was "a tiny bit desperate" because I'd *lost* the woman of my dreams.

My cold continued to get worse, so I didn't go to my bereavement group. I coughed a lot and had trouble sleeping at night. During the day, between tea, naps and over-the-counter cold medicine, I read another dating memoir, this one by a woman. Reading these horror stories had one beneficial side-effect—they made the dating world seem so bizarre and even dangerous to one's health that I felt lucky that I was home alone, sick in bed.

On the 19th of December I was feeling really lousy and afraid I was developing bronchitis. That night I had an incredible dream. Though I'd asked Joy to appear in my dreams, she hadn't lately. But here she was. I could not only see her, I could *feel* her. We embraced and it felt wonderful. The next day I felt much better.

Why had I gotten sick? Was grief-induced depression lowering my immune system? Was I subconsciously using illness as a *"get-out-of-the-holidays"* card, so I wouldn't have to experience the full brunt of my first holiday season without Joy?

I didn't come up with an answer. And it didn't matter. What mattered was that from the moment I dreamt of Joy's embrace, I began to recover.

The weekend before Christmas was jam-packed. Thursday evening I hosted our annual Wisdom Circle Gift Exchange party. Joy and I had been inspired years earlier by attending a "white elephant" party to which, as a joke, we brought a pair of fur-lined handcuffs. To our surprise, our "joke" turned out to be the most sought after, that is, the most "stolen" of all the gifts. And the justifications and negotiations to obtain this "sex toy" were hilarious.

For this year's party I requested everyone bring a gift that was inspired by the letter S since it was the Winter Solstice. So the presents could be *sexy, scenty, sweet, spiritual, surprising* and so on. Still under the weather, I requested the help of other members of the Circle to organize the potluck and MC the game which helped me avoid having to host my first party without Joy. My cold also turned out to be a good excuse for not being in much of a holiday mood.

The next evening I was invited to a holiday party up in the hills near Mulholland Drive. Despite my lingering cold, I decided to give it a try. I wasn't up for partying or dancing, but I knew there would be live musical performances and I felt I had enough energy to be an audience. As I walked from my car up the steep driveway to the party, my still-congested lungs wheezed in the chilly night air.

The house was packed. Dazed by the crowd, I gravitated to people I knew who kept asking me how I was doing. "I'm here," I replied cryptically. Had I been feeling better I would have said more. But this terse response was my truth—just being at the party felt like a major achievement. I was happy to see familiar faces, but I didn't have the energy to engage new people. By the time the musical performances began, it was 11:00 p.m. and I'd had enough.

To my surprise, Angelina was leaving just as I was. Since she had come alone, I walked her down the hill to her car. I asked her why she was leaving so early. "Are you okay?"

"Yeah. I'm saving my energy for the big gala Christmas party tomorrow night. Are you going?"

I didn't know anything about it.

"The hosts are friends—music industry professionals—and they throw a spectacular party every year. You shouldn't miss it."

Another party was the last thing on my mind. "I'll see how I'm feeling," I said. As we hugged goodnight, I thanked her again for everything and wished her a happy holiday.

The next night I didn't feel up to a big Christmas gala, but staying home alone on a holiday Saturday night and watching *The Shawshank Redemption* on HBO didn't seem a great alternative. No matter what I did, it wasn't going to feel good.

The fact that it was Angelina who had invited me to this party tipped the scales. Perhaps leaving last night's party at the same time wasn't a coincidence. I wanted to believe that Joy had a hand in it. So I repeated my mantra (*Yes! I can! Now!*) and decided to go. Angelina would be there, and that would make things easier.

The beautiful hilltop mansion was ablaze with dazzling Christmas lights. As I valet-parked, I overheard other guests describing this as the hosts' 13th annual Christmas party. When I walked into the house, it seemed like I'd stepped into a TV Christmas special. Lavish decorations. Santa Clauses walking around. Beautiful people dressed to the nines. A small choir singing carols by the fireplace. Waiters dressed as "elves" carrying trays of hors d'oeuvres and glasses of champagne among the milling guests. And I knew very few of them.

I was suddenly overwhelmed with the strangeness of being "alone." With Joy, I had always felt "at home" no matter where we were. All these people full of good cheer and I didn't feel connected to any of them. I looked for Angelina in the crowd but didn't see her.

I needed to get some air and went outside to explore the sculpture garden. The gardens were terraced and so extensive that a small funicular transported people up and down the hill. I chose to walk the winding paths instead. I didn't know where I was going, but I had to keep moving.

When I finally returned to the house, I stayed outside on the back deck and through the window watched the singers perform in front of the fireplace. With my nose pressed against the glass, I recalled those classic scenes in countless movies, the picture of *not belonging*. Now that was *me*.

I wanted to leave, to run away from the awful feelings that were gathering like a tidal wave. But then I heard my mantra again—(*Yes! I can! Now!*)—and forced myself to stay awhile longer. I went back inside and made a mad dash for the bar, which was manned by several bartenders. I hadn't intended to drink because of the cough medication I was taking, but this was an emergency. I ordered a vodka tonic. Just then I heard my name.

"Hi, Jerry."

I turned to see who it was. Alongside me stood the woman whose party I'd attended the night before. One of my new "friends." We'd spent an evening or two together dancing, going to dinner and the theater, even massaging each other's feet while baring our souls. Sensing my distress, she began to talk me down from my panic-induced ledge. We got our drink, and she led me to some leather sofas with the excuse that she wanted to hang out with me since she'd been too busy hosting the night before.

She got me talking about my "meltdown." While I sipped my drink, she listened and massaged my free hand. In a few minutes the alcohol dulled the sharp edge of my panic and her tender companionship diluted my feelings of aloneness. I was *with* somebody. By the time I'd finished my drink, I was in a much better mood.

Hearing upbeat music coming from the main room and knowing I liked to dance, my Angel of Mercy led me toward the music. Before I realized it, we were dancing in a crowd of people. Whether it was the dancing or the vodka mixing with the cough medicine, I was catching a buzz. My "meltdown" averted, I managed to enjoy the rest of the party, but left early since my energy was still low. Waiting outside for the valet to bring my car, I felt I'd been rewarded for having said *Yes* to the experience. I'd survived my attack of Sudden Aloneness Shock (SAS) in a crowd of holiday revelers thanks to the kindness of a friend. Somehow I felt stronger, as if I'd passed an important test—even if just barely.

And then, just like the previous evening, Angelina suddenly appeared. She was leaving the party, too. I hadn't seen her all evening, that's how big the party had been. As we waited for the valet to get our cars, I thanked her for inviting me.

"Did you have a good time?" she asked, a hint of concern in her voice.

"It was a little rocky," I confessed, "but it turned out okay."

The valet finally brought her car, so I kissed her on the cheek and said goodnight. She made no mention of the Rites of Joy and neither did I.

As Christmas bore down on me, so did the issue of *gifts*. At first I didn't want to do Christmas gifts because it reminded me of Joy not being here. Then I relented, deciding that the only kinds of gifts I was interested in giving were those that had something to do with Joy.

At the bereavement group I spoke about my gift dilemma. Some of the group had already experienced a spouse-less

Christmas and had chosen to pass on gifts. They were happy they did. The group consensus was that I should do whatever I wanted. I left the meeting feeling that my first priority was to myself, and that whatever I ultimately decided to do about gifts would be fine.

Finally, after agonizing over the Christmas gift issue, I arrived at a partial solution. I announced to Joy's closest women friends that, as a Christmas gift, I was making Joy's closet available to them. Everyone seemed delighted since they'd all expressed the desire to have something of Joy's.

Over the next few days a parade of women took turns in Joy's closet. Jackie brought gardenias, which filled the closet with Joy's favorite scent. After two hours, she emerged from the closet with eyes red and swollen from crying, and told me that more precious than the clothes she chose was feeling how much Joy loved her. Another friend wept in my arms after being in the closet and told me, "Everybody could see that Joy and you were magic."

A dozen women went through Joy's closet and I was gratified to see one friend after another take armloads of clothing. Yet, to my amazement, the closet still looked full. I was happy that Joy's things would be used. Strange as it may seem, I was even looking forward to seeing her friends dressed in her clothes. I couldn't be reminded of Joy enough.

Sharing Joy's closet was a wonderful gift to everyone and, as it turned out, especially to me. Kate, Joy's daughter-in-law, was not only an accomplished poet, watercolorist and *USA Today* "Teacher of the Year," she was also a psychic. Years ago, with Joy's help, Kate functioned as a medium for people who wanted to contact their loved ones on the Other Side. Joy had dubbed these sessions "Dial the Dead." When Kate took her turn in Joy's closet, she received a message from Joy for me which she wrote down on a piece of paper.

"Jerry was the love of my life. We enjoyed all the aspects of relationship that I had experienced one at a time in other

> relationships with men: partnership, sex, dance, intimacy, play, travel, support for my work, and the experience of being equal in a relationship. I loved our passion, and it will carry me through to the time that we are together again."

I wept reading these words—this was the best Christmas gift I could have asked for. I marveled at the way my gift of sharing Joy came back to me in such a meaningful way.

On Christmas morning, I drove to Terri's and sat in my car in the driveway for some time, my eyes stinging, trying to collect myself. When I finally walked in, Natalie ran into my arms. At three years old she seemed to be getting what Christmas was about—*toys*! For me, Christmas morning at Terri's *without* Joy was like mainlining my grief uncut—unadulterated agony. I tried but I couldn't stop missing Joy. I ached so much, I left immediately after brunch.

Despite my pain, I was determined to say *Yes* to every party that came my way, and so that afternoon I went to yet another holiday party. This one was thrown by a woman who lived up near the Hollywood sign in a replica of a medieval castle, complete with turrets, a moat, and a dungeon. There were even shields, swords and heraldic crests on display.

At this party, I ran into many of the same people I'd seen at the other holiday parties and found that I was making some new friends. Musicians jammed while I drank wine and danced. Later, sitting by the roaring fire, I reflected on the irony that a fire is only appreciated when you're cold, and food only when you're hungry. And that when you party every night, you no longer have the experience of *partying*, of something special happening. It was like being full at a banquet—frustrating, even pointless.

Then I had an epiphany. Living a fulfilled life, I realized, required both light *and* dark experiences—the contrast is necessary for the light to be fully appreciated. And the shadows, however painful—like cold and hunger, even death—complete the picture. I saw how this applied to me, how I appreciated

Joy even more while experiencing this Joy-less holiday season. I could also see that I would more fully appreciate new love and new life *because* I'd lived through the agony of this season of grief.

Driving home I had to laugh at myself. I'd complained about all the holiday parties and how exhausting they were, and yet, *Thank God for them!* The alternative of sitting home alone during the holidays would have been much worse. And though going out every day, sometimes twice a day, made me miss Joy even more, it felt like forward movement. I was meeting new people, navigating new social situations, dancing my way through the dreaded holidays! And yet, though the partying was fun, I would have exchanged it all for five minutes at home with Joy.

Exhausted, I climbed into bed with a distinct feeling that some transformation was taking place during this holiday season that I wouldn't fully comprehend for a while. All I could do was trust and say, *Yes...*and *Thank You!*

ℰℴ *35* ℭℛ

Happy? New Year

A few days before New Years, I arranged to have dinner with one of the women in my bereavement group who was having a particularly rough time getting through her first holiday season without her husband. We met at the Coral Tree Cafe in the evening and over dinner shared our holiday ordeals. Her husband had been diagnosed only seven weeks before he died of pancreatic cancer, so she didn't have the opportunity to "pre-grieve" the way I did. She was very depressed. Her grief was palpable.

In the spirit of the impending new year and hoping to change the mood, I asked her what she wished for herself in the coming year. With a straight face she said, "To be diagnosed with a terminal disease."

Knowing she didn't have plans for New Year's Eve, I invited her to a party some friends of mine threw every year. I thought it would be good for her to be with people. I gave her the address and told her I expected to see her there.

As I walked her to her car, she thanked me. I was glad I'd reached out to her. Getting together turned out to be a gift for me, too—it showed me that, despite moments of despair, I was doing relatively well.

For several years, Joy and I had hosted an intimate New Year's Eve party for our friends, the highlight of which was playing UnZipped, the "truth or dare" game we'd created. In the last few years, however, we attended a New Year's Eve party at the home of our dear friends, Judy and Michael. This year they'd asked me to provide dance music, so I prepared a special playlist. I planned to dance my way into the New Year.

At the party I drank a little and danced a lot. Dancing kept my demons at bay. As I slow danced with friends, I glanced at Joy's framed picture, which our hosts prominently displayed. Beneath her loving gaze, I felt as if I'd finally reached dry land, that I'd survived the shipwreck that had marooned me nine months ago on Planet Grief. And I gave thanks that I was among friends dancing for Joy.

At 11:11 p.m. we turned off the music and the thirty or more guests, including my bereavement group friend, formed a circle. People lounged on couches or sat on pillows on the floor. Over the past two years, this New Year's Eve Circle had become a tradition. Our hosts lit the rainbow candles—seven different colors, one representing each chakra—that Joy and I had given them years before and placed Joy's picture next to the candles.

I introduced the New Year's Eve edition of Trading Secrets that Joy had created especially for last New Year's Eve. Questions about the past year and the year to come were written on pieces of paper that were placed in a basket and would be passed around the circle. To start things off, I pulled the first question: *"How do you intend to create more laughter in the new year?"* I joked that this was a problem since I'd already seen all the Seinfeld episodes, then added that I'd spend time with my granddaughter, Natalie, because she makes me laugh.

The basket was passed around the circle and everyone answered a question. For example:

- *What happened last year that made a significant change in your life?*

- *Name one thing that happened last year that made you extremely happy?*

- *What did you do last year that you're especially proud of?*

- *What happened to you last year that was a complete surprise?*

- *What project do you intend to complete in the coming year?*

- *How will you take better care of yourself in the coming year?*

- *What situation in your life would you most like to change in the new year?*

- *What do you intend to do in the new year to create more joy in your life?*

- *In the coming year how do you intend to create more love in your life?*

The sharing was heartfelt, but I was especially moved because I sensed Joy's presence so strongly. It was as if she were at the party helping people bless their past and declare their future. Her game was helping all of us bring in the new year.

The basket of questions went around the Circle and finally came to my friend from the bereavement group, who sat beside me. The last person to go, she reached into the basket and read her question — *What was the worst thing that happened in the world this past year?* I cringed. Her eyes teared up and in a voice choked with emotion said, "In *my* world the worst thing that happened was the death of my husband."

This wasn't the most uplifting way to ring in the new year, so I picked another question, hoping it would take the edge off. *"How did you help somebody last year?"* Despite my best intentions, there was clearly no way we were going to avoid the subject of death. I took a deep breath and answered. "I was honored and privileged to love and care for my beloved wife, Joy, and help her die, help her...." and then *I* choked up.

It was almost midnight and people started counting down the remaining seconds. The moment the clock struck 12:00, everyone shouted "Happy New Year!" and I was deluged by hugs and kisses in an eruption of good cheer.

I couldn't have asked for a more perfect New Year's Eve. Dancing! Joy's game! Everything so perfectly orchestrated, as if custom-made for me! After dreading the holidays, to celebrate New Year's Eve in such a meaningful and fulfilling way seemed almost miraculous. I felt incredibly blessed and looked forward to whatever the new year held in store.

ℰ𝒪 *36* ℭ𝒬

Birthday Quandary

After such a wonderful New Year's Eve, I thought I was home free. But as soon as I put away the holiday decorations and cleaned up the New Year's debris, I looked at my new calendar and saw that January was going to be as challenging as December had been. In fact, January—Joy's and my birthday month—might be like going from the frying pan into the fire.

How did I want to celebrate my Joy-less birthday on January 12th? And how would I celebrate Joy's birthday on the 24th? Since they were only twelve days apart, we often celebrated our birthdays together. I was in a quandary.

The issue of birthdays seemed to be in the air. At the first meeting of my bereavement group since the holidays, one of the women brought a picture of her husband and lit a candle because yesterday was *his* birthday. She'd cried last night worse than she had at his funeral.

If my group was any indication, the new year was off to a lousy start. Some felt their spouse's death was a "mistake," which only compounded their feeling of loss. Another woman was distraught because the memorial DVD her husband's family produced showed no pictures of her sixteen years of marriage with him. A man broke down when he told us his daughter had just been diagnosed with stage four cancer. When he said words like, "Pet scan" and "lymph nodes," I cringed.

At the meeting, however, I came up with a plan that would *kill two birthdays with one party*. The singer-songwriter in the group had a side business catering and entertaining, so I decided to hire him to cater a joint birthday party on the 19th— Joy and I would celebrate together one more time.

My "bereavement buddy" came over the next evening to cook a meal and familiarize himself with my kitchen. He brought two bottles of wine, which we drank as he cooked various dishes and we decided on a menu. He shared some of his devastation at losing his wife of thirty-four years. For many months he drank Bombay Gin every night until he passed out. He was the guy who once was so drunk he walked through a sliding glass door and slashed his face. He admitted having wanted to kill himself. Though for months he was inconsolable at the meetings, the group, he claimed, saved his life.

I shared a lyric I'd recently heard on a country music station that I thought perfectly captured our plight—*"this learning to live again is killing me!"* He laughed in recognition and opened the second bottle of wine. He was six months ahead of me on his grief journey, yet he was as surprised as anyone that he'd begun dating a woman. I told him my grieving heart wasn't all there. "I feel like I'm inside an emotional condom," I told him. "I'm in no place to go anyplace." He laughed and said that was a good lyric for a song. We laughed some more and finished off the wine.

The next day Angelina called to suggest we celebrate my birthday with a Rite of Joy on the 24th, Joy's birthday. I suspected that Joy had something to do with inspiring such an elegant solution to my birthday quandary. And what an incredible birthday gift!

After I hung up, a song came on the radio with the lyric— *"We'll meet someday in that place where there are no shadows."* I took it as a sign that Joy was pleased with "our" birthday plans.

On Friday afternoon, January 11th, I visited my friends Patty and John, to see their newly renovated apartment. When I walked in, I was surprised by a big "Happy Birthday!" Some two dozen friends crowded beneath a bouquet of red heart-shaped balloons. I stood in the doorway and wept, caught completely off-guard by this unexpected outpouring of love.

Since I'd decided on a joint birthday party, my friends didn't want to let me get away with avoiding celebrating *my* birthday. Champagne corks popped. I was toasted and occasionally roasted. When everyone was finished, I choked back sobs and thanked them for loving me through this difficult passage and blessing me with such a wonderful surprise.

I was given a tour of the newly renovated home. In their romantically decorated bedroom, I suggested we play the *2nd Annual Joy Invitational "How Many People Can We Get On John & Patty's Bed"* game.

Last March, one month before Joy passed, John and Patty had thrown a housewarming party after their recent move to their new home. After a while, Joy needed to lie down. Patty took her into the bedroom and some of us followed and got on the bed with Joy. As people came into the room they wanted to get on the bed, too. Someone began snapping photographs. Curious to see what was going on, more people came into the room. And piled onto the bed. It quickly became a "how many people can we stuff into a phone booth" moment. And that's how we transformed what would have been a sad occasion into a game. In that tradition, we all piled onto the bed again—this time in Joy's memory—just the way we had nearly a year ago.

Around 8:00 p.m. I was told to go home and change for a night out. An hour later, friends picked me up and I was whisked away for a night on the town. We ate and drank sake, and danced well past midnight to a five-piece band that played R&B and Funk—everything from Earth, Wind & Fire to Prince.

My first Joy-less birthday was turning into a love-filled celebration. As I crawled into bed that night, I thought to myself, *I'm so damn blessed!*

℘ 37 ℘

Light & Shadow

>———————————————————————————————————⟨

I woke with a slight hangover and dragged myself into the shower hoping the invigorating jet of hot water would work its magic.

I don't know if it was my twilight state or the simple fact that it was my 61ˢᵗ birthday, but as I showered, I drifted in and out of reverie about my life. And not surprisingly, the thread that ran through this impromptu life review had to do with loss and the long shadow the Holocaust had cast over my life.

I was born into the traumatic loss and tribal grief of Jewish survivors of the Holocaust. I was marinated in the womb of a 23-year-old woman who was still a teenager when World War II began and who, by the time the war ended, had lost almost her entire family and endured inconceivable horrors at the hands of the Nazis. For nine months I floated in the grief soup of her womb.

Yet my birth in a refugee camp in Germany after the war was, I'm told, heralded as a minor miracle — the phoenix rising from the ashes. As the first-born son of Holocaust survivors, I consumed with my mother's milk the feeling that miracles were my birthright.

The stories of atrocities, of starvation, of escaping the SS, of being captured and interrogated by the Gestapo, of being hidden by Righteous Gentiles, and of the deaths of most of my family were told constantly. Instead of the horrors of Grimm's fairy tales, I thrilled to my family's tales of survival.

To my impressionable young mind, we were almost biblical, like Noah and his family, survivors not of the Great Flood that had all but destroyed the world, but of the Great Fire known as the Holocaust. Being born without grandparents reinforced my feeling that we were a mythic first generation, post apocalypse, tasked to create a new world once again.

One of my first memories is of living in a dark, dingy basement in Brooklyn that had thin, slitted windows at street level through which, at three years old, I could only see the legs of passersby. Perhaps that's why I longed to have a cloud as a pet.

I knew my parents were different with their immigrant accents, their war stories and the tattooed numbers on their forearms, but I wanted desperately to be like everyone else. So I ran around our new apartment in Brighton Beach wearing a towel as a cape pretending to be Superman. I idolized Mickey Mantle and taught myself to switch hit so I could play centerfield one day for the New York Yankees. And I cried when I learned in civics class that, not having been born in America, I couldn't be President of the United States.

Though I worked hard to be like everyone else, my Holocaust DNA wouldn't be denied. In sixth grade, after we'd moved to a small town in New Jersey, I outed myself with a Show & Tell I called *"How 5 People Were Buried Alive For 9 Months,"* the story of my parents' survival. As a teenager I tested my manhood by smoking cigarettes in the cemetery, shoplifting at the local Woolworth's and jumping trains to ride them through town without being caught by the conductor.

Looking back, I saw how the Holocaust was the fertile soil from which my character grew. I interpreted my parents' ordeal as an ennobling experience, demanding a special effort from me to live as fully as possible. The seed that took root in that soil grew into my reaching, striving, dreaming—something great had to be born from such great loss!

In high school my Holocaust-inspired need to overachieve blossomed, fueling a desire to test myself, to compete, and ultimately to have the largest entry in my high school yearbook. Honors classes. Student government. Newspaper. Varsity sports. Drama. You name it, I did it. I even achieved a storybook moment—a miraculous high school movie dream-come-true.

In the summer of my sophomore year I came down with a kind of mono. The next fall, as a junior, I tried out and made the varsity football team. I didn't know yet it would be months before I fully recovered. Not feeling well enough to play, I had to quit the team. Quitting, especially when I wasn't sick at home anymore, was unacceptable to the coaches. The next summer, fully recovered, I trained every day in a park in preparation for football tryouts. If miracles were my birthright, I vowed I'd be in the starting lineup on opening day. One day, a football coach saw me working out in the park and asked me what I was doing. I told him I was getting ready for football season. He told me I was wasting my time.

I wasn't deterred. When I tried out for the team, I was shunned. Though I was a senior, I was given freshman uniforms and was ostracized in every possible way by the coaches who made it clear they had no intention of considering me for the team and were only putting up with my presence because of school regulations. No matter how hard I worked, I was ignored and at most, assigned to carry equipment for the team. After several weeks of being invisible on the field (not being picked for any of the teams or drills) and sometimes being abused like Richard Gere in "An Officer and a Gentleman," my quest seemed an exercise in futility and I was ready to quit. Again.

Dejected, I was sitting alone in the locker room after practice when one of the coaches came over, put a hand on my shoulder, and whispered, "Keep it up." I listened. Not long after that, I began to be picked for drills, and I was on fire. On opening day I wore number eighty-five and started on the first string varsity football team as an offensive wide receiver and defensive cornerback.

To cap off this high school fairy tale, on a crisp Saturday afternoon in October, I won the Homecoming Day game with a 67-yard touchdown. That very night I opened in the Greek tragedy, Oedipus Rex, in my high school auditorium. When the town newspaper ran a front page story about my incredible Saturday afternoon and evening feats, I began to think I could do anything I set my heart on. With both good and bad consequences.

My childhood ambition of becoming Mickey Mantle faded and I settled on something more practical—becoming a doctor like the ones I saw on TV. Isn't that what a dutiful first-born does for his immigrant family? I studied pre-med in college until I saw the movie, *The Pawnbroker*, starring Rod Steiger. This movie about a Holocaust survivor touched me so deeply, I wound up walking the streets of Pittsburgh all night long. By dawn I'd made a momentous decision: I wanted to *play* a doctor more than I wanted to be one. To my parents' horror, I auditioned and was accepted to Carnegie Mellon drama school.

I was studying playwriting, acting and directing at the best drama school in the country when the June 1967 Arab-Israeli war broke out. The week's preceding what became known as the Six-Day War were filled with echoes of the Holocaust. Israel was threatened by the five Arab countries surrounding it, all of whom had sworn to push the Jews into the sea. And so, at age twenty, I left drama school and flew to Israel, unconsciously answering the post-Holocaust vow, "Never Again!"

It was in Jerusalem that I first heard the Beatle's album "Sgt Pepper's Lonely Hearts Club Band." To the soundtrack of the Doors, Pink Floyd and The Who, I went through the sixties—tuning in, turning on, dropping out—in this 3,000-year-old holy city where every week three Sabbaths are devoutly observed.

While I was acting in Shakespeare by night, by day I was hanging out at the Wailing Wall, strolling along the ancient streets of the Old City, spending contemplative afternoons at the Church of the Holy Sepulcher. The Holy Land became my home for five years where I discovered both my inner artist and began my spiritual quest.

Between running a teahouse, touring with B.B. King, and starring in a musical theater review, I picnicked beneath olive trees in the Garden of Gethsemane, read Rumi's mystical poetry on the Temple Mount, and recited Buddhist mantras as I circumambulated the Dome of the Rock. When I lived with Arabs, I heard the *muezzin* through loudspeakers on every mosque call the faithful to prayer five times a day. In the south I hiked the Sinai desert, in the north I swam in the Sea of Galilee. I was steeped in the sacred. And I awakened.

In Jerusalem I experienced what Hindus call *samadhi*, Zen Buddhists call *satori*, Jewish Kabbalists call the *Splendor*, and I call the *Oneness of the All That Is*. These peak experiences of transcendent states, these glimpses of the Divine Mystery opened me to the mystic vision and the truth of what Shakespeare's Hamlet proclaimed — "There are more things in heaven and on earth than are dreamt of in your philosophy." Not only was my mind expanded, but my heart opened, too.

When I arrived in Jerusalem as an ambitious and idealistic twenty-year-old, I believed that artistic achievement was the most important thing in life and wanted to write, direct and star in plays and movies. By the time I left Jerusalem five years later, I knew without a doubt that the most important thing in life was love.

On this morning of my 61st birthday, I marveled at how the Holocaust had propelled me inexorably toward my spiritual awakening in Jerusalem. And how that fertile ground bore fruit many decades later. That fruit was first foreshadowed by a dream vision about love and sacred sexuality which would ripen until that moment during a lawsuit when, alone in a conference room, I would be asked a question about my life's regrets. And because of that spiritual awakening so many years earlier in Jerusalem, I was able to hear my soul's calling above the siren song of Hollywood, and choose love instead of lucre. And in reward I would find (and lose) Joy.

It boggled my mind that the shadow of the Holocaust, perhaps the most horrible expression of evil and inhumanity the world has ever known, had by some mysterious force led me to the light of Joy and to these Rites, which felt like the most sublime expression of our awakened humanity and the power of love.

However, once I stepped out of the shower's warm embrace, I had to confront the cold reality that I was celebrating my first birthday without Joy.

℘ 38 ℘

Celebration!

>——⟨

I went to the kitchen to make myself some coffee. While waiting for the water to boil, I found myself aching for Joy. Sipping my steaming cup of coffee, I sat down at the computer to listen to a birthday card she had recorded for me several years earlier when she could no longer see well enough to write. As I basked in her voice, her appreciation, and her love, I wept.

> *Good Morning Darling,*
>
> *I woke up thinking about your birthday and about how much you mean to me...and want to tell you some of the things I love most about you.*
>
> *Your humor – the way you make me laugh, the way we laugh together. It's one of the most important things we do...and probably what keeps us young. I just love playing with you. And having fun with you. Singing crazy songs and dancing around. Pretending I'm six years old! Pretending we're both six years old!*
>
> *Your brilliance and insight with other people. You constantly amaze me with the ideas and suggestions and advice and counsel you come up with. You are the best life coach I have ever seen! And I've seen some excellent counselors – I'm one of the them! – and you're better than me. Just naturally. You can change people's lives in five minutes. You give them new*

directions that transform them in front of my eyes. And I've seen you do it so many times. You've done it with me. You're doing it with many of our friends. I know that it feels easy to you, but it is such a gift.

How great you look. Your whole body is just in amazing shape. You look sexy and handsome and healthy. Masculine and strong and yet very flexible. And I'm just so proud to be with you. You look great in your clothes. I just don't know anyone else that turns me on the way you do. So I just wanted you to know that you're my movie star.

And I want to thank you for always telling me that I look good and that I'm the prettiest girl in the room. You have no idea how much that means to me and how much confidence it gives me because I know that you're very discriminating. And I know you mean it. Your compliments are never empty, they're never just flattery.

And I appreciate all the wonderful things you do for me, darling. All the chauffeuring you do without complaint – driving me everywhere, going with me on errands I used to do alone. All the emails you read me. And your patience in sending emails when I can't. Thank you. Thank you with all my heart. For everything you do. Everything you are. And everything you share with me.

I love you more each year...if that's possible. You are a constant adventure to me. And you keep our life exciting. I am never bored with you. I never have too much of you. I never have enough of you.

So I wish you a Happy Birthday, my Beloved, the happiest birthday you've ever had. We're going to celebrate all month... together. We're going to celebrate the whole year...together. And we're going to have a ball! Happy Birthday, Sweetheart!

I love you!

A few days later, one of my friends took me to see the movie, *P.S. I Love You,* for my birthday. It was about a young woman whose husband dies suddenly. She's grief-stricken, but begins to receive letters he's written to her before he died that help her rebuild her life. It was romantic and sappy and I wept. The crazy synchronicity was that her dead husband's name was *Jerry*!

I woke up on Saturday morning, the 19th of January, the day of "our" birthday party, with a sense of expectancy. This was the first party I was hosting without Joy, and my preparations brought back memories of the many times we'd entertained, and especially Joy's ease and grace as a hostess. She loved putting on parties and made it seem effortless.

As I rushed around in a last-minute check of bathrooms, hand towels, etc., I caught myself in the bathroom mirror looking harried and disoriented. And *alone.* Tears welled up. Then my twenty guests began to arrive.

I introduced everyone to my "bereavement buddy" and told them he'd be performing throughout the evening. After drinks and his delicious appetizers, I gathered everyone in the den and thanked them for supporting me, loving me and nurturing me through my grief passage. In honor of Joy's and my birthdays, I played her birthday tape. I thought repeated listening would make me immune, but I was wrong. I wept again.

To change the mood to something more upbeat, I showed a brief video of Joy caught on the TV show *Candid Camera* a few years before. She'd been out shopping with a friend at a local health food store and became one of the "unsuspecting customers" who was told by the cashier at the checkout that she could qualify for a thirty percent discount if she'd participate in a survey. The "size of her discount would depend on how healthy she proved to be."

The survey about her "healthy habits" became increasingly ridiculous. At first she was asked if she used air-conditioning in the sweltering San Fernando Valley where summertime temperatures often top 100°. When she said, "Of course!" she was told that it would cost her five percent of the thirty percent discount since the healthiest customers hardly ever used air-conditioning. Hearing this, she cocked her head more in disbelief than in disappointment. She failed on the sunscreen, she drank coffee (the healthiest customers didn't), and she didn't consume the requisite healthy 8 to 10 pieces of fruit per day. Despite the fact that her "discount" was dropping precipitously she found it increasingly hard to believe that this survey was for real.

Finally she was asked, "Do you wear high heels?" "Oh please," she responded, rolling her eyes. "I love to wear high heels. To a party, to a dinner, to anything. Are you *kidding*?" When she was told that her discount had been reduced to twenty percent, she laughed, "That's fine. I'm not giving up my high heels." Her skepticism grew when asked if she drank 10 to 12 glasses of water a day, wore arch supports in her running shoes, consumed alcohol, and flossed twice a day.

Joy's expression said it all—you could see her impatience competing with her amusement at the ridiculousness of this "survey." When asked, "Do you drive an electric car?" she burst out laughing. With a knowing look at her questioner, she replied with undisguised sarcasm, "Boy, you really have to be *different* to get this thirty percent discount." Then she turned the tables on her questioner—"Do *you* know anyone who drives an electric car?" Sidestepping the question, the cashier asked Joy, "How often do you sterilize your telephone?" To which Joy practically did a "spit-take." Shaking her head she muttered, "I guess every two weeks, when the cleaning girl comes." "Does she actually sterilize it?" the cashier persisted. From the look on Joy's face it was clear she'd reached the end of her patience— "She *cleans* it!" Then with a wave of her hand she signaled she was done. "Okay, I'm down to the regular price. So let's get on with it." She wanted to be checked out. Now.

Of the three "unsuspecting customers," Joy was the only one who came to the conclusion that the "survey" was ridiculous and opted out of the discount. We all roared with laughter.

By the time I finished opening presents, everyone was ready to eat. We devoured the salmon, the pasta and salad. As wine glasses were refilled, everybody settled in to hear my bereavement buddy sing. Then there were the birthday cakes. *Two* cakes. I blew out the candles on my cake first, then I invited everyone to blow out the candles on Joy's.

When the party was over and everyone had gone home, I was getting ready for bed and found myself again staring at my reflection in the mirror. My expression this time was much different. *Our* birthday party had gone so well. Everyone seemed to have such a good time. And I was sure that Joy had, too.

℘ 39 ℂℛ

Joy's Gift

)———————————————————————————(

Despite L.A.'s sunny reputation, the City of Angels can have miserable winters, too. Joy's birthday was rainy, windy and cold. Strangely, a part of me hoped that Angelina would cancel. I would have been relieved. Since it was both Joy's birthday and a birthday celebration for me, my expectations for this Rite of Joy were running so high that, despite many auspicious signs, there were moments when I wanted to call the whole thing off.

A few days earlier Angelina had dropped by to go through Joy's closet, since she hadn't gotten around to it during Christmas. Shorter and more petite than Joy, she didn't find much clothing. But she found a pair of formal, black, arm-length satin gloves that she loved. How appropriate for the woman whose hands were in such special service to Joy.

I wanted to celebrate Joy's birthday by listening to the "memoir" she recorded in the last months of her life. Since she couldn't see, this was her way of "writing" her life story. She was a great storyteller so she asked friends to come by in shifts so she could tell them (and record) her stories. She prepared an outline and practically every day she'd spend a few hours regaling her visitors with stories from her life.

I was unsure how I'd react to these tapes. To my great relief, I loved listening to Joy tell stories about her young life: how even at the age of two she was embarrassed to be photographed topless; how at the age of eight her brother played William Tell with her and tried to shoot an apple off her head with a bow and arrow that nearly took out her eye; and how, as a teenager, she made money collecting coat hangers from neighbors.

Listening to Joy's stories turned out to be the perfect way for me to celebrate her birthday. But as night fell, my anxiety about this Rite of Joy rose.

Despite the stormy weather, Angelina arrived on time.

"You're like the postman," I joked, taking her dripping umbrella from her. "Neither rain nor sleet nor hail keep you from your appointed rounds."

She laughed, then shook herself like a dog who'd come in out of the rain. When she finally unwrapped herself from her raincoat and scarf, I noticed that she was wearing a decorative *bindi* in the middle of her forehead. She explained that it was in honor of our special birthday celebration.

I made myself comfortable on the couch while Angelina warmed her hands by the fireplace. The red heart-shaped balloons from my surprise party floated in the air, tethered by their silken white strings to the glass coffee table. Watching the dancing flames reflected on the balloons' metallic surfaces, I wondered what surprises Joy had in store for me tonight.

As if answering my unspoken question, Angelina turned to me. "Joy told me that this time she wants to express how she feels by *speaking* to you."

I was thrilled. Once again I noticed the synchronicity—I'd spent the day listening to Joy *speak* on tape.

"Joy also showed me what she'd be wearing," Angelina continued. "It was a blue gown, but the fabric was shiny. And there were golden designs on the flowing cuffs with jewels arrayed up the sleeves. Very Egyptian-looking."

It was like Joy to dress up for this special occasion.

I wanted to share with Angelina the recorded birthday card Joy made me, and asked her to hold me on the couch while I played it for her. Though I'd cried the last two times I heard it, in Angelina's arms I didn't dissolve into tears, just a sob here and there. Apparently, being held made the difference.

Afterwards Angelina commented that everything Joy said was true. Especially the part about the way I made everything an adventure. "The two of you are still having an adventure," she said, a twinkle in her eye.

"And now *you're* a part of the adventure, too."

We lit the votive candles and declared our intentions. Angelina's was, as always, to be a clear channel for Joy's love. Mine, besides receiving Joy's love, was to be open to the celebration of our birthdays in any and whatever ways.

For this special occasion Angelina wore a sheer blue top that both concealed and revealed her beautiful breasts. She created a skirt by wrapping silver mesh silk fabric around her waist. She was stunning in her priestess ensemble, as if she'd stepped right out of an Egyptian temple frieze.

In the cold of winter we needed to warm up before the massage, so I played some music and we began to dance. The second song was a slow blues number. Suddenly, Angelina gave me a strange look. "Happy Birthday, Baby!" she said. Then she explained that that was Joy speaking.

Happy Birthday, Baby! sounded just like Joy.

I took off my clothes, climbed onto the massage table, turned onto my stomach and the birthday Rite of Joy began. Soon I was trembling in paroxysms of pleasure.

Angelina announced that she was going to describe her experience of Joy. "Joy is pouring liquid golden light into my hands," she murmured.

I tried to feel Joy's "liquid golden light" pouring from Angelina's hands into my body.

JOYride

In my mind's eye I tried to envision Joy's jewel encrusted gown.

I tried to sense Joy's presence....

The massage definitely had a Joy-quality. Angelina's hands moved in ways that reminded me of massages Joy had given me over the years, especially the special birthday ones. She'd dress up in a black lace negligee, black stockings, garter belt, stiletto heels, the works. She'd serve me finger food delicacies we'd wash down with champagne. And for "dessert" she'd give me a massage from head to toe that invariably climaxed with a "happy ending."

This birthday massage was not only familiar, but so exquisitely sensual, its pure unadulterated pleasure drowned out all other emotions. For the ecstatic moment there was no grief in sight.

"I love you!" I heard Angelina-as-Joy whisper. In my mind's eye I glimpsed Joy bending over me raining gentle kisses all over my back and down my quivering body.

"You're so adorable!" Angelina-as-Joy announced.

Ador-*able*. I was struck by what that word really meant—*able to be adored*. These Rites of Joy taught me how to receive and so made me more ador-*able*.

Suddenly I was transported to our past life 3000 years ago in the Middle East when I was king and Joy was my favorite. Disoriented, I opened my eyes to see where I was. My living room with the blazing fire illuminating the hieroglyphic carvings on our walls looked just like a king's palace.

A wave of recognition washed over me, as if Joy was pleased at my remembering our past life together, and that somehow this life had been a fulfillment of that one so long ago.

"Joy" continued to *adore* me in infinite ways, caressing and kissing every part of me. I surrendered to her loving embraces, to this primal sacrament, to this baptism of love.

229

"Joy" trailed a piece of fur against my skin that sent shivers up my spine and sparks across my synapses. She then gently grazed my flesh with a feather until she was fanning a gentle breeze over my body, feathering me into ecstasy. I marveled at her skill—using the fur to stimulate my physical pleasure and then the feather to arouse my sublime bliss.

Desire awakened in me. As if sensing what was happening and guided by Joy, Angelina moved closer. With eyes still closed, I kissed her lips, sucked her breasts and licked whatever flesh my hungering mouth could reach. I loved squeezing her thighs, relished clutching her hips, savored delicately fingering the lips of her moist well. I *craved* the voluptuousness. I loved feeling the desire...*my* desire!

Afterwards, we relaxed in a candlelit bath and nibbled on birthday cake. We didn't talk, still enthralled by the extraordinary evening. By my count this was the ninth Rite of Joy, and yet I still asked myself—*Was this really happening? Was Joy reaching out from the AfterLife and using Angelina as a channel for her love to heal my grief?* As if reading my mind, Angelina broke the silence and murmured that on her own she could never love like this. The "miracle" of these Rites of Joy silenced us again.

I couldn't fall asleep that night thinking about the astounding way Joy and I had somehow managed to celebrate our birthdays together, just like we always had. First the joint birthday party and then our birthday Rite of Joy.

And the gift of this Rite was finding a woman's body, Angelina's body, so desirable. What progress! Joy had given me the perfect birthday gift—the return of my *DESIRE*!

∞ 40 ∞

It's ALL a Gift

The following wet and wintry Saturday afternoon, I drove up to Ojai. Once again, this picturesque oasis would be the setting for a major milestone in my journey. Virginia, the belly dancer I'd met at the Tantra Reunion, thought I might benefit from participating in a formal grief ritual rooted in African tradition.

I followed her directions onto a muddy dirt road, parked in a field next to other cars and tramped across the rain-soaked ground to a blazing bonfire. Virginia greeted me with a welcoming hug and introduced me to the other people warming themselves by the fire. There were about a dozen men and women. Some were couples, most seemed to know each other.

The chatter ceased when one of the men stepped forward. Grieving, the leader said, is not encouraged in modern Western culture. So it's usually done in private. In contrast, indigenous tribal cultures like those in Africa grieve publicly as a normal part of everyday life with specific rituals that assist and support the grieving process.

This ritual consisted of several elements. The first was *fire*. The bonfire symbolized the "village," or "community." Then there was the *song*. We would sing a simple dirge-like song. (According to legend this song originated long ago, when an African village was washed away in a flood and there were only enough boats to rescue half the village, leaving the other half to drown. The survivors sang this song to express their grief at losing their loved ones.) The song would be sung continuously by those around the fire for the duration of the ritual to anchor those who went to grieve at the *Well of Tears*.

I had walked past the Well of Tears when I first arrived. A wading pool about six feet across, it had been constructed from boulders, rocks and stones gathered from the nearby field. Lined with a blue tarp, it held about a foot of water. The back wall rose higher than the other sides and served as an altar for photographs, mementos, and other relics of loved ones who had passed. Since I hadn't brought anything, I'd reached into my wallet for the small, 1-inch picture of Joy and I that I carried next to my driver's license, and placed it in a niche among the stones.

"At some point during the ritual," the leader explained, "you'll be moved to leave the warmth of the fire and the community of the 'village' to walk alone into the darkness where you will find the Well of Tears."

As we stood around the fire, people introduced themselves, saying their name as well as their "spirit name." One man said, "I'm Richard. My spirit name is *He Who Seeks Wisdom from the Ancestors*." Everyone had a spirit name. When it was my turn, I introduced myself. "I'm Jerry. And if I had a spirit name, it would be either *Dances with Grief* or *Dances for Joy*."

After the introductions, people shared the reason they were participating in the ritual. Most weren't grieving a recent personal loss (one woman had lost her eldest son almost two years earlier), but were grieving all manner of more general losses — their childhoods, their friends, their lovers, their parents and grandparents, even their ancestors. Some were grieving the degradation of the environment, the causalities of the war in Iraq, even the fraying of the fabric of society.

Someone read a poem. One line in particular moved me. *"It's the impediments of the stream that create the song."*

A man beat a drum and those familiar with the dirge began to sing. The song was so simple, it was easy to learn and could be repeated for hours. Though the sunset painted a molten horizon, the temperature dropped. I wrapped my face in a scarf and, with hands covered by fur-lined mittens, pulled a sock cap down over my ears. It was going to be a long, cold evening.

As I tried to keep warm, I wondered, *Why was I putting myself through such an ordeal?* I stood as close to the fire as I could, so close that I felt as if my jeans were burning. Yet my back was freezing. So I kept turning around slowly like meat on a spit. Singing the song and shaking a rattle in time to the rhythm was a way to keep moving and helped keep me warm.

The fire blazed and the singing droned on as we waited for the spirit to move us. Finally, after about half an hour, a woman moved away from the fire and, turning in the direction of the Well of Tears, walked off into the darkness.

We'd been told earlier that to fully empty our tears, we needed to be held, so they could be *poured* out completely. No one, we were told, should go to the Well of Tears alone. Following these instructions, someone else left the warmth of the fire to accompany the "griever."

We'd also been cautioned that as more and more grievers leave the fire and their "holders" accompany them, we needed to maintain enough of a presence by the fire so that those of us still in the "village" could keep the "song" going strong. A balance had to be maintained.

An hour into the rite, half the people had left the fire. Those of us still in the "village" sang even more strongly and rattled more insistently to make up for those who had gone.

I shivered in the flickering firelight, but not because of the cold. Wails rose up out of the darkness. At times it sounded like a pack of coyotes. But these weren't the blood cries of the hunt, these were the wrenching agonies of grief. Now and again the night was pierced by wails so full of pain and anguish it curdled the blood.

Finally, the first griever (followed by their "holder") re-emerged from the darkness and returned to the fire and warmth of the "village." It was important, we'd been told, for those returning from the Well of Tears to be "welcomed" back.

As I embraced the men and women returning from the Well of Tears, I could feel tremors, like aftershocks, rippling through their bodies. Each had been cracked open. Embracing them in welcome prepared me for my turn.

I'd intentionally waited before going to the Well of Tears. I wanted to observe what happened as the ritual unfolded as well as allow it to work its magic on me. After perhaps two hours of singing and rattling and welcoming returning grievers, I felt ready to leave the warmth of the fire and walk out into the cold, dark field to the Well of Tears.

The moment I stepped away from the fire, turning my back on the "village" with its familiar drum and song, I choked up. Though I stopped singing, I continued rattling to the rhythm of the drum. In the dark, I saw a path lined with candles like a jungle landing strip. I walked for several minutes into the darkness—the song of the village growing fainter, the wailing of the grievers louder—until I arrived at the Well of Tears.

It looked very different than the makeshift wading pool I'd seen in daylight. Illuminated by dozens of candles set among the stones, it seemed a magical and mythical *Well of Tears.*

I made out the silhouettes of people huddled on their knees in front of the Well weeping inconsolably. I stepped into a space among the grievers and dropped to my knees. Immediately I started to cry. Like a Muslim bent over in prayer, I put my forehead to the ground and let myself be carried away by the tide of raw emotion rising up in me. With the comforting touch of my "holder's" hand on my back, I began to sob and pour my grief into the Well of Tears.

Wails of grief surrounded me. We were a roiling sea of anguish, waves rising and falling. Loud. Soft. Breaking here, breaking there. It felt good to drown in this ocean of emotion.

When I came up for air, I looked into the Well and tried to see the picture of Joy I'd placed there. My vision was so blurred with tears I couldn't see it. I felt disoriented, lost at sea. The far-off drone of the village song anchored me. With the reassurance of my "holder's" hand on my back, I tried to steady my breathing, to regain some sense of control amidst the chaotic chorus of grief surrounding me. But a plaintive wail from one of my fellow grievers triggered me and I dove into the depths once more. Bending over, I rested my head on the ground so I could pour out whatever grief was left inside me.

This "pouring of my tears" happened several more times. Each time I'd come up for air, search for Joy's picture through my tears, hear the wails of grief around me and the village dirge in the distance, feel the touch of my "holder" and then dive again into the depths of my grief.

Gradually, I realized I was almost done. And not just now, this evening, in this ritual, but done with my grief passage. My tears were almost emptied, my well almost dry. I lowered my head to the ground one final time to pour the last dregs of grief into the Well of Tears.

Suddenly, I heard Joy's voice. *"It's a gift!...It's all a gift!!"* With those words she'd given me a profound teaching. It was all a gift—my love of Joy *and* my loss of Joy! It's *ALL* a gift!

My rational mind found it hard to accept that Joy's death was as much a gift as her life! That her loss was as much a gift as her love. But in that sacred moment, it felt like an eternal truth.

Finally, I was done. I sat up and tried to get my bearings amidst the sea of grief surrounding me. Slowly I got to my feet. My "holder" asked if I needed help. I shook my head. I listened for the beacon of the village song and rattled once again to the rhythm of the drum as I walked back along the candlelit path.

When I emerged from the darkness into the light of the bonfire, I was swept up in one welcoming embrace after another. I felt so vulnerable, so tender, so raw. Like a newborn.

Each embrace restored me to the living and I resumed my place around the bonfire, shaking my rattle and singing the ancient song so that others could go to the Well of Tears and find their way back again.

It grew late. The temperature must have dropped into the low °40's. We'd been outside for hours and even the bonfire didn't temper the cold anymore. But we stayed until everyone was finally done grieving and there was no one at the Well of Tears. The drumming slowed, the song ended, and the ritual was over.

To cap off the evening, Virginia—knowing how much I liked to dance—invited me to join her at that evening's Mardi Gras costume ball. I was emotionally spent and not in any mood to party. Yet I couldn't help but notice how this public demonstration of grieving and dancing paralleled my own private grief work. So I said *Yes*. She loaned me some costume clothes and we drove over to the charity benefit.

In stark contrast to the mud and cold of the grief ritual, over a hundred people wearing fantastic costumes and masks frolicked at this Mardi Gras Ball. I was amazed at how quickly my fatigue passed as I got into a dance groove inspired by a great live band. The costumes and masks enhanced the dancing. The grief ritual had put me into an altered state and my dancing soon became ecstatic. This public dance celebration perfectly balanced the public grief ritual I'd just experienced and reinforced my feeling that I'd completed a significant stage of my journey. At the Well of Tears I'd experienced the depths of grief. At the Mardi Gras I was experiencing heights of ecstasy. Dancing wildly among these costumed revelers after kneeling in the mud and pouring my grief into the Well of Tears, I recalled Joy's voice whispering to me, "It a gift. It's *all* a gift!"

∞ *41* ∞

Thanks for the Harmonies

I woke up on Valentine's Day excited yet apprehensive. My intention to spend the day with Joy was something I desired but also dreaded. Fortified by my Ojai experience of public grieving and dancing, I felt that fully experiencing my first Joy-less Valentine's Day would be another step in healing my grief.

First I listened to the recorded Valentine's card Joy made for me when she could no longer see. This was the third and last recorded card she made that year. I'd already listened to the Anniversary one in July and my birthday one last month. Now on Valentine's Day I'd listen to the last one.

> *Happy Valentine's Day, My Love.... This is the 7th one we've celebrated together. And it feels like every year you've shown me another part of you that has made me love you even more. You are without a doubt the love of my life. And probably the love of all my lifetimes....*

As I listened to Joy showering me with appreciation, whispering sweet *everythings* in my ear, I reveled in her love. Though weeping, I wasn't sobbing. To my surprise, there wasn't much pain or grief. Rather, my tears were the overflow of profound love and immense gratitude.

I was wiping away tears when suddenly Judy Garland began to sing, *"Forget Your Troubles Come On Get Happy!"* I was stunned—that was Joy's theme song. What were the odds that out of 6,000 songs, my iTunes would shuffle from Joy's Valentine to her theme song? I took this musical synchronicity to be a good omen and decided to look through the Valentine's cards we gave each other one last time.

I was surprised to discover that there'd been a theme of *children* in the cards we gave each other. One card pictured a boy and a girl wearing sailor hats at the beach. Shot from behind, they were sitting on the sand facing the water, the boy's arm wrapped protectively around the girl's shoulders. Another card pictured a boy and girl again standing at the seashore with him holding a conch shell up to her ear so she could hear the sound of the ocean.

In many ways we were a combination of wise elders and playful children. Was that the secret of our love?

On one of the cards I'd written—

> *My Dearest Joy,*
>
> *One of the things I've learned through Us is that Relationship is not about "compromise" – the metaphor isn't "negotiation" – where each party gives up something so that each feels diminished.*
>
> *The metaphor is "music" where my note is enlarged and enhanced by your note, and so together we create something more…glorious harmonies!*
>
> *Thanks for the beautiful music!*

Like some geologist of love, I gathered ten years of calendars to take a "core-sample" of our Valentine's Day celebrations. There were dinners and dances and parties, everything from the posh Lakeside Country Club to a Country Western bar where we sang karaoke. Strangely, there was no notation in the calendar for last year's Valentine's Day. And for some reason I couldn't remember what we did. I would soon understand why.

℘ 42 ℚ

The Fifty-Day Countdown

>————————————————————————————————————<

Valentine's Day marked a significant turning point in my grief journey. Just when I thought I was out of the woods, I encountered unanticipated challenges, mostly of my own making.

A glance at last year's calendar reminded me that the day after Valentine's day Joy found out she was terminal. V-Day then D-Day. Love Day then Death Day!

How many days from D-Day to Joy's transition? From February 15th to April 6th I counted approximately fifty. Fifty more days of Joy. Fifty days to complete my year of grieving. And so began what I called my *Fifty-Day Countdown*.

What began as an impulse became a compulsion—to relive Joy's last days. Consulting last year's calendar, I began to track what Joy would eventually call her "Last Adventure." In January we saw the musical *Dreamgirls*, celebrated my birthday at Dance Home, and went to Two Bunch Palms for a joint birthday present to soak in the hot springs and be pampered with massages. Though Joy had less than three months to live, she was still traveling and dancing!

A remarkable event occurred the weekend before Valentine's Day. Joy attended a birthday musicale in her honor. She had attended these musicales for years, but had never gotten up to sing. At this musicale she sang for the first time. And not only did she sing, but Terri joined her in a rendition of "Lullaby in Ragtime." Neither of them knew that in a few days Joy would learn she was dying. Yet something in Joy knew it was time to sing.

D-Day changed everything. The secret was out. We shared a last ice cream cone and Joy sat silently through that evening's Wisdom Circle. By morning she'd been reassured by her guides that dying was "a great adventure." Though she'd gained her equilibrium, I began to drown in despair until she made me swear that her death wouldn't destroy my life because our love wasn't a poison pill.

After Joy's family had been informed about her "terminal condition," Joy dictated an email we sent to our friends.

> SUBJECT: "My Last Adventure"
>
> *Dear Friends,*
>
> *As most of you know I've been dealing with cancer for the past 6 years. Now I seem to be entering the last chapter of my life. On Feb. 15th I learned that the breast cancer has spread to my liver and that the loss of energy I'd been experiencing for the past few months is the result. From the very beginning I've chosen quality of life over quantity. And I am still making that choice. Since I am now 79 I feel that I've had a full and fabulous life. And I'm not afraid to die.*
>
> *From my experiences talking to my Guides and dozens of souls on the Other Side, I'm not fearful, angry, defeated or depressed.*
>
> *After meeting with my doctor last month I experienced a great deal of sadness for the rest of the day and evening as I thought about everything I would be missing in the future. However, the next morning I awoke with an entirely different perspective.*
>
> *My Guides assured me that "dying can be a great adventure"— and that's exactly what I intend to make it. So I am choosing to turn this last chapter into one of the best of my life. I intend to*

use my limited energy in positive ways rather than in fighting and resisting my condition by focusing my attention on trying to find miraculous cures. Of course I am open to "miracles" and feel they are more possible when I am vibrating joy, love, gratitude and acceptance rather than all the negative vibrations that come from fear. And that's where I'm coming from. I'm not TRYING to come from there, that's where I live...that's where I've always lived. Nothing has changed.

I've been a spiritual teacher most of my life and I view these last few years with cancer and blindness as a test to see if I could "walk my talk" in spite of these physical challenges. I've received enormous "gifts" from them which proves once again that EVERYTHING that happens is for our benefit.

Every teacher learns a great deal from their students and I'd like to thank you for all you've taught me. But I will continue learning throughout this last adventure. And beyond. As Yogananda stated—"Death is only an experience through which you are meant to learn a great lesson: you cannot die."

> *With My Love & Blessings,*
> *Joy Mitchell*

Joy's email generated an incredible response. Every day we received dozens of replies and for the next several weeks Joy basked in this stream of appreciation, gratitude and love.

Many wrote that they were going to save her email to inspire them when they embarked on their "last adventure." Others intended to share her letter with friends and family. Remarkably, her email was forwarded around the world and she heard from people she'd never met. She also heard from people she hadn't been in contact with for a long time. It was wonderfully gratifying to receive updates from people she'd given astrological or psychic readings to. Many thanked her for her guidance which had a profound impact on their lives. They thanked her for being a role model. They even reminded her of incidents in her life which she'd forgotten.

Joy was deeply touched and often moved to tears by these tributes. It was hard for her to accept such an outpouring of love, hard to receive such lavish praise and to be seen in such exalted terms. Yet during her life she'd inspired thousands of people and changed countless lives by teaching them how to find their own "path of joy."

We thought Joy had about a year. We anticipated a gradual decline. After all, Joy had recently been dancing and partying. How could we have known she had so little time left?

One afternoon we were sitting around the kitchen table with some friends talking about death and funerals. At funerals Joy and I had attended over the years, Joy had observed how wonderful it would be if the glowing tributes and acknowledgements of love and appreciation being expressed could have been heard by the Loved One while they were still alive, in the flesh that is.

Knowing about Joy's pet peeve with regard to funerals, Genevieve suggested we throw a party so Joy could hear what everybody had to say about her. Joy loved the idea. We'd seen the Monty Python musical *Spamalot* the previous summer, and Joy especially loved the "I'm Not Dead Yet" number. We decided to call it the "I'm Not Dead Yet" Party. We considered dates (Joy wanted to do the party in August; Genevieve suggested April around Easter), discussed a few locations that might be right, and decided on a budget. But the next day, after sleeping on it, Joy nixed the idea. She wanted the party, but thought it was "too soon." How little we knew.

Now, rereading the hundreds of heartfelt tributes to Joy's "Last Adventure" email, I wept. In those last weeks of her life, Joy got her wish—in her own unique way, she had attended her own memorial service. This was yet another sign of the perfection that seemed to be unfolding last year.

In contrast, my *Fifty-Day Countdown* was beginning to take a toll. I became increasingly sullen. Re-reading those tributes to

Joy reminded me how wonderful she was and what a great loss I'd suffered. I found myself inexplicably exhausted. For days I slept in, then wandered around in a daze. I began to wonder if this *Fifty-Day Countdown* was more emotionally taxing than I'd bargained for.

I felt like a comet on a collision course. I'd been moving away from the *dying* all year. Now I was returning for a potentially dangerous flyby. And I could feel the gravitational pull growing stronger and stronger. All this, and I was only one week in. Where would I be in weeks 3, 4, 5...?

One of the women in my bereavement group was approaching the first-year anniversary of her husband's death. She admitted trying to avoid thinking about last year. When I told the group I wanted to relive those days, they couldn't understand why. Clearly, most people do whatever they can to avoid reliving this final chapter. Why was I putting myself through these "last days" one more time?

I told them I wasn't sure why, but that I felt compelled. Since Joy had experienced minimal suffering, and since she wasn't afraid of dying and wasn't in pain, those last seven weeks were filled with beauty and grace that I couldn't fully appreciate at the time. I was in battle mode—stressed and stunned. Now I wanted to honor our great love by revisiting the scene of the battle. By remembering....

Soon after D-Day I bought the book *Graceful Exits: How Great Beings Die*. Late in the evening, after Joy was asleep, I'd read and highlight sections of the book I thought she'd find interesting.

During the next few weeks I'd read these sections to her. She loved the story of a 6th century Chinese Zen patriarch who announced his imminent death to his disciples. When they cried inconsolably, the master told them, "If you knew where I was going you wouldn't be crying." At around that time, I finally told my mother that Joy was dying. She was so inconsolable, I had to give Joy the phone to comfort her.

Another story from the book resonated deeply with Joy. Near the end of his life the Zen master Ikkyu told his disciples, "After my death, some of you will seclude yourselves in the forests and mountains to meditate, while others may drink sake and enjoy the company of women. Both kinds of Zen are fine, but if some become professional clerics, babbling about 'Zen as the Way,' they are my enemies." Joy had no patience for dogma either. No one size fits all. As an astrologer she knew that we all have different "ways" of accessing the divine.

Another book I read to Joy was *Journey of Souls* by Dr. Michael Newton. From thousands of hypnotic regressions he pieced together an account of the soul's journey after death in the spirit world, the "life *between* lives."

The Afterlife was nothing new to Joy. In *Love Ever After*, she asked Bob to describe it. "Can you tell me where you are?" she wrote. "Or is there a '*where*?' I know it's a different reality, but can you give me a description of some kind that I can understand?"

Bob responded. "You're right—there is no '*where*.' Actually, I'm '*everywhere*.' And since there is no '*time*,' I am everywhere at the same time. Your question is like asking where the air is on your planet. It's everywhere. When Jesus said, 'In my house there are many mansions,' he meant 'many dimensions.' And these dimensions all exist in the same general space. Since everything in the Universe is a form of energy, each dimension operates within its own vibration, like a radio or television signal. Many of you are learning to align yourselves with the particular vibrations of some of these other dimensions so you can actually experience them. And when you make the connections you're able to take advantage of the teachers and the wealth of knowledge and experience that is there for you."

Joy looked forward to my evening reading from *Journey of Souls*. One evening, after I read to her about a soul reuniting with a brother who'd died very young in a drowning accident, Joy was struck by the synchronicity that in the morning she'd told friends the story of how her brother had accidentally drowned while fishing off the rocks down in Laguna.

Newton wrote that one of the marks of an advanced soul was someone who showed "extraordinary coping skills." Having lost two children and many other loved ones, having gracefully lived and even thrived with cancer *and* blindness, and now facing the ultimate challenge of dying with such grace and acceptance, Joy was demonstrating what an advanced soul she was. Just how advanced I was about to find out.

One day, I ran into a friend who remarked that I seemed depressed. When I told him what I was doing, he questioned whether my *Fifty-Day Countdown* was such a good idea. "Do you think you're stuck?" he asked me. I tried to explain that it was like "a great cathedral."

"When I visited it with Joy last year, it was at night and a storm was raging outside, so all I could see of the magnificent edifice was by the light of a flickering candle that I held and the occasional flash of lightning. Now, by the light of day, I want to return and behold the awe-inspiring beauty—the metaphorical rose window, flying buttresses, sculptures…the perfection unfolding."

I could see from my friend's expression that he wasn't getting it. So I changed metaphors. "It's like revisiting a battlefield."

On February 29th I was granted an unexpected respite from my *Fifty-Day Countdown*. I wrote about it in my journal.

> Strange. With leap year there's no entry in my "meditations for grieving" book. Nothing on the old calendar either, so I can't track last year's Death Walk. It's as if I've been given a day off. Thank god!

According to my calendar, March 3rd was the "last family day with Joy." On that Saturday morning, seven of us had gathered in our living room—Elliot and Kate; Terri and her husband Paul; Jackie, Joy and me. The poignancy of this day felt very different from the party atmosphere of previous family days.

One by one we acknowledged Joy for the many gifts she'd given us. We thanked her for loving us at our worst and applauding us at our best, for listening without judgment to our fears and doubts while encouraging us with absolute confidence in our ability to meet life's challenges.

Then Joy thanked each of us for the gifts *she'd* received—for the lessons she'd learned, for the ways we'd inspired her and, finally, for the love we'd given her. While this love fest was going on, we took turns rubbing her feet, massaging her hands, arms and neck and, of course, holding her.

There were tears and there was laughter. It was a rampage of love. Though this last family day was bittersweet, knowing it was the last made it even sweeter.

Of all the gifts Joy received that day, the one that stood out for me was the gift she received from her son. Sitting beside her on the couch, Elliot pulled a sheet of notes from his pocket, and for an hour reviewed his life. He explained how he could now see that all the difficulties he'd endured during his 50-plus years—his parents' divorce, the death of his eleven-year-old brother when he was ten, feeling abandoned when Joy remarried, the hard times he'd had with his stepfather, the roller-coaster ride of being a child actor, his failed relationships, his career missteps, his health crises—had all ultimately been a "gift." He illustrated this by describing how his recent lack of work had given him the gift of time to write the music for a new musical based on the life of Judy Garland. He concluded his life review by telling his dying mother, "It was all perfect!"

At my bereavement group I shared my memories of the last family day. Several people said they envied me because they couldn't talk to their spouses about dying. They felt there was so much *unsaid*. I felt doubly blessed.

On March 8th, with thirty days to go, I walked around the lake, enthralled by the cherry blossoms in full bloom. Their yearly appearance was always a treat. Even after Joy became legally blind, she somehow still received immense pleasure from these pink blooms that for a few weeks in Spring created a world of enchantment. Suddenly, I was overcome with gratitude that Joy's guidance had led me from devastating grief to this moment of pure pleasure.

Last year, by mid-March, Joy was slowing down. She received a constant stream of visitors—some to massage her, some to listen to the stories of her life, some to say good-bye. Despite her limited energy, she helped a friend choose a wedding dress while also selecting the music and centerpieces and approving the menus for the memorial service she referred to as her "Celebration of Life" party.

We developed what I saw now was a blessed routine. In the morning, I'd read the new email responses to her "Last Adventure" letter aloud to her and she'd bask in this shower of love. In the afternoon, friends would come by to hear her stories so she could record her memoir. And in the evening, I'd read to her about the soul's journey in the Afterlife.

What an incredibly fulfilling regimen she'd created for her "last days"—in the morning she received loving tributes; in the afternoon, instead of focusing on her impending death, she relived her life; and in the evening she prepared for the journey her soul was about to make.

In stark contrast to the perfection I saw unfolding last year, I was plagued by a gathering wave of regret that threatened to drown me. I kept asking myself—*Did I do enough?* I tried to take comfort in the fact that I gave Joy *everything* I had. Someone else would have different things to give. There was no *best*. We give our gifts. What mattered was the commitment, the willingness, the devotion.

At my bereavement group I shared my one-year anniversary blues. They all said it's common at the one-year mark. I felt like I was in a little lifeboat that was being been rocked by the wake of a big ship that had passed a year ago and I was being all shook up, almost upended but not quite.

A friend who'd studied in seminary pointed out the similarity between my *Fifty-Day Countdown* and the Catholic tradition of Lent, the forty-day period preceding Easter. (Technically, it's forty-six days, but the six Sundays are not counted.) For some reason, I was enduring my version of the ordeal of Lent to honor Joy's last days.

The one-year anniversary was hard enough, but I had *two* dates to deal with. Since Joy transitioned on such a significant day as Good Friday, *two* dates marked the one-year anniversary of her passing—Good Friday (which this year fell on March 21st), and April 6th (the calendar date), almost two weeks later.

I wrestled with this dilemma about the dates for several days until I received guidance from Joy the day before Good Friday during my morning meditation: *"You've done your grieving as gracefully as I did my dying. That's why two dates mark the year— Good Friday is for me, April 6th is for you."*

Now I knew what to do. On Good Friday I'd celebrate Joy's grace-filled transition. On April 6th I'd celebrate the completion of my *Year of Grieving Joy-fully*.

Relieved that I'd found a solution, I rewarded myself with a walk around the lake. I had to brace myself against the brisk wind that was blowing the cherry blossoms off the trees. There were moments when it was *snowing* pink petals. At one point, I stopped before a tree and stood in that pink blizzard and felt inexpressible joy. The last of the cherry blossoms were blowing away and it felt like Joy's "last goodbye."

In preparation for Good Friday, I spent the rest of Thursday poring over last year's calendar. In March the calendar became emptier and emptier. By the 26th there was *nothing*...until April 6th, where I'd scrawled "Joy left."

Holy Week begins with Palm Sunday and ends with Easter. According to my journal, last year's Palm Sunday was a day of firsts and lasts. It was the first time I left Joy since D-Day. She insisted I get a watsu massage and some desperately needed TLC. Meanwhile, she received her last massage in this life from none other than Angelina.

During that watsu, as I was floated in the warm pool, I soaked up the womb-like nurturance in preparation for the inevitable. Looking back I could see this was a kind of "baptism" that marked the beginning of what would become *our* "holy week" filled with the mundane and the miraculous.

On Monday of that week people came by needing Joy's approval regarding the final preparations for her Celebration of Life party. Monday evening was the first night of Passover. This year there would be no Seder for us. However, like a Last Supper, that Passover night marked a critical turning point.

In the middle of the night, on her way back to bed from the bathroom, Joy collapsed. When I tried to pick her up, she screamed in pain and curled up into a fetal position. I grabbed the bottle of morphine hospice had provided and carefully measured out the dosage. I placed the dropper between her lips and gave Joy her first dose of morphine. Within moments, she stopped moaning and I carried her back to bed. I didn't know it at the time, but that first night of Passover was the last night we would sleep together in the same bed.

The next day our bed and night tables were moved to the side of the bedroom to make way for the motorized hospital bed on which Joy would sleep for three more nights.

After I tucked Joy in for her first night in the hospital bed, I lay alone in our bed thinking, *I'll never sleep with her again.* I was dazed by the recognition that we'd arrived at another inexorable place on this journey. Joy was leaving. She was alone and I was alone. We'd been separated into the living and the dying.

A year ago I couldn't allow myself to feel my feelings. I'd had to be strong. But now I could feel them, fully. Now that Joy was safe and I'd been through the worst, I could cry unreservedly. So I cried...and cried...and cried.

Wednesday morning Joy woke up from her first night in the hospital bed and announced she had a poem in her head. She asked for paper and a pen. I propped her up in bed and she proceeded to write *Opening to Joy*, the poem read at her memorial. When she finished writing, she asked me to read it aloud. Beyond my amazement at the beauty of her poem and the message it conveyed—offering to be a "spirit guide" from the Afterlife—I was stunned by the significance of her action.

In *Graceful Exits* I'd read that among Zen masters there was a tradition of writing a "death poem" before dying. I hadn't read those passages to Joy, so she had no way of knowing about it. I began to ask myself, *Who is she?*

For breakfast I served her a small glass of orange juice and a soft-boiled egg. She barely ate. While she still had energy we prepared the JoyStones she wanted given out at her Celebration of Life party. She wanted to use them in conjunction with a meditation she'd written a few days earlier to be read during the service. She saw her death as a teaching opportunity. Even after she was gone, she planned on leading a meditation[4] to help people see the perfection in their life.

Joy slept and rested most of the day. In the evening I sat at her feet in the living room surrounded by family and friends. In a quiet moment I joked with her about my tendency to overdo things. Referring to my loving and taking care of her with such devotion, I said, "Aren't you glad I overdid this?" She smiled, but didn't have the energy to speak.

On Thursday morning, according to my calendar, Joy's temperature at 10 a.m. was 97.4 degrees and dropping. I'd kept track of all her medications on the calendar. On Monday she'd

---

4 See Joy's "*Meditation on Perfection*" at end of the book.

received half a dozen drugs. On Tuesday, she'd been given a drop of morphine at 6 a.m., 10 a.m., 1 p.m., 6 p.m., 10:15 p.m. and 5 a.m. No more medication. Just morphine. She spent most of the day in bed listening to music and resting. In the evening she got out of bed to see Terri in concert for the last time.

Up until a few weeks earlier, Terri had hoped Joy would attend this concert since it was in Los Angeles. Realizing it would be Joy's last, Terri had prepared one of Joy's favorite Berlin songs. But Joy's condition had deteriorated so quickly, she couldn't go. Elliot went to the concert the night before and filmed it, then came over Thursday evening with the video.

I helped Joy out of bed and slowly walked with her into the den, where she sat on her glider chair in front of the big screen TV. Though she didn't have the strength to keep her eyes open most of the time, she managed to watch Terri tell the audience that her mother was gravely ill and that she was dedicating a special song to her.

Soon after, Terri arrived and, together with Elliot, Kate and Jackie, we watched the rest of the concert. Joy's eyes were closed most of the time. Afterward, Joy asked to be alone with Terri for a few minutes since she hadn't seen her in two days. The rest of us went into the kitchen. A few minutes later Terri came in and said, "Mom wants to go back to bed." I helped Joy to the bedroom. She was exhausted. Watching the concert had taken every ounce of strength she had left. I made her comfortable, told her I loved her and kissed her goodnight.

ℰℴ 43 ℭℛ

The Last Goodbye

>————————————————————————————————————⟨

I was sleep deprived, not having slept for several nights. Afraid I wouldn't hear Joy if she needed me, I asked Elliot and Kate if they'd sleep in the bedroom and take turns being on watch while I set myself up in the living room on the sectional couch.

Despite taking two sleeping pills, I couldn't sleep. Not being in the bedroom, not sleeping in our bed, not having Joy sleeping in the hospital bed next to me, allowed my mind to roam more freely than usual, beyond the immediate emergency of my death watch.

Joy's equanimity these past cancer-and-blindness-filled years, these recent terminal months, these past dying days, amazed me. She radiated courage, peace and love throughout it all. She never expressed fear or regret. There was some sadness at times, but on the whole she embraced her destiny.

Who is she? I found myself wondering again.

Neither her aging body nor the mutilation of her mastectomy diminished her confidence. She kept her looks and sexiness well past what was normal. No one believed her age. I remembered a much younger man at a New Year's Eve party just four months earlier who, in the midst of flirting with this terminally ill woman, spilled his drink all over himself when Joy told him she was going to be seventy-nine. I used to kid her that she must have made some pact with the gods, or perhaps the devil, to never grow old. Like the character in Oscar Wilde's, *The Picture of Dorian Gray*, I joked that she must have a painting hidden in a closet somewhere that showed her looking her real age. She'd just laugh and explain that the secret to her uncannily youthful appearance was happiness.

Who is this woman?

Joy knew her past lives and could predict the future, at first through astrology and finally with her psychic vision. Like some oracle, she was constantly being given guidance by non-physical beings she called her guides, who addressed her as "Dear One." She'd recently told me that—besides her late husband, Bob—Isis, the great goddess of ancient Egypt, was also a guide. I remembered her telling me about her initiation by a roomful of non-physical beings who had asked her if she was ready to fulfill her mission on earth to teach joy. When she accepted her mission and started her metaphysical group, The Source, this *Council of Joy*, as she referred to them, promised to help her awaken humans to their true spiritual nature.

Whoever Joy was, the echoes of Holy Week were unmistakable and I felt certain her "passion" would climax during Easter weekend.

Before I finally fell into a drug-induced asleep, I scribbled these words on a piece of paper: "A goddess has walked among us! Her purpose is not *Salvation* but *Celebration*! Hers is not the *Path of Sacrifice*, but the *Path of Joy*."

At dawn on Good Friday I woke up in the living room disoriented. The first thing that caught my eye was a framed painting on the wall of a medieval manuscript that I'd made for Joy years earlier. In big brightly colored illuminated letters it read, *"Joy is the most infallible sign of the presence of God."*

I hurried into the bedroom. Joy wasn't responding. And so began our last Good Friday. It would be filled with extremes—

tears and laughter, singing and crying, grief and exaltation, the mundane and the miraculous.

Soon Terri, Genevieve and Lorraine (Terri's childhood friend and Joy's "spiritual daughter") arrived. We began singing to Joy since she loved nothing better than a show. We also knew that our grief would make her transition more difficult. By singing we were celebrating her graduation.

Over the next several hours, interspersed with reminiscences that made us laugh and cry, we sang at least a dozen songs, some of which Joy had requested for her memorial service—from Genevieve's operatic "Con Te Partiro" (Time to Say Goodbye) to Terri's rendition of the Nat King Cole classic "Unforgettable."

Ever the "musical director," Elliot fired up the computer, located the lyrics online for whatever song was requested, printed and handed them out so we could all join in.

We sang one of Joy's favorite songs from the Monty Python movie "The Life of Brian." *"Always Look on the Bright Side of Life"* was a hilarious production number sung by dozens of crucified men in Jesus-era Jerusalem. Joy loved the song's outrageous satire mixed with simple yet profound wisdom.

Inspired by the musical "A Chorus Line," we danced around the hospital bed singing its signature song "One" (*One singular sensation / Every little step she takes / One thrilling combination / Every move that she makes*).

Between songs and stories there was a sudden concern that Joy wasn't ready to go on her trip with her usually manicured toenails unpainted. "She can't go like that!" Lorraine insisted. Nail polish suddenly appeared and within minutes Joy's beautiful feet were ready for her trip. "Now she can go," Kate said.

We talked about silly things, like the time Joy actually slipped on a banana peel and landed on her ass and, though sprawled on the ground, laughed hysterically at her cartoon moment. At one point Elliot and Terri knelt at either side of Joy's bed, laying their heads on each of her hands as they told their mother how much they loved her.

The hospice nurse who'd been observing us from afar stepped forward and told us how lucky Joy was to have such a loving family and how we were making it easy for her to leave. Most exits, from her experience, were not easy for the dying.

On an impulse I went over to the computer to check emails. I told myself that we might be receiving some urgent communication now that the word about Joy was out. I was glad I did. There was an extraordinary email from a friend who didn't know Joy's critical condition.

> *Dear Ones, during my meditation this morning, I encountered Joy in the White Marble Hallway of the BRIDGE between worlds. She was with her 7 Mentors and they were walking together and talking in a circle. Joy made a joke about the timing of this weekend and the idea of resurrection and Jesus' wonderful demonstration of eternity.*

I read the email to everyone. We were *seven…*in a circle… around Joy. *Here.* And in some mysterious way *over there.* The grace of the moment was palpable. Someone suggested that perhaps we were an escort handing Joy over to a welcoming committee of seven souls who had already left the body. That group included two husbands, two children, and other loved ones.

At one point someone announced, "Her toes have stopped moving."

Kate began to read a beautiful poem by David Whyte entitled, "The Journey." The last words I heard were—

> *You are not leaving*
> Even as the light
> Fades quickly
> *You are arriving.*

I couldn't listen any longer. I felt myself irresistibly drawn to Joy's labored breathing. I embraced her, putting my right cheek against hers so I could be as close as possible. My eyes closed and my breathing immediately synchronized with hers the way it had thousands of times before. The only thing in my world became the rise and fall of her breath. The pauses at the end of each inhalation and exhalation grew longer. I began to experience a blissful state, as if in deep meditation. No words, no thoughts, just riding my beloved's breath. I could have stayed there forever.

I floated on Joy's last breaths like on the waves of a great ocean. The space between breaths grew longer and longer and longer…until finally space was all there was.

"She's gone," Terri whispered.

"There's only love," Genevieve said.

"Yes," Jackie added, "The only thing that matters is love."

Someone said it was noon.

&) 44 (&

A Good Friday Miracle

The rest of the day was a blur. The phones rang. People visited. I stayed with Joy as friends arrived throughout the afternoon and took turns sitting around her bed. Whenever I held her seemingly lifeless hand, I felt a surge of energy flow into me as if I'd touched a live wire. Over the next few hours I was "electrified" by this mysterious current whenever I touched Joy's body. Everyone who saw her remarked how beautiful she looked, a Mona Lisa-like smile on her face. They shared their "Joy stories." I couldn't get enough of them…and the mysterious energy radiating from her body.

At one point Genevieve, who had stood at the foot of the bed while I rode Joy's last breath, took me aside and whispered, "When you were resting your head next to Joy's, I actually *saw* your love swirling around you both, a ring of golden light around the top of your heads that merged into a golden crown."

That was then. On the eve of my one-year anniversary—the next to last day of my *Fifty-Day Countdown*—I couldn't sleep. In a total grief relapse, I wound up hugging Joy's satin pillow for comfort, imagining her spooning with me in bed. The countdown had taken its toll.

When I woke on Good Friday, my mood had shifted—I felt triumphant. I had fulfilled my "promise" to live again and not

257

allow Joy's death to destroy my life. Our love wasn't a "poison pill," it was an incomparable blessing.

Now that Good Friday was here, I wanted to celebrate Joy's grace-filled transition in some special way. Not with love letters, pictures, or music. I'd done enough of that during the past year. As I showered, the idea of doing a shamanic journey popped into my head.

I'd studied the technique of shamanic journeying years ago. Shamanic journeys were like waking dreams. For millennia, shamans would listen to the repetitive rhythm of a drumbeat or rattle, which would induce an altered hypnotic state, so they could *ride the drum* to the invisible spirit worlds. I was taught how to go from our *Middle World* to the *Lower World* to meet animal *allies*, or to the *Upper World* to meet *teachers* and *guides*. The entry one created into the Upper or Lower World functioned like a hypnotic induction. Everyone's entry was unique and custom-made.

Before I could go on a shamanic journey, I had to pack a bag for an intimate Easter weekend with close friends and family. When I finally looked at the clock, it was already 11:40 a.m. Since Joy had passed at noon, it was now or never.

In my office I laid down on my oriental rug, covered myself with a blanket, blindfolded myself with an eye pillow and listened to a CD of repetitive drumming that would induce the shamanic journey.

But the damn phone rang! People had been calling all morning with remembrances, and they were still calling. The only place I wouldn't be disturbed was the bedroom. I grabbed everything I needed, shut the door to my bedroom and silenced the answering machine to have undisturbed quiet. I laid down on the carpet next to the bed, put the drumming CD into the Bose player, blanketed and blindfolded myself again...and prepared to "ride the drum" to my portal into the Upper World.

To reach the Upper World, I'd imagine climbing a mountainside through a fog so thick I had to get down on all fours to feel my way through it. When I finally emerged on the other side of the fog, I'd find myself in a sunny, flower-filled mountain meadow. And the journey in the Upper World would begin.

Since I hadn't done a shamanic journey in years, I was a little rusty imagining my entry into the Upper World. In my mind's eye I finally emerged into the familiar mountain meadow.

But nothing happened.

I waited. No one was there. I waited some more. No teacher. No guide. *No one.* The drum was insistent but there was *nothing*! The meadow was empty. I was alone.

Damn! I was frustrated. I remembered my teacher saying that shamanic journeying is like any relationship—it has to be cultivated. And I hadn't visited in years. I heard a mocking voice in my head—*You don't write! You don't call! You just show up. What do you expect?*

So I lay there defeated. I gave up. *Whatever happens happens....*

Suddenly, I began to experience a strange sensation, as though I were lying in Joy's hospital bed on that last day at around this time, 11:45 a.m. The hospital bed had stood where I was and Joy had been lying in exactly the same position that I was now.

From Joy's point of view I began to sense everyone around me, including *me.* All seven of us were there—Jerry on the left, Terri on my right, Elliot next to her. Kate, Genevieve, and Lorraine were at the foot of the bed. Jackie stood next to Jerry. How incredible! I seemed to be experiencing Joy's last moments!

My breath gradually slowed. I felt Jerry resting his cheek against mine. I felt his great love in a way I wasn't able to while in a body. My children were the fulfillment of my life. His love, our love, was the fulfillment of my soul. As he breathed with me, I knew he would have come with me, but it wasn't his time.

As my last breaths labored with growing intervals between inhalations and exhalations, I felt myself partly in my body and partly out, wriggling out of the cocoon of my diseased physical form, gradually extricating myself from my dying body. Then I hovered in the air, aware of everyone around my deathbed. But now I could see everyone's soul form—a distinct "jewel-like" vibratory matrix of breathtakingly beautiful colors and patterns.

As my dying body labored in the bed and my organs shut down, my spirit was met by my departed loved ones. At first they projected their earthly forms like masks, so that I recognized them. Then gradually those forms became transparent until I saw their eternal soul forms. My return was welcomed with a great celebration. Simultaneously, I experienced the sorrow of some earthly family and friends. The contrast was like two sides of a doorway—one painted black, the other white.

People came into the bedroom to sit with my body while I roamed around the condo visiting with other mourners. I could move about to anyone who thought about me. One moment I was in Washington, D.C., visiting my niece, the next moment I was in Sedona comforting a dear friend. In a flash I was at the beach in the Marina whispering into the ear of another dear soul who was taking her grief for a walk. Time and space meant nothing.

I watched as my body, covered by a red velvet cloth, was wheeled down to the garage by the mortuary accompanied by Jerry, Terri, and Elliot. I laughed when Jerry returned to the condo and announced, "Elvis has left the building." His humor signified so much about our love during this lifetime and beyond. I was so proud of the way my earthly family handled their grief. They'd given me a blessed, grace-filled sendoff.

In some strange way I was both Joy *and* myself as I experienced Joy's grateful acknowledgement of her earthly family—"They set an example of how to *let go* and celebrate the Great Homecoming. Because they were so accepting, I could totally participate in the great Celebration that awaited me. I'm so proud of them. And so grateful!"

Then I-as-Jerry was hailed by Joy's spirit family for playing my role so well. I was reassured that everything was unfolding perfectly and that it was now my time to step forward and share the "miracle of Joy" with the world and teach about love and death and sex.

Just then, the drums stopped and my shamanic journey ended. Disoriented, I lay there for some time trying to digest what I'd just experienced. Finally, I took off my blindfold and sat up to check the clock. The journey had taken half an hour. I was stunned! How was it possible that I could experience Joy's transition? Perhaps riding her "last breath" had been the key.

A few hours later I was sitting in a garden with Elliot and Kate and our hosts for Easter weekend, Gael and her husband Paul (whom I'd introduced and Joy as minister had married). We toasted Joy, sipped wine, and watched the setting sun paint the mountains in the distance. I shared my shamanic journey and confessed that I didn't know if it was real. They said it didn't matter. And I agreed. If my unconscious served up this perfect fantasy for me, I'd take it! I couldn't have asked for a more beautiful way to celebrate Joy's last Good Friday.

Late Easter Sunday, I was alone in my hosts' beautiful garden, lying beneath a magnificent 200-year-old oak tree. It reminded me of my vision during the third Rite of Joy in which I was lying in a woman's lap beneath a tree, hoping but not knowing if it was Joy. Suddenly, I felt Joy's presence and remembered her explaining why there were two dates—"*Good Friday for me, April 6th for you.*" I'd celebrated Good Friday, and now wondered how I would celebrate the completion of my year of grieving Joy. As if in answer, I heard a voice deep within say, *"Ask Angelina if she wants to celebrate by doing another Rite of Joy."*

ℰꙨ 45 ℭℛ

The Last Dance

Back home after my Easter weekend, I began to question whether asking Angelina for another Rite was a good idea. It had been two months since January's birthday Rite. What's more, I'd never *asked* for a Rite before. And I couldn't help but wonder if trying to resurrect the healing magic of a Rite was a mistake. Yet how could I ignore the guidance I'd received?

On March 28th I wrote Angelina an email, careful not to leverage Joy (as in *Joy suggested* or *Joy's guidance is).* It was important that *I* ask for this Rite of Joy.

> *SUBJECT: Rite of Joy?*
>
> *Dear Angelina,*
>
> *During my Easter weekend I was reminded how wonderfully healing the Rites of Joy have been. It got me wondering if we ought to do another one before April 6th as a way to celebrate coming to the end of this momentous year.*
>
> *Check in with your guidance and let me know how you feel.*
>
> *With Love & Profound Gratitude Whatever You Decide,*
>
> *Jerry*

Angelina wrote back. "After going within, I got a big *Yes!* to do a Rite of Joy with you and Joy this week. Congratulations on asking for what you want!"

The only time we were both available before April 6th was Monday evening, March 31ˢᵗ. Angelina arrived just before sunset and we spent a few silent minutes together on the patio savoring the spectacular light show provided by the setting sun. Afterward, I made some tea and shared with her how re-living Joy's Last Adventure allowed me to experience emotions I hadn't permitted myself to feel a year ago. Angelina understood that though it had been healing, my *Fifty-Day Countdown* had probably taken a toll.

"Do you have any guidance from Joy about tonight's Rite?" I asked.

"I was told not to expect anything," Angelina replied. "To open to love and for you to ask for what you want."

We stood before the winged Isis statue in the foyer as we had so many times before. With ceremony we lit both votive candles and declared our intentions for the evening. I turned on the music, and let it shuffle to the first song of the evening— Nat King Cole's "Unforgettable." A shiver ran through me and I swept Angelina into a slow dance, thrilled by the synchronicity.

When *our* song ended, I quickly undressed and climbed on the table. Incredibly, the next song that came on was "Let Me Count the Ways," which reminded me of my Last Dance with Joy. As Angelina began the massage, I sensed that this was going to be the theme of the evening's Rite—our last dance.

As in previous Rites of Joy there were moments of sublime ecstasy, total adoration and, of course, the profound healing and gratitude that comes from being loved so completely.

At one point Angelina-as-Joy said, "Thank You" over and over as she showered my body with tender kisses. At another point, she whispered, "I love you so much," again and again.

There were moments when I felt Joy standing beside me, her hands touching, stroking, caressing my flesh. And moments when her kisses on my back and shoulders, on my thighs and buttocks, triggered memories of our life together. Each kiss exploded into a flashback of the two of us...meandering through the French Quarter in New Orleans; soaking in hot tubs at Esalen that overlooked the dramatic coastline of Big Sur; touring the snow-covered Hopi pueblo in Santa Fe; stumbling upon the butterfly farm on our boating trip around Vancouver; picnicking on our bed in a small hotel on the Left Bank of Paris; hiking up Cathedral Rock in Sedona; climbing the Mayan pyramid in Cancun; and swimming with dolphins in Hawaii.

As Joy/Angelina rained kisses down on me, I saw us in a bed full of balloons and in a bayou full of crocodiles. I saw us laughing so hard we cried, then loving so hard we *died*...to our separate selves.

I saw Joy standing naked on the beach, her body painted with mandalas at each chakra. I saw her dressed as Howard Stern wielding a dildo that she used as a mike to interview people about their sex lives. I saw her dancing with a seven-foot python named Osiris.

I walked with Joy in the gardens of Versailles as she was given a guided tour by Marie Antoinette's spirit (who'd also lost two children) about the raunchy goings-on at this playground for the French aristocracy that ultimately provoked the French Revolution.

As the kaleidoscope of our life together flashed through my mind, I was overcome by its beauty. We had sanctified our love by offering each other our deepest selves. We played every imaginable role with one another—lover, teacher, friend, playmate, confidant, partner. Then the sick, the caregiver...the daughter, the father...the dying, the grieving. I remembered our almost daily exclamations about how wonderful our life was. We were so grateful for the grace and blessing of each other's love and, most important, for the opportunity to love so deeply.

While "Joy's" tender kisses were creating a highlight reel of our love and life together, tears spilled from my eyes. With these magical kisses she was saying goodbye. Yet I also knew that it was the right thing to do. For if I could, I would have done these Rites of Joy for the rest of my life, and I would never have a new relationship. Joy, in her infinite wisdom, was giving me a last glimpse of the wonder and beauty of our love. And I knew without a doubt that this was the *last* Rite of Joy. She would never come to me like this again. It was time for me to move on with my life.

The next day I sent Angelina a "Thank You" email. Her reply was the perfect send-off.

> Dear King Jerry,
>
> I have some things to share to help you paint a more complete picture of last night's Rite of Joy.
>
> As I massaged your body, I saw and felt Joy's energy move through my hands to you. Sparkles of blue sapphire light danced off my hands. When I leaned over to kiss your body, I saw Joy with me as if superimposed over my face. With each kiss, her lips were there. It was as if I could see her and be looking at you through her loving eyes...and be kissing you with her lips.
>
> I was hoping you could feel her presence and her loving energy. And you did, as her kisses sparked memories. That was key, like touchstones. She said several times how much she loves you. She wanted you to feel her love penetrating your very being.
>
> You're one very loved and lucky guy to have had the most amazing experiences with your beloved Joy over these last 10 years...and with her through our Rites for another year.
>
> As you move closer to Sunday, Joy wants you to hold these loving experiences and memories close to your heart to uplift you, to help you on your journey. It's not about clinging to them. It's about filling yourself with these feelings and using them to leap forward into your next life chapter. Joy wants you to know that life holds more magic and love for you in the future, although perhaps you can't imagine that now.
>
> With love and Joy and many blessings,
> Angelina, Priestess of Isis/Joy

ℰ 46 ℭ

Perfection

>———————————————————————<

I'd considered several possibilities about how to commemorate the April 6th anniversary of Joy's transition: doing something with her ashes; leading a Wisdom Circle about her; hosting a luncheon and fashion show in which the women who'd been in her closet would wear her clothes; and even producing a *Joy Film Festival* for my friends, screening tapes of the *Sunday of Joy* and other workshops she'd led.

That was before I realized that April 6th was for *me*. When I told some friends I wasn't sure how to celebrate the completion of my *Year of Grieving Joy-fully*, they suggested I throw myself a party.

I liked the idea—it was simple—and the date fell conveniently on a Sunday. But there was a problem. The water-main break which had driven me into Joy's closet nearly a half a year ago had damaged the entrance to my building. Construction had finally begun only a few weeks earlier and might not be finished by the 6[th,] making it impossible for me to host a party.

Then a friend offered to host it for me.

One of the things my grief journey had taught me was to pay attention to signs. I interpreted the fact that the entrance to my home was under construction as a sign *not* to host a party—not at my home or anyone else's. Perhaps I was supposed to trust that the day would unfold perfectly.

Once I decided not to host an anniversary party, amazing things began to happen. Virginia—the belly dancer who I'd met at the Tantra Reunion and who had invited me to the African grief ritual—offered to give me a massage Saturday evening. Terri was hosting a brunch for the family on Sunday morning. In the late afternoon, Judy and Michael (who'd hosted the New Year's Eve party) were inviting our close friends to their home to plant a "Joy Garden." And that wasn't all.

I had recently contacted Charlotte, the woman who had given Joy and me watsu massages, to find out when she was starting up again since she'd gone on hiatus for the winter. She said that April 6th was her *first* day back and that she had a 2:30 p.m. slot available (which also happened to be the only time I could make!). What's more, she wanted to *gift* me with this watsu session on the occasion of my one-year anniversary.

According to Jewish tradition and other lunar-based calendars, the day begins at sundown—the womb-like darkness of night before the birth of new light. So the celebration of my one-year anniversary actually began Saturday evening with Virginia's incredible massage which employed hot sesame oil, chanted mantras vibrating into my cells, a drum that harmonized my heartbeat, and a gong whose overtones reverberated into the depths of my soul.

There were moments during the massage I wept at how blessed I'd been to have experienced such a profound love. A year ago I didn't think I could go on living without Joy. This extraordinary massage felt like a hero's reward after having survived initiation into life and death, love and loss.

Sunday morning's brunch at Terri's also bordered on the miraculous. As we ate, Terri announced that she'd received a communication from Joy the day before. She read the "conversation" her mother had dictated to her from a piece of paper. "I would like to hear how everyone's grown and benefited from my being away. Because that's what this is all about: growing and benefiting simultaneously. Nothing else."

I was delighted by Joy's words. They not only confirmed my guidance from her, but on this special day her question was the subject closest to my heart.

Terri responded first. "I'm a better woman, mother, and friend. I hid under Mom's branches and, when they fell, I came out into my own, out into the sunshine." Everyone took turns answering the question. As the rest of us spoke about the many gifts we'd received, I was in awe—Joy was still teaching us.

In the afternoon, as I floated in the warm water of the circular watsu pool, I hoped I'd experience contact with Joy. Immediately, I felt a gentle reprimand—*"It's time to stop trying to contact me, time to be present to the **joy of the moment** and not miss it because you're hunting for the **Joy of the past**."*

As Charlotte gently moved me through the water, I couldn't help but surrender to my baptism into the *joy of the moment*. To truly complete my grief journey, I had to stop depending on contact with Joy. I had needed it to get through my first year of grief, but I didn't need it anymore, not if I wanted to move forward and create a new life. Otherwise, Joy would become a crutch that enfeebled rather than enabled.

While surrendering to the joy of the moment and being floated to and fro in the warm water, I was reminded of my vision of the Many-Limbed Goddess that inspired my *Journey of a Thousand Hugs*. Rocked every which way in this womb of liquid love by Charlotte's gentle watsu, I remembered the thousands of different ways I was loved during the past year and was overcome with gratitude.

Suddenly, the once silken water seemed to burn. "That's enough!" my inner voice declared. I was done. With fifteen minutes to go, I stopped the watsu. My new life awaited me.

While I was toweling off, Charlotte remarked, "Do you realize how unusual you are?"

I was flattered, but not sure what she meant.

She explained that she worked with many men and "they're like moving boards through the water. Rigid. Tense. Locked into their masculine roles. Your body is flexible like a dancer's. I usually need to rest after a session with most men because they give so little back. I have to coach them to breathe. You breathe with abandon. I can follow the music of your breath like a dance. I don't need to rest. I'm invigorated. You're so alive and vital. You may be sixty but you're like a man going on forty!"

Was it possible that I'd emerged from my grief journey more vital than when I began? What a wonderful send-off for my new life!

By the time I arrived at Judy and Michael's everyone was already gathered out back in the garden. I counted twelve of us. In tribute, each woman wore something of Joy's—clothing or jewelry—so I had my "fashion show" after all without having to ask for it.

Jackie, who had been at the family brunch that morning, had already shared Joy's question about what gifts we'd received in the past year since her transition. So I was treated to another round of hearing how Joy's passing had ultimately been a gift for our friends. In fact, many claimed they received guidance from her.

I spoke last and listed some of the gifts I had received, including "the love that family and friends have shown me this past year, which I would have never known; memories of Joy, which fill my heart to overflowing; the strength I've gotten from having endured the worst loss imaginable and having survived; my enhanced appreciation of my mortality and the fleeting preciousness of life; and learning to love myself as well as I loved Joy." I spoke about learning to receive. And to trust. I shared my Good Friday vision. But I wasn't ready to tell anyone about the Rites of Joy. Not yet.

In a formal ceremony we replanted the "Joy Garden"—which had been planted with gardenias last year—around a custom-made brick with the word "Joy" carved into it. A poem was read in Joy's honor.

Do not stand at my grave and weep.
I am not there. I do not sleep.
I am a thousand winds that blow.
I am the diamond glints on snow.
I am the sunlight on ripened grain.
I am the gentle autumn's rain.
When you awaken in the morning's hush,
I am the swift, uplifting rush
Of quiet birds in circled flight.
I am the soft stars that shine at night.
Do not stand at my grave and cry.
I am not there. I did not die.
—Anonymous

My *Year of Grieving Joy-fully* had been a painful and, at times, unbearable ordeal. It had also been a profound initiation into the paradoxical truth that *loss brings gifts*. Though I couldn't have imagined it a year ago when I breathed Joy's last breath with her, my *Year of Grieving Joy-fully* had bestowed many gifts: my Journey of a Thousand Hugs, the Rites of Joy, my Good Friday Vision and so much more.

But the irony was that I would have never received these gifts had I not lost Joy. Her words at the Well of Tears (during the African grief ritual) kept coming back to me throughout the day—"It's a gift! It's *all* a gift! The love *and* the loss!"

I'd wanted such an important milestone as this one-year anniversary to speak to this hard-won revelation. How extraordinary that Joy via Terri posed the question about *what gifts her loss bestowed* which became the running theme of the day. Once again the universe had conspired to provide a more meaningful and fulfilling celebration than any I could have produced or even imagined. A healing massage, an intimate family gathering, a watsu baptism into a new life and a formal ceremony with friends. No party I'd planned to host could compare. How could I not believe that this perfect day of celebration had somehow been orchestrated by Joy?

ℰ℧ 47 ℃℞

Grace

>───<

I drove home that evening emotionally and spiritually fulfilled by the banquet of festivities this first anniversary of my beloved's passing had bestowed upon me. Yet my day of celebration wasn't quite over. I was expecting a visit from Grace.

Joy had not only helped heal my grief, she had also guided me to a new love. At times she had prodded, at other times, coaxed, and, when I resisted, she had even *intervened*. I had to be pulled kicking and screaming from the burning building of my grief.

Grace's involvement in my *Year of Grieving Joy-fully* had been relatively minor until very recently. I had met her many months earlier, when I was taking my first tentative steps out into the world, "Yes-ing" my way into a new life. I was attending a lecture by a rabbi who combined tantra and kabbalah into something he called "kabbalove."

"Is that seat taken?" an attractive blonde, blue-eyed woman asked. Still raw with grief and uncomfortable venturing out into public solo, I shook my head and she sat down next to me. Though she resembled an older version of Cameron Diaz, I was in no condition to appreciate her good looks, let alone flirt. I introduced myself by telling her I'd recently lost my wife. She expressed her condolences and then confided that she was "grieving, too." She had just broken up with a lover whom she'd

271

been seeing for the past year. I didn't pursue the conversation and she, sensing I was radioactive with grief, kept her distance.

During the fall, as I slowly made my way back into the social world, I'd run into Grace now and then. Sometimes she was with her lover, other times she was alone because they had broken up again. Whenever we saw each other, we would inquire how the other was doing. Since she was a professional listener—a psychotherapist—I felt comfortable sharing my grief journey with her.

During the party-go-round of the Christmas holidays, I ran into Grace several times. She was always alone. She assured me that her relationship was *really* over. In the course of our conversations I told her that I loved to dance. She said she loved to dance, too. So I invited her over for a playdate. The conversation flowed, but, more important, she was a great dancer!

Grace was fun, athletic, playful, intelligent, and free-spirited, and I enjoyed being with her. Though I wasn't ready to pursue a new relationship, I began to feel a "quickening" between us. For my birthday she gave me a card that read—"Loss demands birth and the two are lovers"—which I taped to my fridge.

In January, just as Grace and I started to date, I began listening to Joy's memoir, which stirred up my grief. So I backed off. It was the old pattern—getting close, then pulling away. I had to wonder: *Was I afraid of loving again? Or was I afraid of losing Joy?* All I knew was that I wasn't ready to enter into a new relationship. Not yet.

In early February I was invited to a birthday party on a friend's yacht. I decided *not* to invite Grace. To my chagrin, Grace had been invited to the party, too. And I had some explaining to do.

While we danced, I apologized for my yo yo-ing behavior and my reluctance to move forward with our relationship. I admitted I wasn't "playing with a full deck" emotionally and that my heart wasn't completely available. "You're very tempting, perhaps too tempting," I told Grace, "but I'm just not ready to be swept away by a new romance. I have to finish grieving first."

Though Grace said she understood, I could tell she was hurt. "I want you to know," she warned, "I'm not going to wait forever."

At that moment I saw Terri (who was also at the party) motioning for me to join her.

"Mom's sitting on my head and wants to tell you something," she began as soon as I sat down beside her. "She's saying, *Get over me!*"

I swallowed hard. This was not what I expected. It was as if Joy had been listening in on my conversation with Grace. "Tell her she's not easy to get over."

Terri closed her eyes for a moment. "She says, *Hurry it up!*"

I shrugged and shook my head in confusion.

Terri was insistent. "Jerry, I've just met Grace and she's great! And a babe! She's not going to wait around."

It was as if they'd all been listening in. "I know," I said, following Terri's gaze across the room to where Grace was being chatted up by two men. I realized I was going to lose this wonderful woman. My grief over my lost love was about to destroy the possibility of new love. Joy's intervention couldn't have happened at a more crucial moment.

I thanked Terri *and* Joy, then got up and asked Grace to dance. As we swayed to the music, I told her I'd had a change of heart. She was pleased, yet cautious, about my sudden about-face. We danced and talked more and promised to see each other again.

Later that evening, as I was getting ready for bed, the phone rang. It was 1:00 a.m. *Who could be calling at this hour?*

It was Grace asking if *I'd* just called her.

I hadn't.

That was strange. Her phone had rung and when she picked up, no one was there. Figuring I was the only person who'd call her so late, she called me.

"Well," I speculated, "the universe [Joy, I thought to myself] wants us to talk...so why don't we?" And it was good we did. We cleared up a lot of the misunderstanding, hurt, and confusion my mixed signals had caused. Our late-night phone conversation, which I believed Joy engineered, solidified the shift that her intervention on the boat earlier that evening had inspired.

As if to confirm the signs I'd already been given, the next time Grace and I got together, as I was driving over the hill to her place in Santa Monica, a country song played on the radio that gave me the chills. The song, "In Heaven," by Suzy Bogguss, was about a widow telling her late husband that she's found someone new and she's moving on. I wept as I listened, especially to lines like: *"I remember when you left me/ You hoped I'd love again"* and *"I'm only flesh and blood/I can't keep talking to a ghost."*

Though my head said I needed to move on, my heart and body didn't agree. Grace and I made out on her couch but, instead of having hot sex, I wound up crying in her arms.

Sex, for the time being, was out of the question. Though Grace was beautiful, whenever I touched her, I couldn't help feeling— *It's not Joy.* Our attempts at lovemaking invariably turned into bouts of grieving for me. Thank god, she was a therapist with the patience of Job.

I told Grace that I couldn't celebrate my first Joy-less Valentine's Day with another woman. She said she understood. During Valentine's Day, I heard Joy say, "Pass it on!" I knew she meant to Grace.

I vowed to make my Valentine's Day absence up to Grace by being more emotionally available. So much for good intentions. After V-Day came D-Day and my *Fifty-Day Countdown.*

Grace was terrific—interesting *and* interested—an irresistible combination. But I didn't want to be distracted from completing my grief journey with Joy. So I told myself that "finding the right dosage" of Grace was the key to whether she'd be *medicine* or *poison*.

My mixed signals drove Grace crazy. And who could blame her. They made me nuts. As my *Fifty-Day Countdown* took its toll, I began to wonder if I—still recovering from an emotional heart attack—was enough "meat on the bone" for her. I wasn't ripe yet; I needed to be put on a windowsill for another few months to ripen. After several more encounters of awkward intimacy, I sensed I wouldn't be able to have sex with Grace until after the one-year anniversary. I told her that I had to complete my grief journey first.

Since Grace and I started dating, I'd wrestled with conflicting emotions—my romance with Grace threatened my grief about Joy, and my grief threatened my new romance.

As I was increasingly caught up in reliving those last days with Joy, I was reminded in so many ways just how wonderful she was, what a great love we had shared, and what a great loss I'd endured. My budding romance with Grace was completely overshadowed

To avoid distraction in the final days, I asked Grace for no contact—no phones, no email, *nothing*—until the one-year anniversary passed. She understood.

During that retreat there were times I questioned whether I could have another relationship so soon, whether I was ready, whether I'd healed enough?

By April 6th I hadn't answered that question. All I knew was that I was so full of Joy, I didn't have room for Grace. And consequently, I didn't know what I felt or what I was going to do. Imagine my surprise when during the anniversary brunch with the family, while sharing her conversation with Joy about "gifts," Terri delivered a message to me. "Mom has one word for you: *Grace!*"

For the rest of the day, during the watsu and the garden party that followed, I allowed my feelings for Grace to re-emerge. The last time we had spoken, we had decided to meet in the evening of April 6th to cap off my anniversary celebration. This would be our first contact since my request for a retreat more than two weeks earlier.

The theme of the anniversary had been the gifts Joy's passing had bestowed on all who loved her. As this momentous one-year anniversary unfolded, I became more and more convinced that Grace was the final gift Joy's passing had brought me. Until I said *Yes* to the most important gift of all—*love*—I wasn't finished grieving. However provocative the gift of a new romance might be, it was time to unwrap it. Grace's birthday card had indeed been a premonition—"*Loss demands birth*," it had said, "*and the two are lovers.*"

My *Year of Grieving Joy-fully* was over.

My *Year of Loving Grace-fully* had just begun.

And it was all thanks to Joy.

Joy

is the most
infallible
sign of the
presence of

GOD

Epilogue

Was I ready for a relationship?

Yes. And no.

At my bereavement group one of the women claimed she wasn't interested in dating. "I created a masterpiece," she said, referring to her forty-year marriage. "I won't create another one in this life. So why bother?" To which I replied, "I created a masterpiece, too. And I probably won't create another one in this lifetime. But I love to paint."

So I "painted" with Grace on most weekends—we danced and laughed and, yes, we made love. Though Grace blessed me with many gifts, I wasn't ready for the kind of relationship she yearned for. Or deserved. To be fair, how could anyone compete with Joy? Looking back, I'm in awe of Grace's courage and compassion. As a widower still madly in love with his "dead" wife, I was no picnic.

I sensed early on that our relationship might be temporary. Never having been married, Grace was on her own quest—to finally find true love. I'd already been to the top of that mountain. One day I half-jokingly said that I wasn't sure whether she loved me or my love story. And that only time would tell. My

Year of Loving Grace-fully brought me many gifts, perhaps the greatest was that I loved, albeit incompletely, another woman.

At about the time Grace and I were considering ending our relationship, Joy confirmed that my Year of Loving Grace-fully was over. At the end of January's Wisdom Circle, a cake appeared for an impromptu birthday celebration. To my surprise, Kate delivered Joy's birthday gift to me—a card Joy had dictated to Terri.

> *To Jerry, the gift you are to me...*
> *by Joy Weinstock*
>
> *You gave me truth*
> *You gave me MY emotions, enjoyment of them for the first time and free expression of them anytime.*
> *You made me young again*
> *You gave me a hot body — yours.*
> *You gave me the best climaxes, with or without you.*
> *You gave me freedom to do what I wanted without judgment*
> *You gave me adventure*
> *You gave me so much more beauty from loving you*
> *You gave me a sparring partner*
> *You gave me a real partner*
> *You gave me all of your time when I needed it*
> *You gave me your love for my kids [Joy was crying here]*
> *You gave me awe and you never tried to hide it*
> *You gave me spontaneity, something I was never good at*
> *You gave me fun, lots of fun*
> *You gave me unconditional love, no matter what I looked like or sounded like or acted like.*
> *You gave me forever.*
>
> *I could go on and on for pages and gush but it would bore your party silly. It bored me silly when you went on and on about me at the Wisdom Circle after I left. [Terri hadn't been there!] So I will leave you with this....*

> *It's time for you to have more partners, not to take my place but to expand your love....*

I was stunned. Joy went on to say that if I tried to recreate what we had, I probably couldn't since any relationship would most likely fail by comparison. What we had was once in a lifetime. And if I was lucky enough to find that kind of love again, I wouldn't learn anything new. I'd been there, done that. It was time for me to explore new ways of loving, new possibilities for love.

Joy had led me to Grace, intervened when I balked, blessed our year together, and now reassured me that the time for Grace was over.

To Grieve or Not to Grieve

How was my grief?

For the most part I was done, except when I wasn't. And I never knew when it would hit me.

On the 11th of November (11/11), for example, I had a strange dream about Joy. I dreamt I was looking at a photo album of our life together, but was horrified to see that all of the photos were *missing*! All that remained were the *captions*. I woke up feeling lousy. Was the dream telling me that the memoir I was writing was all that was left of our life together? Later in the day, I realized that I'd *forgotten* our November 6th Love Anniversary.

At first I was upset, then I rationalized that I'd been preoccupied with the 2008 Presidential election and Obama's historic election. Finally, I remembered Joy telling me that it's always my choice whether I interpret my experience as positive or negative, so I chose to interpret my *forgetting* as a good sign—that I was involved in my present life and that my grief was abating.

A few days later I was sitting in the dentist's chair, when Dr. B, who had known Joy for years and hadn't seen me since the memorial, came in and asked how I was doing. Suddenly overcome with grief, I began to cry.

Joy & I

Do I still communicate with Joy?

Yes. But not as frequently, or as desperately. There were times when I meditated every day and asked for guidance. And periods when I didn't seek Joy's guidance at all because either I was trying to wean myself from dependency on her, or because I'd become increasingly involved in my new life. Yet, I'd often receive a message, a sign, or a dream that helped me navigate the new currents of my life. Joy will always be a powerful presence in my life, guiding and inspiring me.

In a meditation on my birthday in 2010, Joy told me, *"Our relationship outside the body is as important as the one we had in the body."* And it truly is.

Once I asked her, "What's it like for you?" She replied, *"More incredible than you or we could imagine. I can experience all the loves in my life simultaneously. And I can experience all the loves in all my lives simultaneously. The feeling is...indescribable. Beyond ecstasy!"*

Another time I asked, "What are you doing right now?" And she replied, *"I'm exploring new realms of Being. It's fascinating! Wonderful! Something I can't explain. It's like explaining sex to a child. You have no basis from which to understand. There's constant, continual learning and opportunities for growth, depending upon your heart's desire, your soul's purpose, your fascinations, your interests. Everything you can imagine. And more...awaits..."*

After all I'd been through, I still had some lingering doubts about the reality of these communications. One time I said to Joy, "Show me a sign that I'm not talking to myself." I waited for a reply, then I heard Joy say: *"You're always talking to yourself. In the larger picture it can be no other way since we are all One."*

Joy keeps gently guiding me toward the fulfillment of our mission. On Valentine's Day 2009, I lit a candle in front of our wedding picture on that black lava beach in Hawaii. As I meditated on the candle and watched the flame flicker in the picture's reflection back and forth between our hearts, I heard Joy say:

Our "Unforgettable" Love Was and Is a Blessing Beyond Words
Such a Gift of Love Must Be Shared
With Another Individual
With as Many People as Possible.
Our Love Story Wasn't for Us Alone
It was Given to Us so that We Could Be An Inspiration for the
Whole World.
Our Memoir is the Last Chapter,
The Love Ever After Which Never Ends

The Rites of Joy

Joy had continually reminded me that the miracle of her guidance wasn't solely for my benefit. These extraordinary experiences were to be shared. But more than a year after the last *Rite of Joy*, I was still reluctant to share them, still afraid of what people would think. It was shocking enough that my "dead" wife was communicating with me from the Afterlife, but making love to me? How could anyone possibly understand?

An entry in my journal which I'd written over a year earlier explains my ambivalence and was as relevant as ever.

These Rites are so amazing I want to share them and tell people. I want to shout it from the rooftops that I'm experiencing Joy's love beyond the veil of death. But what would people think? I got a massage with a "happy ending?" How could they understand? *He cried and he came.* But it was so much more!....

My fear of people's judgment was keeping me from "shouting it from the rooftops." As far as completing my memoir, I had hit a roadblock. Then I met Heather.

I. J. Weinstock

I was attending a grief conference in San Diego. In the evening I was sitting at the hotel bar when a woman who'd been at another seminar at the hotel sat down beside me and ordered a drink. When I learned she was a massage therapist, I told her about the Rites of Joy, and that I was reluctant to publish my memoir for fear of people thinking I was crazy. She didn't think I was crazy because she'd had a similar experience. I asked her to tell me about it.

"Several years ago I was at a client's home who had recently lost her young husband to cancer," Heather said. "She was lying face down and I was working on her back. Suddenly, I felt the presence of her husband (who I had never met, never seen a photo of). He watched for a few minutes and then asked if he could enter my body and experience her. I considered this for a moment. My heart swelled with compassion and an immediate deep service to these two lovers surfaced. So I agreed."

I wasn't alone! I thought, anxious to hear more.

"His essence entered my hands, and my client immediately began to respond to him. Her back and hips riding the sweet touch. Indeed every cell of her was alive. I experienced their connecting as a third party with deep respect and a profound appreciation of this man's love for his wife. I sensed his relief to feel her again... Her ecstasy in receiving him..."

Her description awakened my memories of the Rites of Joy and tears of recognition filled my eyes.

"He left my body after some time," Heather continued. "I asked her to turn face up and tears were streaming down her face. She said to me in amazement, 'I could feel Chris. I could smell him. I feel like he was here!'"

As I sipped my beer, I wondered, *How many other people have experienced such strange, sacred, sexual encounters with departed loved ones?*

Heather continued, "What I didn't mention was that this client was a devout Southern Baptist Christian. I hesitated to tell her what had just happened because of her 'belief system.'

284

But after a brief deliberation with myself, I told her that indeed her husband had been here and had been touching her, and that she had indeed experienced him."

Heather paused to sip her drink. She hesitated before adding, "This woman was so upset, she asked me to leave and I never heard from her again."

That was exactly the kind of negative, almost horrified reaction I was afraid of! And yet I couldn't deny the uncanny synchronicity that at a grief conference a perfect stranger sat down beside me at a hotel bar to address my fears. This was no coincidence. I was being helped, even prodded, to finish the memoir.

Upon returning home after the conference, I vowed to finish the book despite my fears. As I completed the manuscript, I kept reminding myself that Joy had written in *Love Ever After* that our love had a greater purpose—*"shining a new light on two of the most misunderstood areas of our lives—sex and death."* I would fulfill our mission.

I also realized that *JOYride* was the first installment in the deal I'd made with God.

The Joyful Redemption

A few weeks after I completed *JOYride*, Joy's stepson, Bruce Lisker, was released from prison. It was another incredible synchronicity. In 1983, as a seventeen-year-old, despite his pleas of innocence, Bruce was convicted of murdering his mother and sentenced to life in prison. On August 13, 2009, after a federal judge overturned his murder conviction and, after spending twenty-six years in prison for a crime he did not commit, a forty-four year old Bruce Lisker came "home" to live with me. That's when I began to see that there was more to *JOYride* than I'd realized.

Bruce had been a constant in our lives. Joy and I visited him in prison and spoke to him on the phone almost daily. We lived through the hopes and disappointments of the many legal delays and setbacks. When Joy lost her vision, I took over the practical details of Bruce's affairs—prepping his quarterly packages, ordering books, renewing magazine subscriptions, buying clothes and even eyeglasses, as well as overseeing the construction of his website, FreeBruce.org.

I wanted to harness the public outpouring of support that more than fifty *Los Angeles Times* articles about Bruce's case (including several front pages) had generated. So I built an email list of the hundreds of people who'd responded to the articles and visited the website. For several years, I regularly updated these "Friends of Bruce" on each new development in his case. I had no idea how important this would eventually be.

Joy had "mothered" Bruce for nearly twenty years while he was in prison, and he wrote a beautiful eulogy that was read at her memorial service. During those first grief-stricken months, whenever Bruce called from prison, he would console me. There was a thunderstorm during my last prison visit. As I was leaving the prison, a complete double rainbow appeared, which I interpreted as a sign that he would soon be free.

On that August morning, to the accompaniment of TV cameras and front-page headlines, Bruce walked out of prison. As the TV flashed, "Lisker Freed!" the news anchor announced, "Last week a judge overturned Bruce Lisker's conviction because of false evidence and sloppy defense work. Lisker walked out of Mule Creek State Prison this morning."

In an impromptu press conference outside the prison, Bruce spoke to the media in a voice flooded with emotion. "It's a joyous day—the best day of my life!" As he climbed into the pickup truck that would drive him back to Los Angeles, a reporter asked, "What are you going to do first when you get back to LA?" Bruce thought for a moment, then, with a wistful smile, replied, "Take a swim."

Eight hours later I sat poolside on a hot August afternoon watching a man who'd been caged for over a quarter century take his first swim. And I wept. For Bruce. For Joy. For Bob. For justice. For a dream come true. Joy had been dreaming of this day for Bob after he passed on. And I'd been dreaming of it for Joy. Watching Bruce frolic in the water, I was overcome with an indescribable happiness that I'd like to think was partly due to Bob and Joy celebrating in the Afterlife.

Living with me, Bruce experienced his first taste of freedom and took his first tentative steps towards rebuilding the life he had lost. Joy couldn't be there to witness this nearly miraculous righting of a terrible wrong, but I was. And as I helped Bruce adjust to his newfound freedom, I began to see his story, our story, in a larger context.

Bruce's father's torment about losing his wife and his son, drove Bob—a conservative attorney, former Marine, and Kiwanis president—to attempt to contact the spirit of his dead wife to find who killed her. This set the stage for the channeled communications Joy wrote about in *Love Ever After*.

From the Afterlife, Bob gave Joy a 12-Step program to attract a new love, making Joy and I a "match-made-in-heaven." Weeks after I completed my memoir about the delight of loving and the anguish of losing Joy, I became the "home" Bruce returned to after twenty-six years in prison to begin a new life. *JOYride* was part of an even larger story that began twenty-six years earlier.

Incredibly, out of a murder and miscarriage of justice have blossomed two firsthand accounts of life-after-death communication, in which both Bruce's father and stepmother became "spirit guides." It's wild! It's unbelievable! And yet it's true! And Bruce regaining his freedom was just as miraculous! Why this family tragedy has generated not one, but two testaments to life-after-death and eternal love is a mystery I call *The Joyful Redemption*.

Joy was a witness and chronicler of this redemption during her lifetime. She had no doubt that Bob was somehow responsible for the breakthroughs in Bruce's case. She recorded a channeled conversation she'd had with Bob the day the first *Los Angeles Times* article appeared in May 2005.

> Bob said he's been working very hard on the Other Side to accomplish what's happening now. He cared the most, so he's been spearheading it. But he had a lot of help.
>
> When I said to Bob, "I'm so happy that you're finally going to right this wrong," he said, "It's only wrong on a very small scale. It's 'wrong' because of our perspective here and it gives us the opportunity to turn it around. You have to pull back a long way to get the perspective to see that there are no 'wrongs' and that everything is perfect. Bruce is doing what he came here to do." And so did Bob. And so am I. And so are all of us.

Joy shared her excitement about the breakthrough in Bruce's case at the next Sunday of Joy. Here are her notes—

> Like a lotus which grows in the mud, a murder is at the core of our love story. The gruesome murder of Bruce's mother is the seed from which this spiritual document [*Love Ever After*] has blossomed.
>
> The murder brought Bob and I together. The murder made Bob desperate to seek answers beyond the conventional and to attempt to contact his deceased wife on the Other Side. And Bob's desperation to seek answers propelled him beyond his conventional beliefs about reality…and miraculously awakened his connection to his guides and other dimensions of existence.

I felt an obligation, almost a sacred duty, to honor Joy, and Bob, by telling the world about this miraculous story. I built a website— TheLiskerRedemption.com—which presented Bruce Lisker's "untold story" and where I posted the videos I took of his first days of freedom. I was thrilled when CBS's *48 Hours Mystery* devoted an hour-long episode, "The Whole Truth," to Bruce's case, airing it in Fall 2010 and again during Memorial Day Weekend 2011.

As if to highlight the miraculous nature of The Joyful Redemption, on August 13, 2011, the second anniversary of his release from prison, Bruce married British-born Kara Noble. Having experienced injustice herself when she was linked to a scandal involving the British Royal Family, Kara responded to the *Los Angeles Times* articles about Bruce, becoming a "Friend of Bruce," even contributing to the FreeBruce Fund I'd set up. Who could have known this would lead to a fairy tale romance that would climax with a three-day wedding celebration attended by over one hundred guests?

Their wedding included not only a performance by Terri, but messages from Joy and Bob. Terri informed the bride and groom, who were about to exchange vows, that she'd received these messages from the Afterlife while on the flight to the wedding and that she was "just the messenger."

"She's here," Terri said, referring to Joy, as she read from notes she made, "and she's sorry you don't have her body here. But she wants you to know you will always have her heart." Bob's message to his son confirmed Joy's earlier conversations: "I've never loved anyone more than you, Bruce. You are the love of my life. I'm proud to say I had quite a few hands in your successful release. I don't give up." Bob's final message to Bruce was a hard-won wisdom that applied to everyone at the wedding. "Don't get too logical, like I did. There are mysteries to life that Joy showed me (and all of you) that give life its magic. Let there be magic!"

Bruce's fairy tale wedding, celebrated by the community that had loved me back to life, and which now embraced and loved him back into life, redeemed the Lisker family tragedy and transformed it into a real-life fairy tale with a very *happily ever after.*

From Grief to Gratitude to Haven-on-Earth

Without Joy's help I don't know how I would have recovered from the devastation of losing her. Though my experience being guided from grief to gratitude by the spirit of my late wife was unique, I began to see how the guidance she'd given me could help anyone heal from loss. I began writing a new book that presented what I'd learned as "prescriptions for the grieving heart."

Destiny is a mystery. Soon people began coming into my life who were grieving the loss of a loved one. My heart went out to them. I knew the hell they were going through.

Having been blessed in this life to have found Joy *and* lost Joy, having been initiated into the ordeal of grief and the healing that is possible, having been guided from grief to gratitude, I was inspired to share what I had learned. I had been to Planet Grief and back. I had traveled this brutal and inhospitable Land of Loss. I had already navigated the dangerous bends and turns and pitfalls that await the griever. I was intimately familiar with the terrain. And I'd learned at the Well of Tears that grievers shouldn't go to the Well alone. Without realizing it, I began to function as a guide, a *grief guide.*

I've done many things in my life—acted in films, authored a book that was featured on "Donahue" (the "Oprah" of the time), and created a new cable network. Yet nothing has been as fulfilling as helping people heal their grief. No reviews, no awards, no success can compare to being told, "You saved my life!"

I was blessed during my grief journey in so many ways. Not only did I have Joy's guidance from the Afterlife, but I was surrounded by a conscious community of wise, generous and loving friends, many of whom were healers in their own right, who supported and ministered to me in whatever way I needed. With Joy's guidance and their help, I had created an integrated mind-body-spirit healing program for myself. How could I re-create this experience for others?

I began to envision a retreat with mineral waters, much like Two Bunch Palms, where someone who'd suffered the catastrophic loss of a spouse or child could come to be healed. I call this sanctuary, *Haven-On-Earth*. That's where my *JOYride* had ultimately brought me.

Grief is one of the most devastating human ordeals. For many it's a life-and-death passage, a dark night of the soul. Psychologists rank the loss of a spouse or a child as the #1 stressor in life—the emotional and psychological equivalent of a heart attack.

If grief is comparable to a heart attack, then those who have suffered profound loss deserve the equivalent of a Mayo Clinic! There are *thousands* of drug rehab facilities in the U.S.—1500 in California alone!—yet there is *nothing* for grief.

I envision *Haven-On-Earth* as the ultimate grief retreat and sanctuary—a spa-like oasis of healing where those suffering heartbreak from the loss of a loved one will be supported, facilitated and guided by a world-class staff to embark on their own unique journey of healing. Through residential month-long immersive retreats, combined with year-long outreach programs, as well as week-long and weekend workshops, the grief-stricken will be shown how to transform their breakdown into a breakthrough, their pain into peace and eventually into passion and purpose.

The psychic reading Marcia gave me in those first months of my grief sounded so strange back then—that my grief journey was one of the major purposes of Joy's and my relationship. *"To lose your great love in order to go through the pain to transform yourself. Only in that way can you obtain your knowingness of what pain and suffering and grief is for the work that you have remaining for you to do that may be the greatest work you have done in this life."*

Now I could see that Marcia's reading accurately foreshadowed the events that were unfolding. In fact, during a recent meditation, Joy confirmed this: *"Your vision for these programs and the grief paradigm shift you want to inspire is the passion you have been reborn into. It is your purpose for the rest of your life."*

As I wrote this Epilogue, Joy gave me and *Haven-On-Earth* her blessing—

> *"I'm overjoyed that you've transformed your grief at my loss into these creative pursuits and ideas, into new ways of wonder and appreciation, into a new life.*
>
> *I'm overjoyed that you're looking for ways to celebrate our love by creating gifts that I, we, our memory, your pain, our love, your loss gives to you and to others around you.*
>
> *I'm overjoyed that you've turned your loss into a creative challenge that fills your life with new blossoms, new adventures, new dreams. Every time you creatively act out of the grief, a lotus blooms from the mud. This is the great transformation, the great lesson, the great hope, the greatest testament to our love. Thank you for keeping our love alive in such a gloriously beautiful, creative, life-affirming way."*

Postscript

Just prior to publication, in July 2011, a new and unexpected aspect of *JOYride* emerged. I flew to Minneapolis, Minnesota, where I co-presented a workshop at the national conference of The Compassionate Friends, the largest organization in the country dedicated to supporting families who've lost a child.

More than a year earlier, I'd met Lilly Julien, a woman who'd lost her daughter, Michelle, nearly twenty years before, and had turned that loss into a legacy by founding a grief support organization in New York called COPE. Having received signs and messages from her daughter that had motivated the founding of her grief organization, Lilly was interested in my grief journey. She read an early draft of *JOYride* and was inspired by my *Journey of a Thousand Hugs* and the healing possibilities of non-sexual touch for couples who've suffered the loss of a child. Together we developed a workshop—"Healing Touch for Grieving Couples."

Nearly thirteen hundred bereaved parents, siblings and grandparents attended The Compassionate Friends conference. Over one hundred workshops dealt with all aspects of grieving the loss of a child, including our workshop, which was enthusiastically received.

As I listened to keynote speakers, attended workshops and participated in moving candle-lighting ceremonies, I was struck by the irony that I had come to Minneapolis, home of the Mall of America and the headwaters of the Mississippi, not because I lost a child, but because I lost the love of my life. One of the reasons I was so moved by the conference was the fact that Joy had lost her first two children—Dory and Michael. I began to see that through our love, our *JOYride*, Joy was contributing to the healing of other bereaved parents who've suffered the catastrophic loss of a child. This, too, was her legacy.

I continue to be in awe, wonder and gratitude at the unfolding of our *JOYride* and all of the gifts it continues to bestow.

Meditation on Perfection

A few days before her Good Friday transistion, Joy wrote a *Meditation on Perfection* that she wanted to read at her Celebration of Life memorial service, which she called her "graduation party."

A spiritual teacher most of her life, she saw her death as another teaching opportunity. Even after she was gone, she planned on leading a meditation to help people see the perfection in their own lives.

> *JOY:* Close your eyes for a moment and get comfortable. Take a deep breath and relax. Look back over your life. There were many ups and downs. Let your mind focus on one particularly challenging time in your life. (PAUSE AND REFLECT)
>
> Whatever comes up for you is perfect. Yes, I know that it was painful, difficult, perhaps even tragic for you. And that perhaps you suffered terribly. But I know that when I lost my first child there was a gift in that experience—it opened my heart in a way I could never have achieved before. And so I'm telling you that there is a gift for you in your own experience, if you will take the time to look for it. Cancer gave me many gifts. Blindness gave me many more gifts. Every experience is for our highest good. Keeping this in mind, reflect now on your own experience and ask to be shown the Gift. (PAUSE AND REFLECT)

You may receive an answer now...or tomorrow...
or when the time is right. But know that the answer
will come as you remain open. The certainty that
EVERYTHING is ultimately for our benefit...and that
THAT IS THE PERFECTION IN LIFE has been the
secret to my happiness. And I hope you will make it
your own."

Gently open your eyes and come back to the present....
Know that now and always...All is Well.

I. J. Weinstock

Acknowledgements

────────────────────────────────

My *JOYride* taught me many things, perhaps most important, that loss brings gifts. One of the greatest gifts I received was the love and compassion, generosity and kindness I was shown by friends and family during this dark passage of my life. It takes a village not only to raise a child, but to raise the spirit of the bereaved from the dead.

I was blessed beyond all measure to have been embraced by my community in so many loving ways. I offer my profoundest gratitude, in alphabetical order, to: Amanollah Ghahraman, Annette Cammarano, Basia Tacik, Bruce Lisker, Celestine Conover, Charlotte Holtzerman, Chaz Austin, Christiana Carter, Christina Cassel, Cynthia Richmond, Deborah Gee, Gaelle & Paul Kennedy, Genevieve & Marc Coleman, Gordon Hookailo, Greta Hassel, Herb Slavin, Jackie Cole, Jimmy Yessian, Judith Davenport, Judy Levy, Judy Taylor, Kate & Elliot Anders, Kathleen Rosenblatt, Kevin Larson, Lorraine Marshall, Louise Lanning, Marcia Singer, Marci Javril, Marc Norelli, Mark Hammons, Merrie Lynn Ross, Michael Dawson, Miriam Serman, Molly Schori, R. Morgan Harwith, Patty & John Tierney, Penny & Peter Friedman, Samantha Clemens-Lewis, Sandi Katz, Shama Helena Malin, Sharita Eskridge, Sherry Starr, Stan & Beanie Polsky, Steve Sharp, Suzanne Copeland, Suzanne Shayne, Tara Perry, Terri Nunn & Paul Spear, Thea Soroyan, Vinece Lee, Virginia Lee and Xavier Eikerenkoetter.

Writing this memoir was a grueling ordeal in and of itself. I could not have completed this monumental task without cheerleaders who continually encouraged and reminded me that my *JOYride* could be an inspiration for others. I thank my cheering section who wouldn't listen to my procrastinations, excuses, doubts. From A to Z they are: Anne Taylor, Ann Raisch, Babette Zschiegner, Bari Borsky, Bryan Simon, Cara Brown, Diane Burton, Dido Clark, Dina Routhier, Erin Kinney, Faigy Avnon, Harriet Reiter, Heather Quinn, Joy Lewis, Joyce Alexson, Julia Crouch, Kathleen Gildred, Leah Zahner, Linda Hyden, Linda Ross, Lourdes Colon, Lynne Iser, Marcia Sutton, Marge Engesser, Margie Nunan, Martin Zweiback, Maureen Burke, Melony Hudson, Michelle Menendez, Mikki Fischer Beach, Mirelly Taylor, Mordechai Leibling, Pamela Clay, Rayne Johnson, Rich Ford, Rob Rasner, Robin Connell, Ruth Zoda, Sandra Ruggles, Seth Kadish, Sharon Gibson, Simin Ghasri, Steve Soffer, Stewart Kleiner, Susan Nanus, Susan Zepkin, Tina Morgenstein, Trish Morris and Yvonne Hyatt.

What began as a 500-plus page catharsis required the patience and skill of several readers who gently gave me feedback that helped me edit the manuscript into something readable. I am deeply indebted to: Aurora Winter, Deborah Coryell and Nance McCormick for their input. Bella Mayaha Carter helped edit the raw first draft; Suzanne Sherman's insightful editing helped me take the next step in transforming my cathartic process into what I hope is a captivating read. And kudos are due Dehanna Bailee for designing the book's cover and interior.

A few people deserve special mention, for without the treasure of their love and support this book would never have happened. Thank you from the bottom of my heart: Lilly Julien, Steven & Nancy Weinstock, Suzanne "Butterfly" Strachan and Tatiana Palma.

Finally, a special tribute to "Angelina, Priestess of Joy / Isis" (you know who you are) for "*Joy*-ing me back to life."

About the Author

>———————————————————————————————<

I. J. "Jerry" Weinstock is the son of Holocaust survivors. During his varied career, he's been an actor, artist, producer and author. In the 80's, he co-authored a groundbreaking book about women that the Washington Post hailed as "an important contribution" which became the subject of an entire Donahue Show (the Oprah of its time). In the 90's, his new cable network, The Game Channel, was the precursor to GSN (The Game Show Network).

In the early 2000's, he and his wife, Joy, created and led the "12-Steps to Finding Your Soulmate" workshop that was inspired by the 12-Step program to find new love Joy had received from her previous husband, Bob, after he died. Since Jerry and Joy were a "match-made-in-heaven," they wanted to teach others how they, too, could find the love of their dreams.

When Joy succumbed to breast cancer, Jerry was devastated. But a remarkable thing happened—Joy began communicating with him from the Afterlife. Over the course of a year, she led him on an incredible journey to heal his grief which he recounts in his award-winning memoir, **JOYride: *How My Late Wife Loved Me Back to Life.***

Inspired by his experience of love and loss, he wrote **Grief Quest:** *A Workbook & Journal to Heal the Grieving Heart* which was a FINALIST in the 2012 USA Best Book Awards

On New Year's Eve 2011, Joy once again communicated with him. She asked him a simple yet profound question— What do you love?—which became the inspiration for his new memoir, **The LoveSpell Experiment:** *My Year Exploring Love & Discovering a Secret to Happiness.* He also authored the companion workbook, **The LoveSpell Secret:** *A 30-Day Heaven-Sent Program to Create More Love in Your Life.*

When not leading workshops at bereavement conferences about healing from grief, or giving talks about the *LoveSpell Secret* and how to create more love in your life, I. J. Weinstock writes speculative fiction.

ULTRA BOWL—a sci-fi adventure fable about football, robots and time-travel—is a cautionary tale about the dangers of our Digital Age and the dystopian future toward which we may be heading.

The Secret Sex Life of Angels explores the magic and mystery of sacred sexuality.

I. J. Weinstock lives on Long Island, New York, with his new love Lilly with whom he co-leads a grief retreat every summer. When he's not writing, he spends his time loving more and more of his life and inspiring others to join the Love-O-lution.

He can be reached at DreaMasterBooks@gmail.com or on Twitter @SoulmateGuider. For more information, visit his website www.IJWeinstock.com .

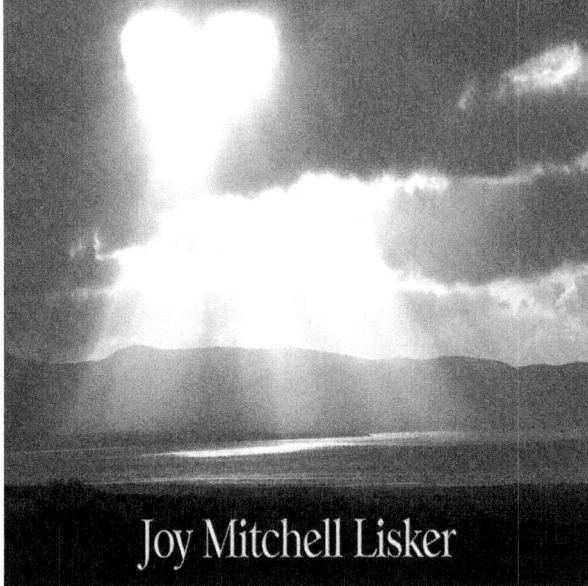

"It's like *Conversations with God*...with an incredible love story! This book will create a healing for anyone who reads it." - Lisa Garr, "The Aware Show" KPFK

Love Ever After

How My Husband Became My Spirit Guide

Joy Mitchell Lisker

"It's like *Conversations with God*...with an incredible love Story! This book will create a healing for anyone who reads it!" ~ **Lisa Garr, "The Aware Show" KPFK**

Find out more at www.IJWeinstock.com

**Available on
Amazon
http://amzn.to/2iIC1H4**

**CreateSpace
http://bit.ly/2j2rSo0**

Love Ever After

How My Husband Became My Spirit Guide

by Joy Mitchell Lisker (I. J. Weinstock's late wife)

It all began with a murder!...

In 1983 Bob Lisker suffered a tragedy of biblical proportions. His wife, Dorka, had been brutally murdered in their Los Angeles home and his teenage son, Bruce, despite pleas of innocence, was convicted of the crime and sentenced to life in prison.

Tormented by the loss of his wife and his only son, this conservative attorney, former Marine and pillar of the community attempted to contact the spirit of his dead wife to find out who killed her. This set the stage for the extraordinary Afterlife communications his 2nd wife, Joy Mitchell Lisker, received after he died.

According to Joy, Bob Lisker was the least likely candidate to be a spirit guide. Yet from the moment he left his body, he gave her a guided tour of the Afterlife that included:

- What happens when we die
- How spirits live and learn on the Other Side
- Reincarnation and the illusion of time
- How the soul chooses its lessons
- How to contact your loved ones on the Other Side
- How to recognize your life path
- How to attract money
- Bob's 12-step program to realize your dreams

This 10th anniversary edition includes an Afterword by Joy's surviving husband, I. J. Weinstock, entitled "The Joyful Redemption" that describes Bruce Lisker's 2009 exoneration and release from prison as seen on the TV show 48 Hours.

JOYride: *How My Late Wife Loved Me Back to Life,* I. J. Weinstock's award-winning grief memoir, is the companion sequel to **Love Ever After.**

FINALIST in the 2012 USA Best Book Awards

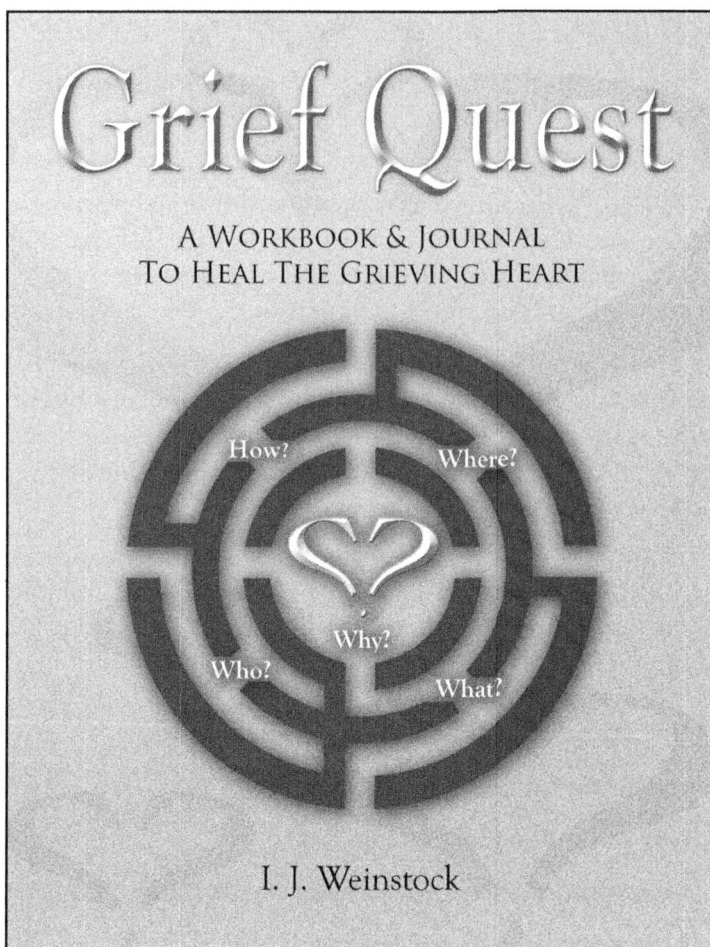

Grief Quest

A WORKBOOK & JOURNAL
TO HEAL THE GRIEVING HEART

How? Where? Why? Who? What?

I. J. Weinstock

Find out more at www.IJWeinstock.com

Available on
Amazon
http://amzn.to/2j59h8c

CreateSpace
http://bit.ly/2jHoks8

LOVE MAY BE THE ANSWER
BUT LOSS POSES THE QUESTIONS

In the agony and inconsolable grief of losing a loved one, we find ourselves asking questions we've never asked before...

When we say we've "lost" our loved one, the truth is we're lost. The world as we've known it no longer exists. The right questions are like a trail in the wilderness that can lead us out of the darkness toward the light of a new life that is forever changed.

THE QUESTIONS DETERMINE THE QUEST

Grief Quest utilizes a unique question-based L.O.V.E. Process—

L — Love your memories

O — Open to your grief

V — Value the gifts

E — Embrace your life

The questions in *Grief Quest* will help you memorialize your loved one. The simple act of recording your memories is a tribute to the love and life you shared.

If you embark on this *Grief Quest* you'll get to know yourself and your relationship with your loved one on a deeper level than you thought possible.

I. J. Weinstock created *Grief Quest* out of his extraordinary experience of love and loss. His award-winning memoir, *JOYride: How My Late Wife Loved Me Back To Life,* tells the remarkable story of how the spirit of his late wife, Joy, gave him *Keys to Healing Loss* and led him on an incredible journey that healed his grief. He leads workshops at international conferences on grief, and counsels the bereaved as a *grief guide.*

My Year Exploring Love
&
Discovering A Secret To Happiness

the
Love
Spell
e x p e r i m e n t

I. J. WEINSTOCK

Find out more at www.IJWeinstock.com

Available on
Amazon
http://amzn.to/2ixxnfL

CreateSpace
http://bit.ly/2jVvbeY

What Do You Love?

by I. J. Weinstock

This simple yet profound question
inspired an extraordinary exploration
into the very nature of Love.

While celebrating New Year's Eve, I. J. Weinstock heard his
late wife, Joy, ask him that simple question—*What do you love?*

His answer became a year-long quest in which
he learned more than 1001 things about love
and discovered a secret to happiness.

The LoveSpell Experiment
is a uniquely intimate document that reveals
a key to unlock the treasure chest of one's life!

A 30-Day Heaven-Sent Program to Create More Love in Your Life

The LoveSpell Secret

I. J. Weinstock

Find out more at www.IJWeinstock.com

Available on
Amazon
http://amzn.to/2hQNUGx

CreateSpace
http://bit.ly/2kb1k5O

The LoveSpell Secret

*A 30-Day Heaven-Sent Program
to Create More Love in Your Life*

Inspired by his *LoveSpell Experiment*, I. J. Weinstock has created a workbook, **The LoveSpell Secret:** *A 30-Day Heaven-Sent Program to Create More Love in Your Life,* to help you develop the habit of asking and answering one of life's most important questions—*What do you love?*

To actually grow the love in your life, you can't just read about it, you have to do it. If you do it for the next 30 days—*Acknowledge, Appreciate* and pay *Attention* to the love in your life—you'll develop the habit of looking at your life through love-colored glasses, receive the amazing benefits of your increased dose of *Vitamin L,* and discover that the power to grow the love in your life is in your heart and in your hands.

"What do you love?" What a profound and necessary question.
Thanks for reminding us to ask the question
on a regular basis. To paraphrase the wisdom in this handbook,
I think we'd all do well to acknowledge, appreciate and pay
attention to this guide!

— Dr. Seth Kadish
*"Pop Your Patterns: The No-Nonsense Way
to Change Your Life"*

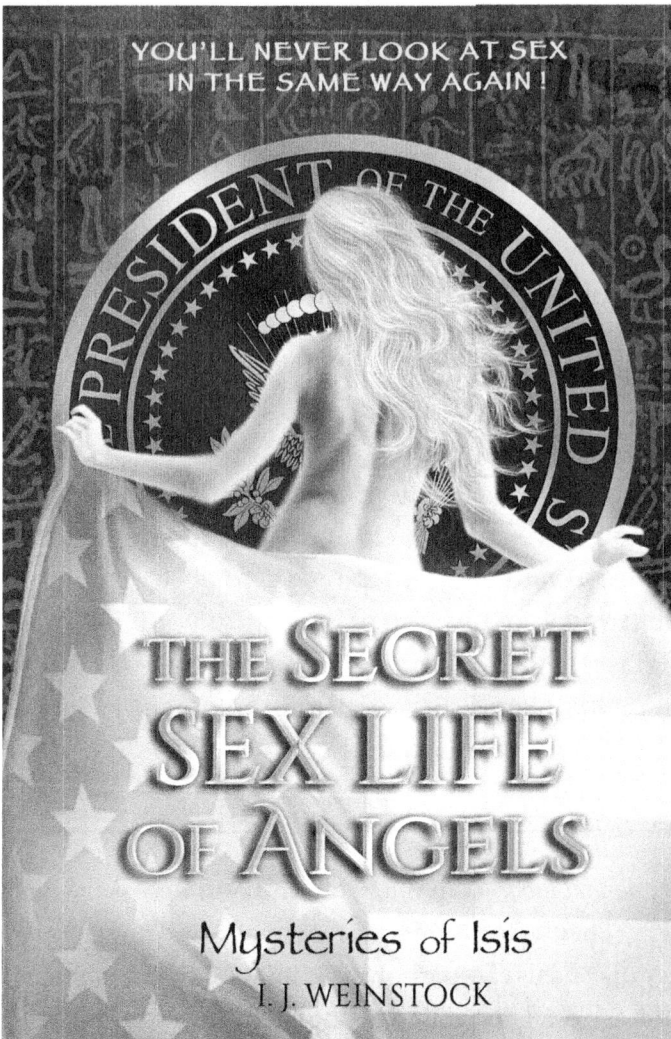

YOU'LL NEVER LOOK AT SEX
IN THE SAME WAY AGAIN !

THE SECRET
SEX LIFE
OF ANGELS
Mysteries of Isis
I. J. WEINSTOCK

Find out more at www.IJWeinstock.com

Available on
Amazon
http://amzn.to/2hFCd93

CreateSpace
http://bit.ly/2jxqiZY

The Secret Sex Life of Angels
by I. J Weinstock

In a world with no future, one man is offered a secret key from the past to unlock the greatest mystery of all.

On the 100th day of his presidency, Adam Hart discovers that to fulfill his oath of office he must embark on a sexual odyssey that could determine the fate of the world.

The Secret Sex Life of Angels combines the intrigue and controversy of *The Da Vinci Code* with the spirituality and eroticism of the *Kama Sutra* in a fantastic saga about the sacred nature of sex.

"Every man needs to read *The Secret Sex Life of Angels.* Every woman needs to have her man read this book."

"You'll never think about sex in the same way again!"

"This is the book everyone will be talking about."

Printed in Great Britain
by Amazon